D1592373

NEST OF
SPIES

NEST OF SPIES

THE STARTLING TRUTH ABOUT FOREIGN AGENTS
AT WORK WITHIN CANADA'S BORDERS

Fabrice de Pierrebourg and Michel Juneau-Katsuya

TRANSLATED BY RAY CONLOGUE

HarperCollins*PublishersLtd*

Nest of Spies
Copyright © 2009 by Éditions
internationales Alain Stanké.
English translation © 2009 by
HarperCollins Publishers Ltd.
All rights reserved.

Published by HarperCollins Publishers Ltd.

First published in Canada by
HarperCollins Publishers Ltd
in a hardcover edition: 2009
This trade paperback edition: 2010

HarperCollins benefits from the financial
support of the Société de développement
des entreprises culturelles du Québec
(SODEC) for the cost of French-English
translation.

SODEC
Québec ⬚⬚

HarperCollins books may be purchased
for educational, business, or sales
promotional use through our Special
Markets Department.

HarperCollins Publishers Ltd
2 Bloor Street East, 20th Floor
Toronto, Ontario, Canada
M4W 1A8

www.harpercollins.ca

Library and Archives Canada Cataloguing
in Publication

Pierrebourg, Fabrice de
Nest of spies : the startling truth about
foreign agents at work within
Canada's borders / Fabrice de
Pierrebourg, Michel Juneau-Katsuya.

ISBN 978-1-55468-450-2

1. Business intelligence–Canada.
2. Industries–Security
measures–Canada. I. Juneau-Katsuya,
Michel II. Title.

HD38.7.P53 2009   658.4'720971
C2008-907959-0

Mixed Sources
Cert no. SW-COC-001271
© 1996 FSC
FSC

Printed and bound in Canada
DWF 9 8 7 6 5 4 3 2 1

To the men and women who work tirelessly
to protect us against spies, terrorists,
and cowardly bureaucrats.

CONTENTS

INTRODUCTION

The clever strategist is subtle, so much so that he is no longer visible.
The clever strategist is discreet, so much so that he can not be heard.
Thus he becomes the master of his enemy's destiny.
—Sun Tzu, *The Art of War* (c. 509 BCE)

In 1996, the Canadian Security Intelligence Service (CSIS) argued in a well-researched study that our country loses between $10 and $12 billion every year to economic and industrial espionage.* That's a tidy haul of a billion dollars a month, which in turn is evidence of professional work by well-trained and specialized spies. At about the same time, the American Society for Industrial Security (ASIS) produced a similar study, which set the monthly cost of corporate spying in the United States at about $24 billion.** Given that America is ten times Canada's size—in both population and economic output—we are

---

* That year, one of the two authors of this book, Michel Juneau-Katsuya, was in charge of CSIS's Asia-Pacific Unit at the Research, Analysis and Production (RAP) Branch. He knows of no other study of this scope having been financed by the federal government, a university, or a private sector company.
** This book will analyze the many categories of espionage.

losing cutting-edge technological information or market share five times faster than the United States. It is no exaggeration to describe this situation as an economic hemorrhage.

Espionage is a multi-faceted problem that challenges our society in many ways. The theft of Canadian cutting-edge research in new products and technologies is only one of them, the visible tip of a vast, submerged and problematical iceberg.

Consider, for example, the "Farewell" affair, one of the pivotal spy cases of the modern era. Ronald Reagan described its principal player, a KGB colonel named Vladimir Vetrov, as "the spy of the century." Vetrov worked for a time in Canada, and later offered his services to France. There he produced a detailed description of Russia's vast global espionage operation.

Or you might wish to consider the hundreds of front companies that the Chinese secret service operates in Canada, each of them harbouring industrial spies. Or the Iranian agents who lurk within the Irano-Canadian diaspora, violently suppressing criticism of the government in Teheran.

These are only a few examples of a worldwide and highly calibrated system of espionage that has been active in Canada since the Second World War. Canadians do not seem to know that the most important cases that deeply affected the relationship between the West and the Soviet Union came to light one day in 1945 when the defector Igor Gouzenko, a cipher clerk in the Soviet embassy, walked into an RCMP office with a dossier revealing a KGB spy operation that affected every nation in the western alliance. Historians believe that the Cold War began with the revelation of what was in Gouzenko's attaché case.

Many of these issues and events are poorly understood by the general public. In some cases, information has been suppressed. A strange silence surrounds the subject in this country.

Why do we say "strange"? Because Canada found itself constantly in the middle of some of the most important international espionage cases and nobody talked about it. But why don't Canadians know about it? Why don't we know that, on the international scene, we are a country with perhaps the highest level of spy activity? A 2005 CSIS study revealed that Canadians had little or no knowledge of their own intelligence service. If some of the most important cases have taken place in Canada, why has nobody ever been charged here for espionage? Consider this: there have been hundreds of prosecutions of spies, including domestic traitors, in the United States, France, and Great Britain during the past fifteen years alone. But there has never been a prosecution for espionage in Canada. Not one.

Clearly, it's time that questions were asked.

The widespread belief that espionage ended when the Cold War ended is unfortunately not true. The fact is, we have moved from a military to an economic confrontation. In recent years, Russia and China have doubled, and in some areas tripled, their efforts in the field. Whether, two decades after the end of the Cold War, we still think of them as "the bad guys" is not really the issue. What is incontrovertibly true is that they are very big players.

They are not the only ones, however. The overall extent of espionage today is much greater than it was during the Cold War. Instead of two politically hostile blocs confronting each other, we now live in a global political and economic configuration where there is cloak-and-dagger warfare of all against all.

Canada's oversized role in this drama is due to four factors. First is our advanced technology (others want our know-how); second is the economy (they want our markets); third is political (they need to manipulate our national and international policies, making certain that citizens of foreign birth do no criticize their homelands).

The final factor is military (they want our secrets, and those our allies share with us).

A complicating factor is the sudden pre-eminence of the war on terrorism since the attacks of September 11, 2001. This new obsession has stolen focus from the greater menace. If it weren't for the fact that terrorists kill people, espionage in Canada would be by far our top national security issue.

BUT WHY CANADA?

Why, of all places, has Canada become the most popular home-away-from-home for the world's spies? It's principally because we are a knowledge-based society. Some of the world's leading research centres are located here, and we operate at the sharp edge of technology in almost all domains. That's especially true of aeronautics, mining, oil and gas, communications, information processing, aerospace, medical and pharmaceutical research—in all, more than fifteen fields of interest to competing nations.

Aggravating this is the fact that Canadian laws are flabbily written and poorly enforced (arguably they are not enforced at all), and the unfortunate truth that our police officers are not trained to investigate in our domain.

And then we must consider one of the dubious consequences of multiculturalism, that wonderful human mosaic, which we rightly celebrate, but which also readily conceals the newly arrived spy. It offers him or her a useful reservoir of potential sources from the homeland, as well as informers anxious to denounce malcontents.

And finally, there is the open-hearted character of Canadians, who welcome foreigners without asking a lot of questions. This propensity arises from our liberal and inclusive culture, and we are proud of it, but it is readily abused by curious visitors: particularly those who intend to leave with intellectual property in their pockets.

Espionage pays! It's vastly more profitable to steal technology than to develop it independently. When the many years of research are accounted for, the cost of a breakthrough can sometimes run into billions of dollars. The thief who absconds with this property, free of charge, can produce it industrially and sell it at a price ridiculously lower than the true inventor can afford to charge.

Given the temptation involved, we now add the further attraction of a country where successive governments of all political stripes have ignored the problem. Canada has lacked the courage, or the resolve, or perhaps the simple ability to grasp the size of the challenge.

Why?

SEE NO EVIL, SPEAK NO EVIL

Given the urgency of the challenge, most people would assume that Canadian authorities must at least have scrutinized the facts and taken measures to deal with them. Any citizen who makes such an assumption is very much mistaken.

Instead, a vicious circle has developed over the years. To start with, senior political leaders do not really understand the extent of the problem. This is partly through indifference (or, in certain cases, conflict of interest) and partly because the civil servants responsible for analyzing the problem and advising the government haven't done their job.

There are three interlocking problems. To begin with, senior civil servants—especially senior people within the Canadian Security and Intelligence Service (CSIS)—have not drawn sufficiently or efficiently the problem to the attention of our elected leaders. Second, government policy and government actions have not been coordinated. For example, both the Department of Foreign Affairs and International Trade (DFAIT, an unfortunate acronym if ever there was one) and the Ministry of Commerce and Industry are guilty of placing their narrow ministerial interests ahead of the common good. Finally, political will has given way to a fear of upsetting powerful individuals and interests that in return will result in lost votes.

That is why, time and again, our federal leaders have avoided the issue. The problem, naturally, continues to grow. But it has never grown important enough (to our short-sighted and calculating political elite) to become a plank in the platform of a major political party. Losing $10 to $12 billion annually is not worthy of being a political issue?

Political leaders believe that average Canadians don't care about espionage. That's why they find it easy to put it off to a tomorrow that never comes. Like the leaky water systems and aging sewer mains of the cities, subjects too dull to capture the attention of voters, our leaders have decided that espionage is not a vote-getter. It lacks the appealing simplicity of a new park or hospital.

Inevitably, senior civil servants understand that this issue will not become a cabinet-level priority. It follows logically that they should not undertake relevant or decisive action. The system is a closed circle where the bureaucracy cannot communicate relevant information to elected officials.

Existing Canadian laws do not protect our country from espionage. But, for the reasons mentioned above, governments in power are not likely to change them. It follows that the legislative branch will not come to grips with the problem either.

Our allies have approached the matter more effectively. After the Soviet bloc collapsed, most western countries—the United States, France, Russia, and the United Kingdom, among others—within a few years passed laws to protect themselves against economic espionage. With less fanfare, they also gave themselves authority to practise economic espionage.

Canada waited until 2001 to pass its first legislation acknowledging the problem. Unfortunately, the legislation in question was the Anti-Terrorism Act, a clumsy omnibus bill that contains a truncated version of the old Official Secrets Act. It has only two sections that deal specifically with economic espionage and other forms of improper interference in domestic affairs by foreign governments.* These provisions are so weak that, in effect, law enforcement agencies are obliged to fall back on the Criminal Code when they uncover foreign interference and threats to Canadian citizens. The Criminal Code, however, does not specifically cover this kind of activity. To put it mildly, the framework of Canadian law is inadequate.

Nor do law enforcement officers possess the resources and training necessary to investigate the offences. If they did, they would still be hampered by the fact that there is little legal framework to authorize such investigations. And even if that framework were in place, they would find they lacked the resources for the job. Canadian police forces already lack the funds and expertise to investigate everyday white-collar crime (commercial fraud, money laundering, and other financial chicanery). Confronted with the nightmarish complexity of espionage cases, they are terribly ill equipped.

Canada's business community contributes to the problem. Commercial enterprises often delay the dreaded telephone call to the police or to CSIS or the RCMP until it is too late. The theft has occurred. Their intellectual property is gone. At this point, the police have no recourse except to the Criminal Code, which limits them to indicting offenders with charges such as "theft over $5,000" or fraud.

---

* These two sections, 19 and 20, have never been used. They are also buried within the proposed law C-36, which became a sort of catch-all for the Anti-Terrorism Act.

The penalties attached to these charges are, as a rule, a suspended sentence or a small fine. Absurd!

This leaves Canadian businesses and Canada's ethnic communities with no choice but to fall back on their own resources when threatened by professional spies. Corporate directors do their best to decide what measures to take, but they are hampered by a lack of information. Many decide to treat it as somebody else's problem. By default, this "somebody" is often the police. And since business leaders don't hear from the police, they assume that all is well. Thus the vicious circle continues.

Should any particular CEO decide to take action to protect his enterprise, his decisiveness will come to nothing when he learns that there are few security specialists available to help out. Too often he finds himself in a "spy store," plunking down money for James Bond gadgetry that has little relevance to the problems he faces. A professional could tell him that tracking devices and security cameras are nothing more than tools. They are the carpenter's workshop without the carpenter. In any security system, the weak link is always the human factor.

This is a problem with two dimensions. There is the issue of human resources, and there is the issue of information management (a much bigger matter than "information technology," or IT, with which it is often confused). These challenges can be met only through a change of business and organizational culture. The enterprise must rethink its interface with the larger economic world. Employees will need to internalize a series of security reflexes. This does not, however, mean turning the company into a sealed bunker.

WHAT WE PROPOSE

If Canada wishes to become a leading economy in the contemporary world, the problem of espionage must be confronted. As it is,

corporate resources are principally directed to finding new markets and developing cutting-edge products. Specialized employees
and research scientists find this challenge utterly absorbing, as they
should. Who could expect them to look up from their desks and
peer into the shadows, where they might discern a small army of
foreign agents nimbly appropriating their work and dealing decisively with anyone who threatens to expose them?

This book will attempt to throw a little light on the world of
espionage, identifying the players and the stakes. We hope the public will come away with a better understanding of the threat.

At the same time, we wish to acknowledge our limitations. This
work is not meant to be a scientific or academic study. We are not
scientists and we are not academics. All that we can do is present
the evidence and turn attention to the subject. We hope that we can
raise Canadians' awareness of the danger and, above all, encourage
decision-makers to take action.

Each country analyzed here might in itself be the subject of
another book. We are thinking of China and Russia in particular,
and that is why we have devoted the larger part of our attention to
them. The resources these countries devote to clandestine operations on our soil are the legitimate concern of every Canadian.

We also wish to pull aside the curtain of silence that federal
and provincial institutions draw tight around themselves when the
subject is broached. Every one of us has the right to know how big
the problem has become. How else can we deal with it? How else
can we help the business community to deal with it?

The reader will certainly notice our anger and indignation at
the many senior officials who have placed self-interest ahead of the
public interest. These men and women have endangered private
citizens and undermined important sectors of the economy. We
are calling them to account only because the people who should

have done so—our leaders and our law enforcement agencies—
have not.

At the same time, we acknowledge and honour the work done
by the thousands of men and women who carry on in spite of
bureaucratic indifference and daily frustrations. They can be found
within the intelligence community, inside police agencies, among
customs officers, throughout the military, and in every organization charged with the enforcement of Canada's laws. Their tireless
labour, within a system that serves them poorly, protects us and our
country. We would like to dedicate this book to them.

A final word concerning sources. We have met personally with
informants from all walks of life. Where possible we have named
them. Others, for reasons not difficult to understand, have asked
that their identities not be revealed. We have also made use of all
available documentation, whether in the form of media reports,
official documents, or books on the subject. These have been cross-
checked for accuracy.

At the same time, espionage is a subject that does not give up
all its secrets. Some matters can't be verified, no matter how reliable
the sources who have brought them forward. These sources are, to a
reasonable extent, entitled to the benefit of the doubt.

As for those who have done reprehensible things, they—like
politicians—are not in the habit of answering questions. They do,
from time to time, condescend to deny everything. The reader must
form his or her own opinion of them.

CHAPTER 001

How the "Tired Old Whore" Became a Brand-New Menace

You're very naive about Russia and her intentions. You think, now the USSR is gone, that Russia is your friend. You're wrong.
—Sergei Tretyakov, former Russian spy

It's the ninth of November, 1989. Around the world, television screens are filled with dramatic images of the Berlin Wall as it shudders under the sledgehammer blows of ecstatic East and West Germans.

A somewhat different euphoria, perhaps no less intense, reigns over Parliament Hill in Ottawa, thousands of kilometres away. On the twelfth floor of 340 Laurier Street West—according to a witness who was there that day—officials in the offices of Assistant Deputy Solicitor General Wendy Porteous tossed back fake champagne from plastic cups. It was a lapse of good taste, certainly, but an understandable one. The slurred toasts were raised not in a spirit of triumph, but more of simple exhaustion and great relief. Although the Warsaw Pact had not yet officially been dissolved, there were more than a few Canadian bureaucrats who felt it soon would be. The moment had come to close the book on the Cold War and move on.

Over at the Canadian Security Intelligence Service (CSIS), however, a rift had already appeared. On one side were those who likewise wanted to close the books and redeploy the agents long assigned to countering the USSR and its allies. The other camp was wary, thinking it a mistake for Canada to lower its guard so quickly.

While this debate was underway, several dozen Soviet citizens named in a surveillance order signed by the solicitor general wondered whether they were off the hook. The consensus among them was, yes, they were.

In fact, it was clear to most people with an interest in the subject that Canadian authorities were tired of the Cold War. They wanted things to go back to normal. The error was to assume that the Soviets wished to do the same.

"Once you learn to swim, you never forget," said a Russian spy, twenty years later, when a European secret service agent asked him about this. The question he was answering was: Had Mother Russia diminished its espionage activities after the fall of the Berlin Wall? Had the spies truly come in from the cold?

The Russian's metaphor was droll and to the point. The Russian Federation, successor to the Union of Soviet Socialist Republics, had not stopped swimming for a moment. After decades of turbulence and humiliation in which the countries of the North Atlantic Treaty Organization had moved aggressively to undermine the USSR's satellite states, the new federation had only one obsession: to win back its former authority.

Warning signals had been going off for some time. Western agents trying to co-operate with their Russian opposites in the new and supposedly mutual war against terrorism faced endless harassment. One CSIS agent, exhausted by bureaucratic obstacles and petty intimidation, was ready at the beginning of 2009 to abandon his Russian post and return home.

Businessmen visiting Russia were also aware of this tension. They learned that they were seen not as legitimate competitors in the free market sense, but rather as hostile competitors in the old Cold War sense. They had to learn to watch out for themselves. In the months preceding the CSIS agent's complaint, several business visitors had been followed, sometimes ostentatiously, throughout their stay in Moscow. Other countries, such as China (see Chapter 004), had also been quick to confuse normal business with spying, and put visitors under observation in order to protect what they saw as their fair share of the market. The same thing occurred even in the so-called "friendly" countries. At the beginning of 2009, British military intelligence placed the Russians and the Chinese at the top of a list of twenty nations guilty of economic and industrial espionage, out ahead of Syria, Iran, North Korea, Serbia . . . and France and Germany! The only difference was one of style: the "friendly" countries were a little more discreet in their methods.

Meanwhile, European Union states were complaining that the number of spies hidden in Russia's embassies and consulates had risen to levels not seen since the Cold War. They came from Russia's military intelligence agency, GRU, as well as the civilian spy agency, the Sluzhba Vneshney Razvedki (SVR), which had replaced the former and much-hated KGB.

"They're back, and as busy as ever," complained a former high-ranking officer of an American intelligence agency. This was in 2005, when the Americans were already getting nervous about Russia's renewed efforts to pilfer military or dual-use technology. They had learned some new tricks, too, such as hiding their "front" companies in a country other than the one where the espionage was being carried out.

But the "return" of the Russians came as no surprise to Canada's intelligence community. "They never left," said one.

Recent observations in Britain confirm that there are now about thirty Russian secret agents in London alone, working for either the GRU or the SVR (Line X in particular) under different cover identities. That is about the same as it was at the height of the Cold War. Speaking in Manchester in 2007, MI-5 Director General Jonathan Evans expressed exasperation that, "nearly two decades after the end of the Cold War," he was having to commit more and more of MI-5's financial and human resources to fighting technology theft. Russia and China in particular, he observed, were treating it like a national sport as well as a top priority. "They not only use traditional methods to collect intelligence, but increasingly make use of sophisticated technical attacks, using the Internet to penetrate computer networks."[1] It would be helpful if Canadian security leaders were inspired to imitate Evans's straight talk.

Evans's disappointment was all the greater because his agents now had to fight a war on two fronts: international terrorism and espionage. This undermined the war against terrorism, which Evans felt was the more pressing menace to the safety of the British population, as well as Britain's allies.

The Canadian government reportedly refused admission to no fewer than four Russian "diplomats" in 2008, believing them to be GRU and SVR agents. They were identified through "Trace Requests" sent to the intelligence agencies of friendly countries. Fearing a loss of face, and angered by Canada's deportation to Russia in 2006 of the alleged spy Paul William Hampel, Russian authorities responded with the above-mentioned campaign of harassment against the CSIS liaison agent in Moscow.

The return of Russia to the forefront of western security concerns led our counter-espionage service, CSIS, to spend most of 2007 and 2008 studying the problem classified as "High Priority." It found that Moscow was sponsoring a wider than ever range of spy activities, in Canada and elsewhere, and that these activities were managed from its diplomatic missions. The Russians were looking for all kinds of information, whether economic, scientific, technical, or political. Russia's agencies are extraordinarily powerful and well financed. They have the resources to corrupt new information sources, and are able to operate even within Canadian government ministries, particularly Defence. For the Russians, putting a mole into the highest echelons of our government is mere child's play.

A top-priority Russian target was the huge project to modernize the Canadian Air Defence Sector operations at North Bay in Ontario. This strategic establishment occupies nearly 10,000 square metres and is a crucial element of the North American Aerospace Defense Command (NORAD). The rebuilding took from 2003 to 2007, and the many security gaps in the areas where construction was taking place made it relatively easy to infiltrate. According to the Auditor General of Canada there were security failures with respect to: building blueprints, which were placed in the public domain when they were made available to interested contractors; physical access to the site, which was under only limited control; and management of work crews, none of whom was cleared by security to work there.[2] Incredibly, neither the Department of National Defence nor Defence Construction Canada ever completed security clearances for the twenty or so foreign and Canadian companies working on the site of the new NORAD complex and having access to the plans. It was an astonishing oversight. As a result, the shiny new complex was left empty and unused for many months after completion while checks and modifications were carried out.

Similar cases of the new Russian aggressiveness have been observed around the world. In Japan, for example, counter-espionage agents struggle to cope with the combination of new SVR agents trying to enter the country under diplomatic cover and the ones already implanted. One agent wreaked havoc for nearly thirty years while adroitly slipping from one false cover to another.

Of course there's another side to this story. The West continues to deploy agents to monitor Russia, and the Russians are offended by this. Though regarded as the traditional "bad guys," they point out (quite justly) that they are not the only players in the contemporary version of the Great Game. Alexander Bortnikov, the head of Russia's internal security service, announced in December 2008 that his agency had thwarted 150 spies and informants of all descriptions, including 48 full-time agents employed by foreign security agencies. Nine were expelled.

This autumn will see the twentieth anniversary of the fall of the Berlin Wall. The world has certainly changed, though you wouldn't know it from the obsolete political insults still exchanged between East and West. Where espionage is concerned, the change is two-fold. The first is that military espionage has indeed declined. The other part, the important part, is that its resources were redeployed to the small but expanding specialty of economic espionage. What began as small and intermittent theft of industrial research has now grown into a vast and destabilizing form of economic warfare.

After 1989, the political elites of the democratic countries were seduced by the policy of "perestroika" (or restructuring) of Yuri Andropov, followed by the "glasnost" (transparency) of Mikhail Gorbachev. The West failed to understand that, within the ruins of Communism, the remnants of Russia's intelligence agencies were already recovering from the collapse. It had become very obvious to them that their homeland was technologically primitive by comparison with the western powers. That was why they had lost the Cold War. How could they now ever achieve economic equality? Given Russia's poverty, the only possible route was through the wholesale theft of advanced technology.

Though the shattering of the Berlin Wall, followed by the shattering of the USSR, was theatrically impressive, on a profound level it had changed nothing at all. Russia still needed what the West had, and was now perhaps more determined than before to acquire it.

It's often forgotten in the West that Mikhail Gorbachev, while still a rising Communist functionary, was an advocate of scientific and technological espionage. As far back as 1984, while visiting the Soviet embassy in London, he did not conceal his enthusiasm for the successes of the Line X agents from the KGB's Directory T. Their specialty was technology and scientific information, and it can be presumed that he continued to support their efforts when he became secretary general of the Communist Party only weeks after his London visit.

These agents, often working in tandem with colleagues from Soviet bloc countries, sharpened their skills as the years passed. Eventually they plucked thousands of components, mechanisms, and sometimes entire technological systems from western nations. As early as 1980, an agent code-named "Farewell" was recruited by the French security service DST (Direction de la Surveillance du Territoire). Over the next two years he provided literally thousands of documents showing the extent of Soviet infiltration into western economies.

Interestingly, Farewell (whose real name was Colonel Vladimir Vetrov) had the habit of dismissing the KGB as a "worn-out old whore." French agents working with him at the time, still in thrall to the myth of Soviet omnipotence, did not quite understand what lay behind Farewell's disillusionment. Few imagined that the collapse of the Soviet system lay just a few years in the future. Some, such as a West German agent who in the mid-1980s jumped the Berlin Wall in the wrong direction, still thought that Communism might triumph. This was less than five years before the Wall came down.

"We're still sorting out the Farewell business," admits Rémy Pautrat, who was the director of the DST at that time. He adds that, within the agency, "we didn't imagine that everything would come apart so quickly and that the geopolitical equilibrium would be so decisively overthrown." Farewell, who at one time had worked in the Soviet consulate on Boulevard Pie-IX in Montreal, ended his career as a double agent in 1985 when he was apparently executed by a firing squad in Russia. Line X, most of whose agents he had revealed to French intelligence, collapsed, along with much of the Soviet Union's espionage capacity.

Despite these reverses, there were still those within the Soviet sphere who saw a glorious near-future for Russian espionage. Nikolay Holushko, head of Ukraine's KGB, told the newspaper *Pravda Ukrainy* that perestroika would provide a wonderful environment for the KGB—a statement he made a mere two months after the fall of the Berlin Wall. To Holushko the KGB was far from a tired old whore: on the contrary, it was the "gauntlet and shield" (a reference to its insignia) that would make new conquests by infiltrating the world of capitalist business.

Holushko described an evolving KGB. Its new mission would be to plant agents in foreign corporations. These would harvest proprietary information and pass it along to Soviet businesses competing in the same markets. Apart from bestowing an unfair advantage on Soviet companies, commercial espionage would permit a weakened Russia to avoid the purgatory of signing co-operative agreements ("ententes harmful to Soviet interests") with western countries.

In the interests of fairness we should point out that American and French agents had created the template for this kind of espionage some years earlier by passing on Soviet aeronautic research to Boeing and Airbus.

EXTREMELY ODD BUSINESSMEN

In this new espionage, a favoured tactic would involve joint ventures with western companies wishing to set up operations inside the USSR. The Soviet (or, later, Russian) company that offered a welcoming handshake was almost invariably a creation of the secret services. The few that were not were heavily seamed with intelligence agents, right up to and including their executive suites.

In 1999, Robert James Woolsey, a former CIA director, took evident pleasure in recounting to the U.S. House of Representatives how these arrangements worked.

> If you run into a suave Russian, wearing a three thousand dollar suit and Gucci loafers, in the restaurant of one of the expensive hotels along the shore of Lake Geneva, and he says that he is an executive in a major Russian firm engaged in the export of high technology, he may be what he says he is. Or he may be a Russian intelligence officer operating under commercial cover. Or he may be a senior member of some Russian organized crime group. But the really interesting point is that he may well be all three—and that none of the three institutions he works for has any problem with that.

Perestroika greatly facilitated the work of Russian agents by opening their country's frontiers with the West. All they had to do was sit at home and fawn over the planeloads of western businessmen and scientists who descended on the dying USSR to whip up business. An additional benefit was that these agents could work undisturbed on home turf, safely beyond the reach of western counter-intelligence services.

CSIS quickly took note of this "new orientation." A Soviet bloc expert at its Research, Analysis, and Production (RAP) Branch issued this early warning (1990) to Canadian companies: "Canadian business people who deal with Soviet firms should be told to be very guarded with their counterparts, and to be certain of the safety and confidentiality of their information and their negotiating strategy."

To show themselves in a better light, the Soviets gave the United States the flattering designation "Principal Target" (that is, competitor), replacing the previous tag "Principal Enemy." They would soon do likewise with China and the other NATO countries.

But this was only so much window dressing. Their qualitative goals and procedures, most authorities feel, remained the same. Remarkably, they carried out this ambitious project at a time of economic and political chaos when they possessed only a fraction of the tens of thousands of people who had in the recent past worked for the KGB.

Former diplomat Vladimir Fedorovki, now a prolific writer, often cautions western critics to beware of oversimplifying matters when trying to understand the political situation in the former USSR. At one time the interpreter of Soviet leader Leonid Brezhnev, Fedorovki later became a member of Mikhail Gorbachev's inner circle. His task was to promote perestroika in Europe during the second half of the 1980s. When embittered Communists attempted a putsch in 1991, Fedorovki took advantage of the chaos to ingratiate himself with new leader Boris Yeltsin.

We reached him in Paris, where he gave us his analysis of the situation. He is little impressed with the West's infatuation with Mikhail Gorbachev, which he calls "Gorbimania."

> At the time, Gorbimania was blown up to be more than it really was. It was a public relations masquerade, usually driven by opportunists with their own agenda.

Don't forget that the entire country was developing very rapidly at that time, and that this had little to do with Gorbachev's influence. There was immense progress in governance, including—and this is just one example— universal suffrage. Seen in this perspective, far from being a smokescreen, perestroika represented a genuine change which altered the world.

However, the true believers in Communism had not accepted defeat, particularly the followers of Yuri Andropov, who had run the KGB from 1967 to 1982 before becoming general secretary of the Communist Party. Against them were ranged the newly powerful faction that wanted to see a decisive break with the Communist past.

Fedorovki argues that the old guard retained control in several crucial domains. Agents from FSB, responsible for the country's internal security, tightened their hold on power thanks to the adroit intervention of Vladimir Putin, an ex-lieutenant-colonel of the KGB. Putin's first loyalty is still to the security services, whether he calls himself president or prime minister. Fedorovki refers to him as "the ghost of Stalin."

Putin is a student and admirer of Andropov, who ran the country until Gorbachev's arrival. In a sense, Putin has dragged Russia back into the Andropov era. Fedorovki, with typical puckishness, likes to compare the current regime with SPECTRE, the nasty organization that never ceases to set traps for James Bond. Certainly Putin has cemented the new authority of Russia's secret services.

The mafiosi and the oligarchs grew fat during the chaotic years of the USSR's collapse. Today they are held in contempt by average Russians, but that is only because they successfully seized a good part of the country's riches through the purchase of state companies at derisory prices. At the same time, the security services ransacked the treasury of the Soviet Communist Party and used the booty to set up more than 600 overseas corporations. This new structure was essentially in place by 1993.

Since then there has been a golden age of collusion among organized crime, legitimate business, bankers, and corrupt politicians. In a 1994 report, CSIS alluded to the disappearance of billions of dollars in value from the Russian economy in what it called a "criminal revolution." This was the period when the term "parallel economy" entered western intelligence jargon. And "enter" isn't just a figure of speech. The parallel economy entered the West in a literal way, as well. Not too long ago, a well-placed Canadian bureaucrat was suspected of taking bribes to facilitate the activities of the "Red Mafia" in Canada.

With the aid of Vladimir Putin, scores of agents from the old KGB (the KGB was split in two: SVR, responsible for spying abroad, and FSB, responsible for internal security) infiltrated the worlds of politics and business. A Russian sociologist reported in 2005 that around 80 percent of key positions in the corporate and government hierarchy were occupied by *siloviki*, a sinister term referring to senior police and military officers now tricked out with bespoke suits and attaché cases. Olga Krychtanovskaia went on to describe the new Russia as a "militocracy."

One notable exception, however, is the technocrat Dmitri Medvedev, now president of the Russian Federation. Medvedev has no military connection: he is a former head of the Gazprom energy conglomerate. But Fedorovki views the realms of intelligence and energy resources as nearly completely integrated today. "The two keys [to power] are oil and gas, together with the secret services," he asserts.

It might be more accurate to speak of a triumvirate made up of government economic power, the secret services, and the Russian mafia. But it's misleading to think of them as three well-defined groups. Nobody really knows where the boundaries are, or even if the groups can any longer be separated. They do, however, represent the most profound development of the post–Cold War period, and a formidable challenge to western counter-espionage efforts.

In Canada, meanwhile, the budgetary allocation for CSIS agents monitoring the arrival of the siloviki was melting away like a Montreal snowdrift on a warm spring day.

The CSIS organization was created in 1984. At the time, nearly 80 percent of its operational employees worked in counter-intelligence. Only one in five worked in the then-nascent field of anti-terrorist activities.

During this time the countries most actively involved in economic and political spying included

- China
- Cuba
- East Germany
- France
- India
- Russian satellites, particularly Czechoslovakia and Romania
- South Africa
- United States
- USSR

During the following decade, Canada became the target of a dozen countries actively involved in political/military espionage, together with more than fifteen that practised economic spying.

More than twenty had developed the capacity to interfere directly in Canada's domestic and foreign relationships.

A number of countries were especially prominent in the CSIS analysis of the new problem: China, India, Russia, and Israel. Each was active in all varieties of information gathering.

Nor had classical spying been forgotten. Here we find more or less the same actors who had been present ten years earlier:

- China
- India
- Iran
- Israel
- Morocco
- Romania
- Russia
- South Korea
- Taiwan
- Ukraine

Russia had been particularly aggressive in changing the nature of its activities. Its formal espionage stations (called *rezidentura*) had been shut down throughout the world, particularly in Africa, Asia, and South America. In other western countries, including Canada, SVR agents put an end to most of their political espionage operations. They also let go of ideological propaganda, the so-called "active measures" much loved during the Cold War era but now (clearly) obsolete.

Having cleared the decks, they installed the new heavy artillery of economic espionage. *The Foreign Intelligence Collection Act*, ratified by Boris Yeltsin in July of 1992, restored the morale of the former Soviet (now Russian) intelligence agencies. For one thing, the act allowed them to keep their military rank, even though they would now work in suits and ties and have no military duties as such. Of course this was on the condition that their loyalty to the new Russian state remained beyond reproach.

From that moment forward, these former Communist agents presented a new kind of challenge to Canadian spy-catchers. They were neither fish nor fowl. It was hard to tell which of them had repented their Stalinist past and which had not. It would have been pleasant for CSIS to invite them all in for a lengthy fireside chat, but the agency didn't have the luxury of doing that. It also had to deal with a new generation of active Russian agents. These showed up with business visas, and many of them were associated with perfectly legitimate joint ventures.

Some ex-Soviet agents didn't hesitate to disembark in Halifax or Montreal, even though they were perfectly aware that their CSIS files were still tagged "Known KGB/SVR." One of these was the remarkable Vladimir Lavrentiyev, who had been a security officer in the USSR's Ottawa embassy as recently as 1990. Less than a decade later he emerged from an Aeroflot jetliner as a highly placed Russian bank director, complete with a business visa stamped by Canada's Ministry of Citizenship and Immigration.

Lavrentiyev's arrival caused something of a commotion at CSIS's head office. A young intelligence officer was sent out to interrogate him. Shortly afterward, the agent slumped home to report that the Russian wouldn't talk to him. "Not that I mind talking to CSIS," Lavrentiyev later declared. "But why did they send a boy?" One can doubt, however, that he would have been more forthcoming with Methuselah.

The military information service GRU, like the KGB, survived its participation in the ill-fated three-day putsch against Mikhail Gorbachev's government in 1991. It is a hard-line operation that emphatically rejects co-operation with western agencies in the war against terrorism. Nor is it much troubled by the proliferation of weapons of mass destruction. Instead it continues to amass intelligence at an impressive rate. A few years ago Canada identified no fewer than nine of its agents, in diplomatic or corporate guise, industriously gathering data on NATO and the United States. Their favoured method was cyber-attacks on government information systems, though they were not above the old-fashioned recruiting of sensitively placed government employees.

Canada is, for the Russians, an easier target than the United States or Great Britain. That is an inference based on the fact that Pentagon officials, in restricting our access to cruise missile research, have been known to compare Canada's military security to a kitchen strainer.

Whichever agency they work for, today's Russian agents continue to seek out local informers and turncoats, which, in the craft's jargon, are described as HUMINT (human-sourced intelligence). Cold War–style cover identities are once again fashionable, ranging from the slovenly journalist to the stylish commercial delegate. Others impersonate the harried translators at the International Civil Aviation Organization in Montreal. Still others, such as Paul William Hampel, take up residence disguised as everyday Canadians. They don't wear a costume as such, but they are usually concealed behind somebody else's birth certificate.

Since the advent of the Internet, electronic information gathering (SIGINT, or Signals Intelligence) has become nearly as important as HUMINT. Like the Americans' ECHELON network, the Russian listening systems, usually concealed in their embassies, draw down so much power as to tax the local electrical services. In friendly countries like Cuba they are openly installed in rented premises. The Russian electronic systems are designed to pick up the chitchat of bureaucrats and diplomats, which is often not even encrypted. But they also snoop indiscriminately.

Modernization has affected these operations. After becoming president of Russia, Vladimir Putin shut down the huge electronic listening post in the town of Lourdes, near Havana. The Cuban government was outraged, since it relied on the annual $200 million rental fee the station had commanded. Putin had decided that the money was better spent on spy satellites.

But most of these antennae are still active and still aimed principally at North America. They try to pick up industrial information, whether of a civil or a military nature. They are also still useful for monitoring diplomatic activity. In some cases they have learned the position of the Canadian government on international issues well before most of its employees knew it. The listening posts' most notorious success involved a Belgian-Canadian communications satellite that relayed telephone and telecopier messages around the world. This kept the Russian Federation fully briefed on every detail of NATO activities.

Even as a newly invigorated Russia ramped up its espionage program, CSIS's counter-intelligence budget was reduced to less than 44 percent of its overall expenditures. Bureaus in the former Soviet satellite nations were closed, apart from the one in Albania. The Chinese bureau struggled along, developing a reputation as a graveyard for employees on their way out.

This was especially galling at a time when the number of Chinese diplomats posted in Vancouver, Toronto, and Ottawa had skyrocketed. CSIS was in no position to respond to this development. In a classic example of bumbling political interference, the federal government, frightened by the threat of the 1995 Quebec independence referendum, instead ordered CSIS to devote a portion of its budget to reopening the old Front de libération du Québec (FLQ) surveillance office in Montreal.

By this time—the mid-1990s—the shrinking role of counterespionage could be seen in CSIS's annual public reports, where it was now rarely mentioned. Instead, resources were shifted to counter the new threat of terrorism. These attacks, unleashed by unfamiliar and difficult-to-identify enemies, forced the western security services to re-examine their priorities.

The era of terror began, in Canada, with the planting in 1985 of a bomb on an Air India flight. All the passengers were killed. The event had no connection with East-West rivalry and signalled that, for Canada at least, the era of searching for spies in black coats was over.

A contributing factor in the new "war against terror" was the proliferation of weapons of mass destruction—in particular, nuclear weapons. Pakistan, Iraq, Israel, Iran, India, Libya, and China were all suspected of building nuclear weapons. Monitoring this new threat further depleted the resources once devoted to East-West rivalry.

Finally, to anybody who worked for CSIS, it was apparent that the organization had lost political favour. It had become a favourite target of ambitious politicians who declared it a costly relic of the Cold War, which—as everybody could plainly see!—was over.

Today, a former CSIS officer recalls the thoughtless and unexamined "frenzy" to reduce the service's budget and spend tax dollars on more fashionable priorities. The marginalizing of CSIS was a popular cause in the media and in front of parliamentary committees, to the despair of agents who saw new threats arising—and strongly suspected that the old threats had not gone away.

Such a development is understandable in a country with Canada's unusually peaceful domestic history. There is no Canadian tradition of necessary espionage. Perhaps the only people with strong views on the subject were French Canadians, who had not forgotten the October Crisis of 1970, when hundreds were unjustly imprisoned. This unfortunately left them with a visceral dislike of domestic intelligence activities.

For these reasons, the Canadian government has always refused to celebrate whatever success CSIS may have enjoyed. The French, the Americans, and the British mythologize their secret services. Even the Dutch and the Japanese have a lively domestic tradition of celebrating undercover exploits and denouncing the perfidy of their enemies. Canada has never been part of this tradition.

After the events of September 11, 2001, however, the other countries of the western alliance also turned their backs on the old Cold War template. Overnight most investigative resources were shifted to Osama bin Laden, to the great satisfaction of the growing army of Russian and Chinese undercover agents.

Today, from the Arctic to the Rio Grande, the sealing of borders and airways against terrorist militants has become a costly obsession. The dollars devoted to this project monopolize virtually every agent and every surveillance budget—with the enthusiastic support of voters. They can easily identify with people like themselves who were trapped in the World Trade Center. In the words of a former CSIS agent, the popular feeling now is that it's "better to let a spy slip away than to miss a [terrorist] attack."

Three thousand people work for CSIS. By 2008 only a minority—fewer than 30 percent, though precise figures can't be obtained—were working on counter-espionage. Today, at least half their time is devoted to China alone. This allows near-complete freedom to manoeuvre for Russia, which annually increases the budgets of both its military (GRU) and domestic (SVR) espionage agencies. Other countries go unmonitored, in spite of evidence that their activities are also hostile.

Nothing has escaped the cutbacks. This applies especially to the elite agents assigned to shadow and monitor suspect foreigners. The painful choices that they are forced to make occasionally take on a near-comical air. For example, in Canada these counter-espionage agents no longer work on weekends in the big cities. Wal-Mart is open, but the spies are home watching the game. Not the Great Game: the football game.

Russian agents have an exquisite sensitivity to this kind of situation. For example, they're aware that global positioning technology allows CSIS to monitor the location of their vehicles at any time. But on a Sunday afternoon there isn't a single flesh-and-blood CSIS agent on the streets of Montreal to go and look at the automobiles themselves. So the spies park them in front of a subway station and hop on a train.

The following day the Canadian agents shuffle on down to the office to check out the GPS data. They duly record that a Russian vehicle was parked outside a Metro station all Sunday afternoon. They are well aware that its driver was probably at the other end of the city. But that is no longer their concern.

Raymond Nart, the former number-two of France's DST intelligence agency, has given a good deal of thought to the consequences of reduced counter-espionage. Best known for having recruited the Soviet double agent "Farewell," Nart is familiar with Canada through frequent liaison with our security services. He is best remembered here for his involvement in the Hugh Hambleton affair (Hambleton, an economist at the University of Laval, was eventually exposed as a Soviet mole).

In France, says Nart, "we really fought quite hard against this tendency [to reduce counter-espionage] back in the 1980s." Paris had experienced a number of bloody terrorist attacks at the time, and had at least as much motivation as Canada to shift resources away from Russian agents and into the new fight against extremism. But the DST instead declared that its specialized Cold War staff would remain a high priority. "For example, we were at great pains to keep translators on staff. It's disastrous to demobilize highly trained people."

According to a reliable source, the French were so suspicious of the Russians that they found fresh money to launch a new division devoted to counter-espionage against the old Eastern bloc countries. Located outside Paris, it was given the highest possible priority.

Even so, the war against terrorism has consumed more and more French intelligence resources. Today, counter-terrorism may have taken the upper hand by a 60–40 proportion. But the remaining 40 percent is enough to protect the core of its anti-espionage operations, in Nart's opinion.

What about the situation in Canada? Time will tell whether former CSIS director Jim Judd's concerns (expressed in the 2007–2008 annual report) will be taken seriously, or set aside and ignored: "Espionage dominated the work of security agencies through the 1990s. But its importance did not disappear with [the events of] September 11. Very much the contrary: it has taken on new urgency, continues to evolve, and has become even more aggressive thanks to new technologies."

THE DEFECTORS COME CLEAN

The spectacular arrest of Paul William Hampel, a long-implanted Russian spy, took place at the end of 2006.

Those in the world of espionage who study these matters believe that Hampel's downfall (like the 1996 arrest in Toronto of a Russian couple who masqueraded under the name Lambert) came about through a defector's testimony. Their belief is based on the coincidental fact that Hampel was arrested shortly after the Americans brought Sergei Tretyakov, a highly placed Russian spy posted to the United Nations in New York, to Canada to be interrogated. Tretyakov had defected to U.S. authorities in 2000. During his time in Canada he shared extensive information with CSIS agents. A former CSIS employee who is convinced that Tretyakov fingered Hampel says, "Without these defectors, we weren't worth five cents."

We feel, however, that Hampel was identified by Canada's own spy services after a series of tactical errors by Russian undercover agents here. Once on his trail, they expended considerable effort in identifying him. This involved painstaking sifting and collating of records at Passport Canada, together with examination of the files of the Canada Customs Agency.

The point of the Hampel story is that counter-espionage breakthroughs can occur through hard work, but also through happenstance and good luck. Some years ago, another Russian illegal was identified through nothing more than the alertness of his next-door neighbour. The neighbour found it strange that broadcasts on his FM radio were sometimes interrupted by Russian conversation. CSIS found these "atmospherics" extremely interesting.

There was also the case of an eighty-year-old Montreal woman who had in her youth been involved in the Spanish civil war. This elderly Ibarruri, apparently above suspicion, had lived in Verdun for decades. It was found that she had been spying from the day she arrived in Canada, a feat that she sustained through the final decades of the Soviet Union and into the new era of the Russian Federation. Denounced in 1996 by the same source that helped identify the Lamberts, she spilled the beans with Olympian composure to stupefied CSIS investigators. The old doll, still proclaiming a deep belief in Communism, didn't hold anything back. She was eventually persuaded to retire, after being told that she would not be further troubled out of consideration for her age . . . even if Canadian spies then lost the trail of a suspicious Bulgarian diplomat who lived on the Île des Soeurs in the same part of town. Perhaps it was just a coincidence.

Then there was the traitor Hugh Hambleton. It's said that he was denounced by his wife, after their thousandth marital shouting match came to blows. CSIS called the CIA, which called the DST in Paris. It was a welcome lead for French counter-espionage, which for years had been desperate to identify a spy they knew operated inside NATO. All they had previously possessed was his code name.

This time it really was a Soviet defector, a colonel using the name "Rudi Herrman," who put them on the trail of the mysterious agent. "Hambleton was an extremely important case," recalls Raymond Nart, who arrived in Canada at the end of the 1970s in order to interrogate him. "It was said that he allowed himself to be recruited for no better reason than his father's connection to the Soviet Union." Hambleton was spared prosecution on the grounds that he hadn't spied on Canada itself. But he then committed the misstep of visiting England, on which he had spied, and where he was sentenced to ten years. At his trial he said his proudest moment had been meeting Russian leader Yuri Andropov.

Defectors are in short supply today, mostly because the dream of a better life in the West is not so tantalizing as it once was. Now, when a defection occurs, it's more or less a cash proposition.

Underpaid Russian agents have found a new way of monetizing their know-how. They quit, emigrate, and then sign a publishing contract to write a tell-all memoir.

But it is still dangerous to turn one's back on the Russian secret services. In an earlier day they did not hesitate to eliminate colleagues who became overly talkative. It's no exaggeration to say that once in the KGB, you were in for life, if you liked your life. Rumour has it that the organization even circulated a memorable black-and-white training film that depicted a man strapped to a steel gurney, howling in terror as he was rolled, feet first and ever so slowly, into a crematorium oven. The turncoat's pension plan, so to speak.

The years following the collapse of the Wall and the rise of Boris Yeltsin were a golden age for recruiting double agents. Whether junior or senior, these individuals had made the difficult decision to change sides. Sometimes for family reasons, or because of the unsettling changes in the USSR, or due to the nasty nature of spy agency office politics (especially, one imagines, when located near a crematorium), these were the men and women who bundled secrets under their overcoats and defected to the West.

During this era, however, Canada's appetite for recruiting double agents diminished noticeably.

Gorbachev's arrival in power and his commitment to reforming the Soviet system was deeply troubling to the KGB's Canadian agents. Although the "empire" had long been disintegrating at the edges, from East Germany to Poland—not to mention the loss of Hungary and the humiliating defeat in Afghanistan—hardcore KGB people at the beginning of the 1990s still found it difficult to accept that the end was near. Nervous and frightened and thousands of kilometres from home, they raged against history. Once seen as the inexorable bringer of socialism, their homeland had betrayed them. When not suffering on this high philosophical plane, they also noticed that money was becoming scarce.

Some employees in Russia's Montreal consulate were forced to return home when they could no longer pay the rent in the nearby apartment towers of Boulevard Côte-des-Neiges and Avenue Docteur-Penfield. CSIS agents enjoyed going out to the airport to bid them farewell on the tarmac where their Aeroflot flights awaited. It came to the point where the recently appointed *rezident**, Baturov (replacing his disgraced predecessor Vadim Rubtsov), also turned around and went home because of the unreliable arrival of operating funds.

"The fruit could not have been riper. You could catch it as it fell," complains a former CSIS agent, who at the time identified many "turnable" Russians. But Ottawa did not even wish to hear the names of potential collaborators, going so far as to reject a source as important as Sergei Tretyakov. These political decisions were justified by earlier experiences with fake or planted double agents. Less creditable, however, was the simple desire to economize on the security budget and to downgrade the importance of espionage.

To some extent this reflected Canada's historically nonchalant attitude toward defectors. In 1945, poor Igor Gouzenko had to beg and plead to be taken seriously by the Canadian government. This unimportant cipher clerk at the Russian embassy ultimately proved to possess a tremendous amount of knowledge about Soviet spy networks. But by the 1970s Canada had once again returned to its habitual indifference, allowing Vladimir Vetrov ("Farewell") to slip through our fingers. He supposedly reported to his French controllers that the Royal Canadian Mounted Police's information-gather-

---

* Russian term for head of mission. See Glossary.

ing abilities were very unimpressive. One can understand his attitude, since he had been approached on behalf of the Mounties by
counter-espionage officer Sergeant Gilles Brunet. Brunet, who led a
life of conspicuous consumption, was later revealed to be himself a
KGB mole. He was the only one ever officially identified, yet he was
never prosecuted.

The torment suffered by Mountie agents who took their work
seriously can be felt in the words of a veteran from that period. He
observes: "The thing they kept telling us, and they never stopped
saying it, was that the Russians were ancient history."

While the frustration of exemplary agents is easy to understand,
it is also true that not every would-be defector possessed valuable
information. Less emotional professionals had learned that a few
words over a glass of champagne at some forgettable embassy reception might pry more information out of the *rezident* than a low-
level defector could hope to offer. The head man, not his poorly
groomed enforcers, was the quarry worth pursuing.

Another consideration, not so obvious to outsiders, is that a
defector was no more than a quantity of unverified data in human
form. Herculean labour was necessary to verify his or her information, composed as it usually was of uncertain memories, rumours,
deliberate fabrications, things already known, and outright fantasies.

The decision to more or less entirely abandon defectors, however, had disquieting consequences on the ground. A CSIS observation post near a Russian consulate was, by the end of the 1990s,
completely empty at nighttimes and during the weekends. Reports
written by agents conducting surveillance on the Russian embassy
itself went unread.

Many of the agents interviewed during research for this book are bitter about their experiences. They frequently describe their overseers as floundering and amateurish, motivated by little but careerism and whatever incidental benefits might arise through their position. One notoriously alcoholic operational chief took home classified files in the saddlebag of his bicycle. Predictably he took a tumble and they slid across the street.

This story was repeated not for its own sake, but rather in the context of concerns about the penetration of CSIS by double agents. Why else would an officer take documents out of the office? How many Gilles Brunets had there been? Like Brunet, James Bennett, a one-time head of the counter-espionage department, was forced to resign under a cloud of suspicion. However, he always denied the allegations and was never charged.

Canada was considered by the Russians to be a weak player on the espionage chessboard. The KGB found that generous quantities of cash, together with what it called "operational psychology," were effective in undermining the Canadian system. The Mounties, and later CSIS, were particular priorities. The KGB wanted to know what the Canadian services knew and the methods they used for investigations. As one ex-spy put it, a spy agency's first target is always the other side's spies, "who are supposed to know everything about you."

Every western intelligence agency at one time or another came under attack from double agents, most particularly Russians, though other nations were also involved. The United States, which took the matter seriously, arrested the CIA's Aldrich Ames in 1994 and the FBI's Robert Philip Hanssen in 2001. Four years after Hanssen's arrest, a senior U.S. intelligence official was quoted in *Time* magazine suggesting that other Russian moles were still carrying on clandestine activities. This he had surmised, he confided, because there were still too many strange and unexplained things taking place.

Former CSIS people spoke to us in similar terms, telling of the sudden disappearance of people who were being shadowed, or people under suspicion who acted as if they knew they had been exposed, and similar occurrences. Some may say that it is paranoid to assume such activities occur in Canada, given the smaller number of high-level arrests here. Realists might reply that we don't arrest many moles because we don't try very hard to find them.

By the end of the 1980s, a Concordia University student, originally from the Indian subcontinent, applied to join CSIS. He was found, after a polygraph test, to be a Soviet mole. His controller went by the initial R. Some years later, a junior employee in the service was surprised in the act of rummaging through files outside of his operational area. Though fired, he escaped prosecution for lack of evidence. Two other apprentice agents were caught red-handed in similar activity during the same period.

And, while it doesn't prove anything, CSIS personnel still wonder if undiscovered moles were responsible for the ability of one *rezident*, from Soviet military intelligence, to demonstrate a continuing awareness of when he was being followed and who was shadowing him. Nothing else in the activity of this Far-From-Perfect Spy was remotely as impressive.

THE MAN WITH THE SILK SOCKS

Our greatest failure concerns Sergei Tretyakov, who was code-named "Comrade Jean." This is the same Tretyakov who later defected from the United Nations in New York. In the early 1990s, before his service in New York, he was sent to replace Leonid Ivanovich Ponomarenko ("Comrade Pietr") as head of KGB operations in Ottawa. However, Tretyakov was not given complete authority right away: he was named acting head of operations, for a time sharing the function with Vladimir Lavrentiyev. Lavrentiyev, officially described as a mere security officer in the embassy, was described by Canadian agents as an intimidating, argumentative, and arrogant individual. After investigation he was identified as a spy by both the RCMP and CSIS.

From the pinnacle of his six feet, two inches, Comrade Jean (Tretyakov) looked out on the world with a brutish expression, owing to his alarming gaze and, more particularly, to the fact that his facial features appeared to have been carved with a dull knife. Nevertheless, he could be a charming if self-centred companion. He was lazily elegant, invariably showing off long silk socks and speaking eloquently in both French and English. His wife, Helen, was equally impressive and worldly. Tretyakov was a graduate of the Foreign Language Institute in Moscow and had profited from a long stay in France during the 1980s, under cover of being an exchange student.

His specialty was the recruiting of what were called "involuntary" (that is, unaware) informers. He befriended intellectuals, bureaucrats, and scientists, together with members of peace groups, disarmament lobbyists, and other believers in a woolly-minded dream of Soviet-Canadian friendship. In this respect Tretyakov was in the tradition of manipulating what the Russians called, in a phrase attributed to Lenin, "useful idiots." Westerners who felt that our military secrets should be delivered to a disadvantaged Russia in the name of fair play were especially prized.

At a later date the Chinese security services also made use of this technique when political fashion delivered a crop of "China groupies." The phrase described well-educated westerners with a profound naïveté about what was really taking place in that country. Chinese agents hunted for them in various political networks, in particular those of benevolent groups that "twinned" Canadian individuals or organizations with their Chinese counterparts.[3] Even the Confucian Institutes were transformed into key institutions for projecting soft power.

Comrade Jean, from the moment of his arrival in the national capital, expressed a lively interest in plans for the aging fleet of Canadian submarines. Tretyakov was not particularly interested in their antique propulsion systems, apart from a dutiful desire to know who might wish to purchase them from us. His real interest was in the submarines that Canada planned to acquire, in particular their technical specifications and strategic capabilities. He knew that we intended to purchase from European contractors. His objective was to obtain technical specifications so that the SVR could pass them on to Russian naval authorities. They, in turn, would design detection systems capable of monitoring the run-silent-run-deep movements of these vessels.

A secondary interest for Tretyakov was to know the capabilities of Canada's military surveillance system in the far north, particularly in the coveted and strategic Northwest Passage.* It was not surprising that the Russians wished to know this. But it was surprising—and proof of his influence—that a KGB-SVR man like Tretyakov had been assigned the dossier, which properly belonged to GRU, the military espionage branch.

---

* This demonstrates Russian interest in a region of vast energy resources. Seventeen years later it would be long-distance Tupolev TU-95 bombers caught penetrating Canadian air space. The two countries sent out more than 20 interception missions against them in 2006 and 2007. In the summer of 2007, Vladimir Putin ordered the resumption of systematic patrols by bomber aircraft in this strategic zone. This was a practice not seen since the Cold War.

It's the old game of two roosters sticking out their chests at each other. Once it gets started, anything can happen. The day before newly elected President Obama's first visit to Ottawa, in February 2009, two Russian Tupolev-95 bombers were intercepted by Canadian F-18 fighters while trespassing in Canadian air space. Just a routine flight, insisted the Russians, who went on to denounce "Russia bashing" and a return of the Cold War mentality.

Tretyakov was a diplomat's son who had grown up in the world of espionage. His life was a comfortable one, but he belonged to a group of sophisticated agents who felt that the chaotic Russia of the post-Communist era had little to offer them. Its economy was obsolete and uncompetitive, while its republics struggled with unending low-level civil wars. Nor could he have failed to notice that thousands of agents much like himself had been dismissed from the service without notice.

It is only realistic to acknowledge that potential defectors like Tretyakov were by and large mere opportunists. They were terrified of losing a job that offered a good deal of status and privilege in the impoverished Russia that existed after the fall of the Soviet system. Their life in Ottawa was clearly more agreeable than the life they could hope for at home. While this was obvious in terms of creature comforts, the Russians also enjoyed Canada for less obvious reasons. For example, groups of Russian agents made a habit—in the lull between spy operations—of setting out on the Ottawa River to fish for sturgeon. There, right behind the Parliament Buildings, was a staggeringly rich fishing ground of which Canadians seemed, as they did in so many matters, to be completely unconscious. If the comrades happened to hook a female sturgeon they returned to the embassy in raucous good spirits. There they dined on fresh caviar, washed down with generous lashings of vodka.

When contemplating Boris Yeltsin, Russia's new leader, Tretyakov could not help but be aware of the great man's contempt for the SVR. Yeltsin did not hesitate to describe its dispatches as "shit."[4] Returning the favour, Tretyakov concluded that Yeltsin was little more than an alcoholic propped up by a well-organized group of oligarchs. These boyars were slicing Russia into little pieces for their personal consumption.

Finally, on a personal level, Tretyakov had to contend with the bureaucrat who had been sent by the SVR's high command (the so-called "Centre") to replace Ponomarenko. This individual set himself up as a sort of imperial envoy in Ottawa's Russian community. Tretyakov, marginalized and very angry, began to signal CSIS agents that he had no desire to return to Russia. The message was immediately relayed to head office.

The answer from CSIS headquarters was no. Categorically nyet. There were no resources to process yet another defector. There was nobody available to debrief him, nobody to parse his statements word by word, nobody to investigate and verify, and certainly nobody to organize the costly and obligatory jaunt that would show him off to the English, French, and American espionage services.

It was a bad moment for Tretyakov. And it was soon made worse by Anatoli Gayduk, a SVR operative from Line X who had worked in the commercial bureau of the embassy on Wurtemburg Street in Ottawa. Gayduk defected. His terms were $1 million for the documents he had conscientiously copied on his daily visits to the *rezidentura* concealed within the fortress-like Russian embassy. Gayduk's code name was Poppy, and Poppy dribbled lovely black juice. But the juice was costly to process. Moreover, CSIS could not pass him on to the Mounties because the Mounties had already turned him down.

Before the Gayduk affair became too troublesome Tretyakov was lifted out of the Canadian morass and transferred to the Russian mission at the United Nations headquarters in New York. In 1995 he became part of its well-known espionage operation. On paper, his title was first secretary in charge of media and communications, but in fact he was joint *resident* of the domestic intelligence service, the SVR. In this capacity he was the controller of a swarm of Russian moles masquerading as diplomats and journalists. He also managed a substantial number of United Nations employees who were feeding information to the Russian secret service.

Tretyakov's office was located on the eighth floor of the Russian mission, in a windowless bunker that was supported on shock absorbers and equipped with walls that vibrated in order to frustrate listening devices. To enter this sanctuary you needed a special coin or ring. This activated a mechanism permitting entry into an empty chamber that served as a vestibule. Since there's no such thing as being too careful, even a visitor with the magic ring was obliged to remove his coat, his telephone, his digital recorder, and anything else electronic. Anything that could potentially record or transmit.

This concealed espionage department contained twelve offices, one for each "line" of espionage, together with an archives room.

The man with the silk socks was ordered to monitor foreign missions at the United Nations, especially those of the United States, China, France, and other countries of interest. Deploying the wiles he had developed in Ottawa, Tretyakov became a fixture at events involving the Russian community. He moved easily in the political, academic, and financial worlds of New York.

He also had a new role: spreading disinformation. Armed with anti-American propaganda, together with information sheets containing distorted and partisan views about issues of concern to the Russian Federation (such as the war in Chechnya), he made certain that the American media were well aware of the views manufactured by the SVR's propaganda arm back home. Depending on the issue at hand, he also made certain that appropriate material was forwarded to advocacy groups such as environmental organizations. This material, much subtler and more professionally edited than the clumsy propaganda of the past, came from the same modernized SVR that had created and inflated the infatuation with Gorbachev.

By 1997, with economic chaos mounting in Russia, Tretyakov once again toyed with the idea of treason. This time he had better luck: the Americans accepted him as a double agent. He surreptitiously began to send documents to U.S. authorities. By the time he was done he had passed on as many as five thousand files, from telegrams to lengthy reports.

Then, one panicky day in October of 2000, Tretyakov abandoned his official apartment in the Bronx, together with his wife, his daughter, and their grossly overweight white Persian cat Matilda. He knocked at the door of the U.S. authorities.

Within a short time he had turned over the names of agents and contacts in both the United States and Canada. These contained, according to sources, the profile of a double agent who had been operating inside the FBI for fifteen years, Robert Philip Hanssen (though Tretyakov himself has since denied this).*

Two months later, after his defection, Tretyakov was followed by Yevgeny Toropov, the first secretary of the Russian embassy in Ottawa. Toropov was, of course, yet another security agent. He was immediately whisked into the arms of the American authorities.

In exchange for his collaboration, Tretyakov (who, to the great amusement of his interrogators, claimed he had acted out of conviction and not for lucre) pocketed a sum estimated at several million dollars. This allowed him and his wife to lead a princely life on the proceeds of their investments. They bought a superb mansion, in which the Persian cat dined well. In the garage was a Porsche Boxster and an oversized Lexus SUV. It was the American dream, delivered on a silver platter. Unhappy memories of brown coal smoke and broken-down Ladas were banished forever.

---

* Hanssen spent twenty-five years working for the Soviets and later the Russians. He delivered tonnes of confidential information, above all the names of double agents who were subsequently executed. Arrested in 2001, he served a life sentence in a maximum-security penitentiary.

It was quite a change from the miserly payouts offered to defectors back in the 1980s. Think of poor "Farewell," Vladimir Vetrov. Back then, in exchange for three thousand pages of ultra-secret documents concerning KGB spy technology, he received in sum total 150,000 French francs ($35,000 Canadian) and a fake fur coat for his mistress. For this he also threw in a list of 250 Soviet agents posted to various world capitals.

Vetrov certainly didn't get good value for his merchandise. But others did worse. During the same period, Major-General Dmitri Poliakov, the GRU *rezident* in New York, traded twenty-five years of collaboration with the CIA and the FBI for a collectible historic rifle and a set of gardening tools.[5] Perhaps he consoled himself with his code names: "Bourbon" and "Tophat." They at least had an aristocratic air.*

In 2007 Tretyakov's story was published in Pete Earley's book *Comrade J*, in which he energetically declared that Moscow had infiltrated Parliament Hill in Ottawa.[6] This account included the astonishing allegation that an anti-Communist Conservative member of Parliament had been recruited in 1992 because he was short of money for his election campaign. The officer of the KR line who claimed to have recruited him was Vitali Domoratski, officially a Russian diplomat to the Canadian government. "Grey" (the code name for the member of Parliament) was alleged to have been paid approximately $10,000 in $100 bills during a secret rendezvous in Ottawa's Gatineau Park. The M.P.'s name was revealed in Earley's book. He denied all allegations.

The book also claimed the successful recruiting of five other Canadians in Ottawa. These were described using their code names: Arthur (a nuclear weapons authority), Ilya, Semion, Lazar, and

---

* Poliakov was executed in 1988 for espionage after being denounced by Aldrich Ames, the KGB mole within the CIA.

Kirill. Three of these allegedly worked for a think-tank, founded in 1983, called Le Centre Canadien pour le Contrôle des Armements et le Désarmement. It has since changed its name.

Comrade J enumerated more than a hundred other informal sources within the political, media, and diplomatic communities. Those who monitored Tretyakov's activities at the time, however, are very skeptical about the length of the list. They forget, perhaps, that having an informal Canadian "source" or a "contact" is not the same thing as recruiting a Canadian to become a Russian agent.

Finally, Comrade Tretyakov boasted of his ability to manipulate the United Nations' "Oil for Food" program in Iraq. Intended to relieve the distress of civilians at a time of widespread sanctions against Saddam Hussein's dictatorship, the program, Tretyakov alleged, had been easily undermined. He had diverted a good part of its budget to Russia.

Curiously, he didn't say a word about his activities in recruiting Canadian agents. But his many other accusations certainly provoked a reaction. Within CSIS, the book was dismissed as "bullshit." James Warren, a deputy director of the agency at the time, described it as mere fantasy. Russia's SVR, using its own particular rhetoric, described it as "self-promotion supported by treason."

We tried to find out what happened to the four sources cited by Tretyakov when Earley's book was published. Had they at least been identified and questioned? Did they even exist? CSIS refused then, and continues to refuse, any comment on the subject.

Tretyakov himself replied to our inquiries with a sarcastic message asserting that he had never tried to defect during his time in Canada.

> I have never approached any Canadian official with [personal] complaints or concerns. Why? First, and obviously,

because Canada is an insignificant country. It's a lovely peace-loving place with remarkable scenery. Moreover, it has always been my policy to take action rather than complain. Had I wished to defect [while in] Canada ... I would have gone straight to the American embassy. Without talking to a single Canadian. Throughout my entire career I have never been approached by an official of any government. Nobody has tried to recruit me. And I'm fairly certain that Canadian authorities have neither the audacity nor the know-how to do such a thing.

I'd like Canadians to be aware of what Russia's spies have achieved in their country, and how the Canadian authorities were not able to lift a little finger to stop it. I'm very fond of the people of Canada, and I'd like to offer them some advice: Don't mess around with Russians who know what they're doing.

Tretyakov has a selective memory. He appears to have forgotten the note, scratched in his own handwriting with blue ink, that lists his personal and work telephone numbers on the back of a Canadian secret agent's business card. Perhaps by now somebody has reminded him. In any case, one of these "please call me" numbers is still legible. It's the phone number of the embassy of the Russian Federation on Charlotte Street in Ottawa.

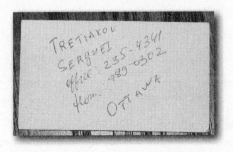

There's always a Canadian, whether code-named "Arthur" or something else, who is ready to sell himself to the Tretyakovs of the espionage world. They'll do it out of greed, naïveté, or simple stupid-
ity. Two years after Tretyakov's defection in 2002, a Russian military
attaché, suspected of spying for the GRU under diplomatic cover,
was ejected from Canada by the Department of External Affairs.
Moscow acquiesced without making an issue of it.

The diplomat in question, Vladimir Androsov, had been very
busy during his brief posting in the nation's capital. His assignment:
to procure classified information about Canada's national defence.
His method: to attempt to corrupt a highly placed Canadian official.
If accomplished, at the cost of many thousands of dollars, he could
achieve access to the information his employers needed. His tradecraft
was impeccable. He usually managed to evade his shadowers, and he
never approached an informant except after painstaking preparation.

CSIS shut him down just before his intended informant
could slip him a CD-ROM containing the agreed-on information.
Androsov was able to leave the country, presumably to undertake
further adventures. His informer was not punished. As seems to be
customary, he was quietly shifted to a job where no damage could
be done.[7]

A similar affair came to light in Austria in 2007. On June 11 of that
year a fiftyish Russian, Vladimir V. employed by his country's space
agency (RKA), was arrested in Salzburg under suspicion of being
an agent of the GRU. His local contact, an air force officer assigned
to a combat helicopter unit, was also detained. Harald S. had care-
lessly spent far more money than could be provided by an Austrian
air force salary. He had sold himself, it emerged, for $35,000, agree-
ing to steal design information on Eurocopter's cutting-edge battle
copter, the "Tiger." It was a joint French-German project, making
the leak highly awkward for the Austrian government.

Androsov unfortunately walked free. He had been jailed for as long as possible before his diplomatic immunity worked its magic. During this time he confessed nothing.

His expulsion meant that he couldn't honour his commitment to attend an upcoming NATO conference on the peaceful use of outer space. This makes an amusing anecdote, but it has a less amusing side. We learned that ten days before his arrest this GRU spy had also helped to host a Moscow conference jointly organized by the Department of Foreign Affairs and International Trade (DFAIT) and Russia's International Centre for Science and Technology. Its theme was Russian-Canadian co-operation in the aerospace industry. The light-fingered Russian agent had socialized at leisure with senior people from Pratt & Whitney and the National Research Council. We don't know whether CSIS's Moscow agent was aware of the situation.

Tretyakov's is far from the only story of a would-be defector who was refused by Canadian authorities. A number of Soviet citizens attempted the same thing, and encountered the same indifference.

One of them was Alexandr Alexandrovich Fedoseyev, a GRU colonel with a background in science and technology. Posted to Ottawa, he could have been an important catch. His motive for treason was humanly understandable and unusually urgent. His granddaughter had been gravely injured in a Moscow car crash and he was convinced that she might live if she could be brought to a Canadian hospital.

One day he approached a CSIS agent with the question: "What do you think you can do for me?"

"That's up to you," replied the agent, using the customary badinage that let the other know he understood perfectly well what was going on.

As usual after a first contact, a report went to CSIS headquarters in Ottawa. A staff psychologist sifted through Fedoseyev's file with particular attention to his past career. Apart from his granddaughter's plight, they sought any other possible motivation for his decision to contact Canadian intelligence.

Months dragged by. Finally, when news reached headquarters that Fedoseyev and his family had purchased Aeroflot tickets to return home, CSIS roused itself. An order to approach him at Mirabel Airport was sent out. But on that fateful day Fedoseyev was not alone at the airport. When the CSIS agent approached, hand extended in welcome, the Russian signalled with frosty politeness that it was too late.

"Thank you so much," he said, rolling his baggage wagon ahead of him in order to fend off the unwelcome handshake. The agent understood by this that he was not to embarrass Fedoseyev in front of his watchful escort.

One target that CSIS did attempt to approach was the secretary of the KGB's powerful Ottawa *rezident* Leonid Ponomarenko. Here again they missed their chance.

Same thing with a GRU agent in the embassy whose delicate task was to manage Russians illegally present in Canada. This one was approached while he and his wife navigated through the international zone of Mirabel Airport. But the man's boss, Alexandr Kozhurin, hovered nearby and prevented the contact from taking place. Rumour has it that Kozhurin wouldn't take the agent and his wife to the airport unless they paid for the gasoline, suggesting that the gentleman was already under suspicion. He had in fact vainly tried to arouse CSIS's interest, and left Canada with tears in his eyes.

In Canada's defence, it must be noted that other countries sometimes adopted the same bizarre indifference toward would-be defectors. In 1992, by way of example, a KBG archivist named Vassili

Mitrokhine fled to the Latvian capital of Riga in order to throw himself on the mercy of the Central Intelligence Agency. He was given the bum's rush, on the grounds that he was too junior an employee to be of any use. Mitrokhine, however, had admirable self-possession— and a better understanding of his value. He took himself off to the British embassy, where MI-6 put him on the next flight to England.

Rémy Pautrat was the director of the intelligence agency DST before French Prime Minister Michel Rocard asked him to take charge of his personal security in 1989. He recalls the "tidal wave of defectors" that overwhelmed French intelligence after the fall of the Berlin Wall:

> In the Aeronautics Hall at Le Bourget Airport [the Paris
> site of an important aerospace show] we couldn't find
> enough agents to debrief the defectors. . . . It was clear,
> of course, that most of them were looking for money.
> Whether spies or high-level scientists, they had noticed
> that [back home in Russia] just about everybody was
> looking for a way out of the country. There was simply
> no personal fear any more. It has to be said, though,
> that many of them were haunted by the thought that
> the Russian nation itself might collapse.

Some of our recruitment efforts did succeed. But these defectors were then interrogated in a manner that should leave Canadians ashamed. Consider the case of "Citizen X," a low-level employee of Aeroflot. The airline was known, as we have seen, to conceal spies among its legitimate employees. Citizen X was therefore invited to join a CSIS agent on a fishing trip, where he was persuaded to change loyalties and turn over valuable information on Aeroflot's station master in Canada, Yuri Gorodnichev. As agreed, he spent some time compiling a methodical photographic record of Aeroflot activities. After a short stay in an Eastern Townships safe house where defectors were interviewed, he was moved to a secure facility thousands of kilometres away for further interrogation. For many weeks he underwent an exhausting debriefing.

During this time, certain agents adopted a clumsy (and, we might say, dim-witted) attitude toward Citizen X. They decided, for whatever reason, to treat him as a prisoner of war. A retired agent who was unable to prevent the abuse recalls his colleagues throwing money in Citizen X's face when he reminded them that he had been promised funds to start a new life in Canada.

Citizen X had made it crystal clear from the beginning that he had always earned his living and could not bear the thought of living on government handouts. He wanted a job in Canada, and a job was promised. But when the interrogation was over he was thrown into the street without employment.

Soon Citizen X became clinically depressed. Why did his interrogators not see this coming? The obvious answer is that they failed to understand the pride of defectors like Citizen X. These men and women did not see themselves as traitors. They wished to transfer their loyalty to a country they had come to respect. Instead, they were squeezed like lemons and tossed into the garbage.

A WELCOMING FIRE

To err is human, says the poet. And the world industriously proves him right day after day. This was particularly evident on the morning that Montreal's Soviet consulate caught fire: January 14, 1987. The senior people at the consulate, including the *rezident* himself, made a splendid display of human error.

If forgiveness is divine, though, there wasn't much available to the Soviets that day. Despite the consular staff's best efforts, Canadian agents greedily watching the cooling embers were able to harvest a bumper crop of intelligence. The events that led to this outcome have passed into the annals of western intelligence history.

It was, in fact, one of the few espionage-related events in Canada to inspire briefings and conferences around the world. British and American agents made pilgrimages to Montreal to gaze upon the spot.

"That fire represents the secret dream of every secret service," chortled France's Raymond Nart. Twenty years later, the consulate fire is perhaps the only case on record in which western agents rummaged in comfort through a mountain of Soviet files and artifacts without fear of being disturbed.

It was around ten minutes to eleven that Wednesday morning that residents of Avenue du Musée, which climbs the flank of Mont Royal, looked up the hill in some surprise. A throng of Russians had burst out of the consulate building, tripping over each other while shouting loudly. Some waved fire extinguishers while others carried lengths of garden hose. Still others hurriedly dipped plastic buckets into the snow.

Within moments a thick blanket of smoke was belching from the second- and third-floor windows of the venerable limestone building, which had stood since 1911. The conflagration, which had begun with an electrical short in the basement, rapidly climbed through the upper storeys of the building before bursting through the snowy roof.

The Russian staff did not call the fire department. They were determined that no outsider should enter the burning building. Instead, they tried to control the fire with the puny means at their disposal, all the while surely knowing that it was hopeless.

One particular group of neighbours was fascinated by the surreal spectacle: CSIS agents observing the scene from their nearby hidey-hole. Concealed in a ten-storey apartment building across from the consulate, they had a peerless view of the Soviet staff as they swarmed about the scene during the following days and nights. They recorded every movement of staff members as well as visitors, jotting down the licence number of every vehicle known to be associated with the consulate. Wielding flashlights, they took special care to record the mileage on the odometers of the cars that brought in additional people to guard the site during the night.

Whenever CSIS's watchers on Avenue du Musée needed to be in touch with their colleagues who were shadowing the Soviets on foot, they had to make use of a secure phone. This was decidedly inconvenient. For security reasons, it was hidden in a metal box bolted to the stone wall of the Grey Sisters' convent a kilometre away.

The ruined heritage building had concealed much, much more than one would find in a typical Soviet consulate. Within its three-storey limestone walls, together with a trio of attached buildings—the entire compound purchased in 1970—was located one of the KGB's (and the GRU's) largest operating bases on the North American continent.* Immediately to its north, Avenue du Musée came to a dead end, meaning that any pedestrian who ventured close to the building, whether working for one side or the other, became a person of interest. No stranger had a plausible reason to be loitering nearby. Overlooking the consulate, and accessible only via a steep stairway leading upward to Avenue des Pins, was Pierre Elliott Trudeau's spectacular art deco mansion (now an historic monument). It was an enviable redoubt. The Russians are still there today.

Opposite Avenue du Musée, at the corner of Avenue Docteur-Penfield, is the Molson mansion. It was the home of lower-ranking

* The final Soviet property acquired on this street was purchased in 1985 for $2 million in cash.

consulate employees, together with a certain number of Aeroflot crew members. Some of these junior employees also lived inside the consulate enclave, under the close surveillance of a security officer from the KR Line.

The consulate staff was enormous, especially when one added to the members of the diplomatic corps the many chauffeurs and cipher clerks. Once a medium-sized operation, as diplomatic posts go, it had become very large indeed.[8] Routine duties were overshadowed by the resources devoted to espionage (as appears to be the case again today). At five thousand square metres, it was far larger than any consulate needed to be—particularly one located in an unprepossessing Canadian city.

Within the consulate were at least sixteen employees with full diplomatic status—a remarkable two-thirds of the number enjoying similar status at the Soviet embassy in Ottawa. That winter, at least seven of these supposed diplomats, consuls, and vice-consuls were registered as belonging to the protocol service—far more than it actually required.

The other institution that sheltered a significant number of spies was the Soviet commercial mission in East Montreal, located at 4368–4370 Boulevard Pie-IX near the Olympic stadium. At all times both the GRU and the KGB (later SVR) maintained an agent there. At the beginning of his illustrious career, it was the home of Vladimir Vetrov, alias "Farewell."

During the Cold War the agents of the commercial mission were assigned a wide range of duties. They had to monitor Canadian activity in fields as diverse as aerospace, pharmaceuticals, electronics, computer products, and of course military research. Among the many domestic corporations involved in these various businesses, the Russians focused their attention on three in particular: Canadair; Paramax, which designed operating systems for Canadian military frigates and later became Lockheed Martin Canada; and CAE, which manufactured flight simulators for the civil and military market. A fourth company receiving nearly as much attention was Canadian Marconi, a builder of systems for navigation, surveillance, and tactical communications, as well as radar.

And of course they watched CSIS.

A final but compelling advantage of having this operation in Montreal was the city's proximity to the United States. It was seen as a safe rear base for agents dispatched to American destinations. More than that, the Soviet consulate provided the perfect location for an ultra-sophisticated system for intercepting radio and electronic communications. For that reason, Yuri Andropov, when he was director of the KGB, approved the costly undertaking. Only fourteen other cities in the world boasted such Russian facilities. These were New York, Washington, Paris, Rome, Teheran, Beijing, London, Belgrade, Mexico City, Athens, Bonn, Salzburg, Reyjkavik, and Tokyo. All were built on a single order given by Andropov in the spring of 1970.[9]

This powerful yet invisible listening post captured countless thousands of coded messages and ultra-confidential telephone conversations between the president of the United States and members of his administration.

As soon as they saw the smoke, the CSIS men in their post across the street ran to the secure phone and contacted CI-1, the group in charge of consulate surveillance. CI-1 was a CSIS regional office located inside RCMP headquarters at 4225 Dorchester Boulevard in

Westmount.* It was responsible for monitoring all Soviet activities. Since CSIS's regional office in Montreal was not yet built at this early date, CI-1 was obliged to borrow space from the Mounties.

Given that CSIS was still a young agency, this was a tremendous opportunity for its newly minted spies to get a close look at what was going on inside the consulate's walls. It was, in fact, an opportunity unlikely to occur again during their careers.

Unhappily, their enthusiasm was not shared by their boss, Gilles C. As head of the Soviet Consular Desk, he, at least initially, took a relaxed view of the situation. The fire had inconveniently broken out in the late morning and he hadn't yet had breakfast. Plenty of time to alert his superiors later on. The anxious surveillance people, hopping from one foot to the other in their hurry to get to Avenue du Musée, were furious.

"Get back to me when the fire burns out," he said, imperturbably, to his dumbstruck staff.

This didn't go down well with Joe M., the head of Special Operations. Disregarding the boss, he ordered his best men to proceed immediately to the disaster site. These included skilful trackers and shadowers who were instructed to lose themselves in the growing crowd of bystanders, cops, journalists, and firefighters. They were discreetly to photograph everything photographable and write down whatever wasn't.

An hour later, things weren't going well at Avenue du Musée. Hundreds of firefighters stood helplessly on the sidewalk, like so many storks in a swamp. They had been called by local residents, of course, and not the Soviets themselves. Now the firefighters had learned that the blazing building was not, technically, located on Canadian soil. Alexandre Yereskovski, the consul general, possessed

---

* Together with CI-2, it was in charge of the USSR's satellite countries.

consular and diplomatic immunity sufficient to prevent them from setting foot on the property.* They could not even fight the blaze from ladders hovering above the ground. Yves Bineau, the fire chief, shared his frustration with journalists: "We're really not used to standing around watching a building burn down."

A strange dance was underway inside the consulate. While some employees fought the flames with fire extinguishers, others flung armloads of secret documents into the blaze. Boxes and filing cabinets were hustled out the back door and crammed into the trunks of cars in the private parking lot. Some personnel, together with their families, were seen calmly letting themselves into a nearby house, where their children attended school during the daytime.

Fifteen minutes of strained negotiations between the fire chief and consular authorities took place before the firefighters were at last able to attack the flames. But new difficulties awaited them. While breaking windows in order to insert fire hoses, they discovered that one had been bricked up on the inside. And once inside the building they found themselves surrounded by security guards who firmly informed them that, no, they couldn't go through this door or that door, but maybe they could use the door over there. Several firefighters found themselves in a secret tunnel that didn't show up on the building plans.

By sunset the consulate had been reduced to four scorched and blackened walls. Heaped up inside and out were tonnes of plaster and still-smoking debris. According to Soviet practice, the

---

* As a historical footnote, Yereskovski's wife was carrying on an affair with KGB Colonel Vitaly Yurchenko. Yurchenko defected to the CIA in August 1985. Four months later, he rejoined the KGB under improbable circumstances (claiming he had been drugged and locked up by the CIA). The real reason was that his mistress didn't want to live in America.

debris should have been loaded as soon as possible into dumpsters by cleanup teams sent specially from Russia. Once lifted aboard a Russian ship, the containers would be carried far out into the Atlantic Ocean and dumped overboard. Against all expectations, however, Montreal's KGB station chief, Boris Lumpov, decided to have the debris hauled to local landfill sites. It was an inexplicable error in judgment from an experienced officer with a chestful of medals.

As the situation, and the opportunities it presented, became clearer, CSIS's special operations staff in Montreal urgently petitioned Ottawa headquarters for extra resources. They had come up with a plan for getting the debris off the consulate property and into their laboratories.

Headquarters brusquely turned them down. Persisting, they were refused again. The reasoning of the great minds upstairs came down to this: that anything valuable had either been spirited away and concealed elsewhere, or else it had been destroyed in the fire. These were assumptions, of course.

THE INCREDIBLE "OPERATION F"

The investigators on the ground in Montreal understood the difference between facts and assumptions. On their own initiative, they decided to do some dumpster diving. "Operation F" (for "fire") was underway.

There are two contradictory accounts of what happened next. According to one—the one made public at the time—eighteen dumpsters loaded with broken limestone and blackened lumber were eventually emptied by the Russians into a clandestine landfill located on Mohawk territory at Kahnawake.[10] This is where CSIS teams supposedly used teams of sniffer dogs to separate the useless garbage from shredded or carbonized documents that might be of interest. But they learned, to their sorrow, that the clever Communists had thrown them off the trail by sending a number of trucks to other landfills.

The other story is the one that we pieced together from confidential sources. In this version, CSIS agents audaciously disguised themselves as firefighters and emergency cleanup crews. They succeeded in this nighttime pantomime even while the consulate's hyper-alert security staff monitored them closely. Very likely, the CSIS planners hired a number of rough labourers to impersonate dumpster crews: silent men who were paid in cash. A variant on the story suggests that a legitimate industrial cleanup company agreed to do the heavy lifting, again for a premium price and on condition that no questions were asked.

Most of the heavily loaded trucks were directed to a weathertight hangar at Mirabel Airport, near the Turcot freeway interchange, which had been rented by CSIS. But a smaller number of vehicles, whose cargo was thought to be more valuable, drove directly to a laboratory at CSIS headquarters in Ottawa. The senior officers who had initially been so skeptical had changed their minds after receiving Joe M.'s preliminary reports.

The project was managed in the manner of an inquest after an airplane crash. Over the course of the next year a handful of specialists—chemists in particular—reassembled countless puzzle pieces. Reports have it that the laboratory building was stuffed to the ceilings with boxes of documents and heaps of debris. With monkish patience the specialists collated slender strips of shredded paper and glued them back together. They were able to make burnt papers speak again by plastifying them so that they would not crumble when handled. Some of these documents were written in everyday language. Others were in code. The most exacting task was to connect a given document with its author.

Other specialists analyzed traces of various chemicals, as well as reassembling scraps of metal that had been twisted beyond recognition by the heat. By degrees, the wreckage yielded its secrets, and as it did so British and American intelligence services began to demand access to the laboratory. Sniffer dogs from French intelligence worked their way through the debris and identified the odour of a French engineer who had been suspected of collaborating with the Soviets. Already arrested in a spy scandal concerning France's Ariane space rocket, the man was apparently a "walk-in" (or "volunteer" in the jargon of the trade) who had offered his services to the Soviet Union. His name was eventually located in the Montreal consulate's carbonized visitors' book.

CSIS people subsequently flew overseas to share their information with foreign colleagues. It covered a dazzling variety of topics.

For example, specialists had been able to build a life-sized reconstruction of the isolation room that had existed inside the consulate. This "Faraday Cage" blocked any attempt at electronic snooping or magnetic interference from outside the building.

Investigators also identified keys and locks, surveillance and counter-surveillance equipment, and, somewhat mystifyingly, a sophisticated military scuba diver's mask and cartridges (investigators wondered if it had been used to bring an "illegal" into Canada). There were pharmaceutical ingredients, perhaps linked to the sinister Biopreparat operation (more on this later), as well as syringes and related medical bric-a-brac.

In a class of its own was the appointment book of Boris Lumpov, the *rezident*. Its pages were filled with notes about meetings with various "Bob"s and "Dan"s, evidently pseudonyms for people whose real names CSIS would have preferred to know. But it was highly useful nonetheless.

And then there were the operational plans. This is where the names of Canadian moles such as Gilles Brunet came to light. And there were, in addition, long lists of occasional informants who very likely had no idea they had been talking to a Soviet secret agent. These were often well-meaning idealists who thought that a conciliatory attitude toward a Soviet in a restaurant might hasten the end of the Cold War. For them, learning that they had given useful information to a determined enemy was probably punishment enough.

AND IF RUSSIA HAD WON THE WAR . . .

There was worse to come. The sniffer dogs came across evidence of Soviet plans for the population of Canada in the event of a final and total war between East and West. These involved chemical and bacteriological warfare on our territory.

So oblivious were the Soviets to the discoveries made in the rubble of the consulate that, several years after the fire, three specialized agents of the KGB's Line V were still stationed in Canada. Their specialty was assassination, together with sabotage of energy and transportation networks. The great electricity-generating dams of Hydro-Quebec, as well as its sprawling network of high-tension power transmission lines, were on their list of potential Canadian targets. It also included oil pipelines. The list had been prepared a decade before the fire by KGB agents who had been smuggled into Montreal under pretence of working at the Russian pavilion at Expo 67.

One proposed secret plan involved placing deadly chemicals in the city's drinking water system. This helped explain why the Montreal consulate was apparently equipped for chemical and bacteriological warfare. It was also well supplied with the protective clothing its employees would require if they were to carry out such an order and survive.

This is perhaps the place to mention that every *rezidentura* located in the western nations possessed a plan to terrorize the civilian population of the country in which it was located. These were usually described as plans of revenge or reprisal against the West, for unspecified prior acts.[11]

All of this helps to frame an event that took place some time earlier. Agapov, a GRU officer posted to Montreal, had targeted a professor at Macdonald College, a part of McGill University. This man was a renowned microbiologist working in the area of epidemiology. Agapov approached him in the guise of an admirer, pretending to be fascinated by his research and his skill. He dangled the possibility of a generously funded research position in the USSR.

Agapov's real purpose was to learn whether the microbiologist had access to certain biological cultures, and whether he had the authority to remove them from the laboratory. CSIS got wind of this and sent agents to warn the professor about Agapov's real identity. At the same time, of course, they wanted to know what kind of questions the Soviet had been asking. Above all, they wanted to make sure that the Canadian scientist understood the danger of any kind of "collaboration" with the Soviet.

Far from being convinced, the professor was indignant. He demanded that CSIS leave him alone. He took the view that counter-espionage agents were probably spy-obsessed fantasists who were imagining things.

While these events were unfolding, Agapov, the GRU agent, kept in touch with the professor and bit by bit put his cards on the table. During their third meeting he handed the researcher a list of the specific biological cultures that interested him. The man finally understood. Shocked, he called CSIS. When the agents arrived at his office he was as white as a sheet. He said that Agapov had asked for samples of extremely dangerous laboratory cultures. One in particular was potentially capable of killing everybody living within a fifty-kilometre distance of the St. Lawrence River.

It will never be known whether the Soviets intended to use this merchandise during some future conflict in North America, or simply to advance their own research. As for Agapov, the affair went into a file that was already stamped "For Action" and he was soon expelled.

This leads us back to Biopreparat, a biological weapons program started in 1973. Since the USSR had signed a treaty to ban biological weapons less than a year before, it was always publicly described as a routine pharmaceutical research project. It remained one of the best kept secrets of the Cold War. Difficult to track because it was decentralized in a string of laboratories scattered across remote regions of the USSR, Biopreparat was scaled to produce an armoury of fully usable weapons derived from toxins, deadly viruses, and bacteria.

For all the resources devoted to it, this dark program depended on infusions of information from the advanced laboratories of the West. According to Alibekov, the second-in-command at Biopreparat who had defected to the United States, it was the job of the KGB (code-named Capture Agency N1) to steal these toxins and viruses and send the samples back to Biopreparat. Alibekov revealed how agents from the highly secretive Department 12 of Directory S were posted around the planet in order to expedite the business. They used the diplomatic bag from various Soviet embassies and consulates to transport laboratory phials filled with dehydrated germ cells, cultures, and assorted potentially deadly substances that they had acquired from their collaborators. These plague bags travelled in the pilot's cabin of Aeroflot jetliners.

Agents linked to Biopreparat targeted in particular the Defence Research and Development agency at the Canadian Air Force base in Suffield, Alberta. The mandate of this highly classified operation is to create medical treatments and systems of defence against both chemical and biological attack. It was a place entirely fascinating to Soviet authorities, and only a simpleton would imagine that they are any less interested today.

All doubt on the matter has, in any event, been put to rest by another Soviet agent who decided that life in the West might be more congenial. Alexander Kouzminov, a KGB biologist living today in New Zealand, ran the Special Operations section of the agency's Directory S from 1985 to 1995. His mission was to recruit well-qualified Soviet scientists, train them as agents, and then smuggle them under "deep cover" into Canada and the United States. Their final destination was either Suffield, Alberta, or the military research centre at Fort Detrick, Maryland—two biological laboratories working in close concert.

Other agents controlled by Kouzminov made their way to softer targets, such as university laboratories working on early detection of emerging or highly infectious new diseases. His work continued on into the new Russian era, by which time it was focused on obtaining vaccines offering protection against salmonella, clostridium, and bacillus, the latter a rod-shaped bacterium that, among other diseases, causes anthrax. The Russians believed that they needed this protection in case the West used such disease agents against them. But there is ample evidence that they also intended to modify these pathogens in order to increase their resistance to treatment—that is, to use them as offensive agents.

Unhappily, CSIS failed to publicize the Agapov story, as it should have, leaving the country's research centres and their employees in the dark. It still has not done so, though the story is often repeated over a glass of wine in the agency's inner circles. A shame, since the people who need to hear it are the country's medical researchers. They are a prime target for today's new breed of technological spy.

Not too long ago, should anybody think the Biopreparat story a relic of another era, the British security agency MI-6 caught Russian spies lurking near a biological research centre. Their objective was to steal ampoules containing anthrax and ebola virus.

That was in 2007.

A WAVE OF EXPULSIONS

The intelligence revealed by seizing the remains of the Soviet consulate led to an unprecedented wave of expulsions. In a single week, starting on June 15, 1988, Brian Mulroney's government signed deportation orders for nine Soviet diplomats, six of them in Montreal. "Good work!" he exclaimed at the time to CSIS. Ten others who had already left the country were declared *personae non gratae*. The great winnowing included consuls, vice-consuls, secretaries, delegates to the International Civil Aviation Organization (ICAO), the highest-ranked military official in the Ottawa embassy, an Aeroflot manager, and a journalist employed by a press agency.

The expulsion of at least four can be traced directly to the fire. But at the time, the connection was muddled by rumours that the deportations, which had taken place in mid-June that summer, were linked to a Russian defector, Yuri Smurnov, who had turned himself in at the beginning of the month. Smurnov was a translator at the ICAO. Today we know that Smurnov, nicknamed The Rat, was a minor character unconnected to the consulate affair. "The information he gave was worthless," says a source today. "He denounced people already well known to CSIS without adding to what we knew about them. Some people in Ottawa were sure Smurnov was a double agent and avoided him like the plague."*

Another event that summer further worsened Canada-Soviet relations. In mid-June, a twenty-five-year-old Canadian was arrested in a Newfoundland hotel and accused of being a Soviet spy. Stephen Joseph Ratkaï had in his possession documents stolen from the U.S. base in the town of Argentia, which controlled the routing of submarines.

As usual, the USSR responded with the face-saving expulsion of a dozen Canadian diplomats in Moscow. Others were given warnings. Soviet authorities then withdrew twenty-five of the thirty-nine employees working in the Ottawa embassy. Yuli Vorontsov, the Soviet deputy minister of foreign affairs, went on to accuse Canada of behaving like a bad actor in a soap opera.

Two days later things had calmed down. Joe Clark, at that time the External Affairs minister, had met the Soviet ambassador, Alexei Rodionov, for a formal thirty-minute encounter described as a "frank conversation." During the same two days a team of peculiar tradesmen arrived from the USSR and began the reconstruction of the destroyed consulate. Their building materials also came from the home country, shipped under diplomatic protection so they could not be examined. If Canada had wished to make an issue of this it had the means at hand, because the tradesmen arrived with out-of-date work permits. Joe Clark decided it was better to be magnanimous, creating a moral obligation that he could call in from the Russians another day.

---

* Historical note: at the end of June, in 1988, Smurnov was transferred from Montreal to Ottawa, but in the personal vehicle of a CSIS officer rather than the private airplane customarily used for reasons of security. The CSIS man simply wanted to pocket the twelve cents per kilometre mileage allowance, while at the same time helping his daughter move out of her university residence.

Behind these superficial manoeuvres was a growing determination on the Soviet side that they should never again be outdone by Canadian trickery. The bitterness was ill concealed in a public statement claiming that they had brought workmen from home to rebuild the consulate because, given that Canada had sent "so-called firemen and so-called cleanup crews" to the burned building, why should they not expect that "so-called electricians and so-called plumbers would not profit by the opportunity to cram the [new] building with hidden listening devices?"

It must have done them good to get it off their chests.

Cuban diplomats also had good cause to denounce Canadian spycraft. Their consulate on Avenue des Pins burned down the March after the Soviet fire, fanning suspicion that Canadian agents had taken up a sideline in arson.

The fire not only killed three Cuban employees, it also revealed that the structure had been wired with listening devices when it was built. Ottawa's agents had somehow got hold of a shipment of interior doors intended for the new consulate building and delicately concealed remote-control microphones with five-year batteries inside them. Since the Cubans sent wiretapping experts from Havana to inspect the consulate periodically, it was a simple matter to turn off the microphones while they were in the building.

After their fire, the Cubans made sure that the debris was shipped back to the homeland.

One of those expelled from Canada in the summer of 1988 was Igor Aleksandrov. Not surprisingly, Aleksandrov had come to Canada under the benign cover of working for the International Civil Aviation Organization. ICAO was known as an espionage threat, along with overtly Soviet companies like Aeroflot, Intourist, and a Russian-owned farm machinery maker on the south shore of the St. Lawrence River.

Aleksandrov's job was to fabricate identities for future Russian moles. It suited him. He was an enthusiastic visitor of cemeteries and parish offices, where he purported to be fascinated by birth and marriage records. In the consulate ruins were discovered Aleksandrov's work notes, including the record of an encounter with somebody in the village of Hudson. This individual gave him the name of a local child who had died in infancy. The notes also contained the names of Lumpov and his successor, Rubtsov.

Because of his high rank, the unfortunate Lumpov was certainly going to be recalled to Moscow by his fearsome bosses and made to account for his clumsy handling of the fire. Mistakenly seeing an opportunity, CSIS tried to recruit him before he left Ottawa. It was a poorly conceived undertaking, and it led to an outcome for Lumpov that was not only embarrassing but so dangerous as to arouse sympathy.

As the KGB's chief *rezident* in Montreal, Lumpov was responsible for all KGB operations in Quebec as well as the Maritimes. This made him a critical player in the organization's plans for Canada. When his bosses understood the full extent of his bungled management of the consulate fire—we can hardly imagine their reaction to the news that he forgot to take his personal agenda when he fled the building—certain consequences became inevitable. The order for his return to Russia would have been worded in such a way that his final ride to the Montreal airport would have been a very anxious one.

The operation to recruit Lumpov was secretly launched in CSIS's Ottawa headquarters without informing the agents who had known him in Montreal. Instead, Ottawa assigned the delicate task to "one of the boys" who, it was felt, had all the makings of a hotshot spy. This "cowboy" had done well in counter-espionage, especially on the Brunet and Hambleton cases, but he had a small shortcoming that the Ottawa people had overlooked: he couldn't speak French. This limitation in itself wasn't fatal. But when considered alongside the fact that Lumpov could not speak English, one might have thought the problem would become obvious. To make things worse, Lumpov had learned a very elegant French in Paris, absorbing at the same time the Parisian antipathy to those who speak the language of Molière badly.

One can imagine the scene that took place on Boulevard Saint-Laurent. Lumpov is moving with stately stride from storefront to storefront, window shopping and enjoying a pleasant afternoon. He is unaware that on all sides the pincers of the surveillance and counter-surveillance teams are inexorably closing on him.

The brash anglophone spy approaches. "Hey, Lumpov!" he cries.

The response is silence. Lumpov is, after all, an elegant and experienced diplomat as well as a spy. His usual haunt is the decorous official salon. He looks on quietly, his face registering mild surprise.

The CSIS man sidles up and utters his carefully crafted opening remarks. "Hi, I'm Agent P and I work for CSIS. Hope you don't mind if I speak English."

"Oui," replies Lumpov, bemused. "Je ne parle pas anglais." (*"Yes* I do. I don't speak English.")

Things are going swimmingly! Ottawa's agent obliges the Russian by switching to a badly butchered version of the French language. He explains that he has important information for the Russian and he wants to share it with him right away. Deploying the universal gesture of masculine self-assurance, he lifts one leg and places his foot on the wheel of a parked car. In doing so, he unintentionally pops the hubcap, which strikes the pavement with a clang and rolls uncertainly into the middle of the road.

Lumpov looks on, stupefied. The unknown gentleman is now running after the hubcap. Perhaps, he thinks, I am dreaming that I am in a very bad movie.

The moment passes. Lumpov begins to feel that it would be worth knowing what this important information is. They agree to decamp to a nearby coffee shop. Agent P then shows the Russian a page taken from his lost daybook.

"We have your agenda," confides the CSIS man. "We know everything. We know who 'Pretty' is."

"Ah, oui," replies Lumpov, nodding sagely. "Vous avez decouvert qui est Pretty?"

"Yes," rejoins the agent. "She's talking to us. We know everything about your activities. Arrests are imminent."

"Ah, oui," continues Lumpov, still nodding. He leans forward and repeats his question. "You have discovered who Pretty is, and you are talking to her?"

"Exactly!" exclaims the apprentice recruiter.

"Well," continues Lumpov, who has now adopted a frosty tone, "if you've found out who Pretty is and she's talking, then you haven't discovered anything at all."

With that, he politely stands up and exits the coffee shop. The turning of Boris Lumpov has failed.

When the story of the coffee shop encounter reached CSIS's Montreal office—the one that was not consulted about Agent P's mission—there must have been great shouting and rending of garments. After all, the CSIS people in Montreal knew who "Pretty" was. She was not the Mata Hari of Agent P's fantasy. "Pretty" was the Soviet diplomatic pouch. "Go on out to Mirabel and pick up Pretty," would have been a typical assignment. More lamentations ensued.

A SPY SAYS "NO!"

"Operation F" made the headlines three years later, in an unexpected way. In June of 1991, a former CSIS agent launched a lawsuit for $150,000 in Federal Court. Guy Chamberland was a twenty-nine-year-old researcher originally trained in the RCMP's forensic science laboratory. He possessed abilities much coveted by secret services everywhere. Today, on its website, CSIS permanently advertises for graduates of physics and chemistry studies, stating explicitly that such "scientists may be required to travel and to make use of their training in operational situations where conventional laboratory facilities may not be available. They must demonstrate an ability to innovate and be creative in the application of both skills and training."

The range of abilities expected from these recruits is considerable. They should be virtuoso analysts of clandestine documents. For example, they must be able not only to open other people's mail and to tease out the hidden information within, but also to disable any harmful traps, and, having done all these things, put it all back together so the recipient never guesses. They should also be able to recover the information on a burned sheet of paper, as well as to detect and decipher invisible ink, and to do both of these things while poised for a quick escape, should they be doing them in a place where they shouldn't be.

Guy Chamberland, by now a doctoral student in biochemistry in Montreal, claimed that he had become infected with tuberculosis while working for CSIS. Since this disease is endemic in Russia and all but nonexistent in Canada, and he had worked at deciphering the debris of the Soviet (and Cuban) consulate fires, he held his former employer accountable. How else could he have been infected with bacteria that attacked his lungs, as well as causing lesions and other skin abnormalities? His life had become one of unending pain. Endless consumption of antibiotics did not prevent endless fevers.

He was convinced that he had been infected with Biopreparat toxic agents stored in the consulate and later on extracted from the fire debris by investigators. It's possible, of course, that he had merely touched a facial tissue thrown away by a consulate staffer who, himself tubercular, had coughed into it. Nobody will ever know for certain.

Those who contract tuberculosis are legally obliged to report it. It is both deadly and highly contagious. Chamberland's problem—like one of those contrived philosophical dilemmas that haunt the pages of espionage novels—was that he couldn't possibly have tuberculosis because, officially, "Operation F" did not exist. This absurd fiction frustrated his efforts to claim medical coverage or insist on his rights under the Canada Labour Code. He tried every possible avenue. He regularly suffered intimidation from CSIS, even after leaving the organization. So did his personal physician when CSIS learned that Chamberland had asked him for a medical certificate.

CSIS refused to share Chamberland's medical history even with its own doctors, and even where this information was critical to his treatment. He was also warned that he could not discuss his ailments with any party for any reason. All of this notwithstanding the fact that he hadn't become aware of the precise nature of his illness until after leaving CSIS in 1989.

Chamberland's relations with the intelligence hierarchy became stormy and then descended into outright hostility. He received death threats. Typical was an episode in May 1988 when Chamberland, already ill, showed his CSIS supervisor a doctor's letter expressly demanding that he be withdrawn from "Operation F."

"You know what you can do with your letter?" snarled the supervisor as he crumpled it into a ball and tossed it into the garbage.

Chamberland had always understood that he risked his health when working with dangerous substances. But he had assumed that his employer would do everything possible to help him should that dreadful circumstance arise. Instead, both he and his illness had become a state secret. He remembered that one of his officers had gone so far as to tell him that he must be ready to accept death rather than reveal secret information. Was that what the man had meant when he said, "A good secret agent must be prepared to die for his country"?

Over the next two years Chamberland's hospital visits multiplied. His legal struggle led to questions in the House of Commons. Phillip Edmonston, MP for Chambly, took up Chamberland's cause and sent out a press release in mid-October 1991. It asked the following questions:

> Is there not a direct violation of the Canadian Charter of Rights and Freedoms when people go digging in other people's garbage pails? Are government employees such as M. Guy Chamberland poorly protected because of arbitrary budget cuts? . . . We need to know how many other people might have been infected while carrying out similar operations. If others may have been contaminated with toxic agents, the federal government must take steps to ensure that the general public is not exposed.[12]

Edmonston resumed his attack in the Commons on November 7, 1991, recalling in Chamberland's own words the grievances that the ex-agent had expressed during a visit to his riding office: "Listen, I asked CSIS for compensation and I also asked to know the name of the substance which had contaminated me. Was it a bacterium, or some kind of product from the USSR which contaminated the papers and furnishings that burnt in the fire?"

Chamberland's legal struggle even made the headlines in the Soviet Union. In mid-October 1991, *Pravda* described the woes of "poor Guy" in a sarcastic article signed by a certain V. Shelkov, its Ottawa correspondent.

> We also "supplied" the Canadians with high-quality ashes (which may have contained the residue of our personal secrets), but it appears that any danger they presented was created by the Canadians themselves. Perhaps they didn't store them properly. . . . It may be that the people of the West who complain about the health hazards of polluted smoke from our country are correct.

Guy Chamberland was also isolated and psychologically tormented by the campaign against him. Fearing similar treatment by the agency's senior cadres, his former colleagues shunned him. Even to be seen speaking to him was dangerous. A rumour began to circulate that he had caught tuberculosis from members of his own family. Some versions of this preposterous story claimed that Chamberland had been "pushed out into the street like a trash can," after which, realizing that his career was over, he had resigned from the service with a heavy heart.

Chamberland's remaining friends defended him, recalling that he had been raised in a military family and that, as a scientist, he had brought to his work a soldier's sense of honour. He was devoted to the cause and to his country. Three years later, in 1994, he accepted an out-of-court settlement.

Chamberland wasn't the only victim of the scandal. The supervisor who had thrown his doctor's letter into the garbage, a chief of operations in Ottawa, was forced into retirement. Another was bullied into silence. Two of his colleagues, one of them a woman, also fell ill. That meant that three of the five people in the scientific operations unit were affected. It was a shameful outcome that permanently tarnished an otherwise exemplary counter-espionage operation.

Today, a number of important details about this operation are still under the seal of secrecy. One of the most troubling is the death of a technician who was brought out of retirement by CSIS to study the Faraday cage and other cutting-edge Soviet technology recovered in "Operation F." He died from lung cancer. His family sought legal advice on suing the federal government, but took no action.

TRETIAK: THE GOALIE WITH A SECRET IN HIS GLOVE?

On January 29, 2007, goalie Ken Dryden's hockey sweater was about to join the numbered uniforms of immortal Canadiens like Maurice Richard, Guy Lafleur, and Jean Béliveau that were hung in the raftered heights of the Bell Centre in Montreal. The applause was deafening.

Among the celebrated guests gathered on the red carpet that day was Dryden's rival in the 1972 Summit Series, his Russian alter ego Vladislav Tretiak. The immortal Tretiak had unhesitatingly accepted an invitation to travel all the way from Moscow for the ceremony. He was clad in his historic sweater, on which the letters CCCP (Cyrillic characters meaning USSR) were still clear after the many years that had passed. So was the famous "20" stitched on the back. Also very evident was the crowd's adoration for a man who had single-handedly thwarted the best efforts of Canada's most brilliant skaters.

Tretiak was fifty-five years old at the time of the Bell Centre event, and he had led an exhilarating life. During the two decades when he was in his prime, he had collected a staggering number of prizes, including ten world championships and three Olympic gold medals (in 1972, 1976, and 1984).

Watching that evening's ceremony on his television set, a former CSIS agent could not help smiling. He was seized with nostalgia, though not necessarily for the medal-bedecked hockey superstar lovingly followed by the TV cameras. His fond memories were of a different Tretiak, who had worn different kinds of medals. One, for example, was the 1978 Order of Lenin and another the 1984 Red Flag, given to a worker who has laboured on behalf of the people. And Tretiak had laboured mightily: hockey player, Red Army lieutenant-colonel, and . . . person well acquainted with the KGB.

The great Tretiak was quite a celebrity in his day, and not only among hockey fans. CSIS was also an avid Tretiak-watcher. A number of good sources inside the organization have told us that Tretiak was "ticketed" at the time. That means that he was believed to be a "co-opted" individual, somebody who had been recruited as an informer and was being paid or recompensed in some way. There were hundreds of these back then, especially among Soviet citizens like himself who had received job offers outside the homeland.

But there was also the hypothesis that he was more than a simple informer. Had this been the case, then the note "K/SVR" ("K" standing for "known") would have appeared beside his name in the CSIS computer system. Placing a "K" is not something done lightly. It happens only if there is reliable information to support it (for example, corroboration by allied security services). And a "K" has consequences, including the possibility of the person being placed on a "*persona non grata*" list. A notch lower than "K" is the "S (S/SVR)" status (S standing, of course, for "suspect").

The former CSIS agent watching Tretiak on TV that night recalled that the hockey legend was identified quite late, not until the mid-1990s. The agents who worked on his case had come to feel that the talented goalie was, in spite of everything, a "bon gars"— a good guy. Based on available evidence, the consensus was that Tretiak was a "talent scout," a recruiter of new agents who reported to the PR or KR Line.

Hockey people don't believe any of this. Those we spoke to hotly recalled that Tretiak was refused permission to leave the USSR in 1982, when the Canadiens had wanted to recruit him and bring him to Canada. Why would Moscow keep a secret agent at home when he had just been offered the perfect cover for a life in the West?

Historians will recall that Tretiak's name was once associated with that of Michel Bordeleau, a young Quebecer who lived in Moscow during the 1980s and earned his living as a translator. Bordeleau worked for Dan Rather of CBS as well as Radio-Canada's Bernard Derome when their work took them to Russia.* He also made his services available to Pat Quinn, coach of the Vancouver Canucks, when he went to Moscow to meet famous players like Igor Larionov.

It was frequently reported that Bordeleau, in his own words, was the "exclusive agent" of Vladislav Tretiak. And certainly his smiling face was often seen beside Tretiak's when the Russian made his annual trek to the Quatre Glaces arena in Brossard, Quebec, where he ran a school for promising young goalies. Tretiak's business partners at the time were José Theodore and Martin Brodeur.

When Bordeleau was a seven-year-old kid in Shawinigan he witnessed the Summit Series and developed a boy's infatuation

---

* Bordeleau has appeared in recent months on Quebec television sports shows, where he has fiercely defended the reputation of Russian hockey players.

with Tretiak and his gang. He was still a boy five years later when he met Tretiak coming out of an elevator in Quebec's historic Château Frontenac.

But Bordeleau's boyhood was already behind him when, as a politically passionate nineteen-year-old, he went to Moscow in 1985 for the Twelfth Annual Festival of Youth and Students. He joined thousands of others from around the world in chanting "Peace, Friendship, and Anti-Imperialist Solidarity!" The festival had been organized since 1947 by the International Union of Students, an organization dominated by the KGB for the purpose of spreading propaganda and disinformation. The young Bordeleau persuaded the organizers to give him a scholarship to study Russian at the Pushkin Institute in Moscow.

"Obviously not just anybody can go there," he acknowledged in an interview at the time. "I got in because I had met an interpreter at the [Youth] Festival who endorsed me. From that moment I knew that I was going to live for quite some time in Russia."[13]

Bordeleau stayed there for nearly two years, until the summer of 1988. Then, once again, a kindly soul appeared out of nowhere and helped him to realize another dream. According to his own testimony, a teacher at the Pushkin Institute introduced him to the fitness coach of a team of workers in a Moscow pencil factory called Sakko and Vanzetti (or Sakko i Vantcetti). The coach offered Bordeleau a privilege rarely accorded to foreigners. Would he like to play for a second-division Russian hockey team?

He certainly would. And from that time onward Bordeleau began to call himself Mikhail Bordelov.

It happened that his team practised on the same rink as the Red Army team. That was where he met future stellar players like Igor Larionov and Viacheslav Fetisov, who were just then on the point of moving to North America.* As Larionov's confidant, he was invited in 1989 to holiday with the player and his family at a Russian resort featuring thermal baths, saunas, and freely flowing vodka.

A year earlier, when Bordeleau was about to return to Montreal to begin law school at McGill University, he had received an unpleasant visit from the KGB. The undercover men ordered him downtown to be interrogated. Here is his account of what happened, as told to journalist Réjean Tremblay: "I just had time to call Evelyn Prexley, from the Canadian embassy. But I still had a pretty tough interrogation. They told me I'd changed dollars for rubles on the black market. And then I'd gone to Leningrad without an internal visa. . . . The idea was to intimidate me."[14]

The KGB released him, but followed him relentlessly until he boarded the airplane home. His chief interrogator took him aside at the airport and hoped Bordeleau would remember him fondly.

What really happened? As far as we have been able to ascertain, Bordeleau the Russophile had been blackmailed. He told CSIS investigators that, after the interrogation, he was advised that he could rectify his unfortunate indiscretions by doing a few small favours for Mother Russia. It's a favourite method in totalitarian countries. Not long ago, an employee of a prominent aeronautics company was on a business trip to China when, responding to the warm embrace of a young prostitute, he found himself surrounded by police officers. The Chinese call it "the honey pot trap."

Bordeleau's odyssey, exotic at first glance but all too familiar to CSIS people, was the product of an era in which Communist

---

* Larionov played three years in Vancouver (1989–92) before being traded to several NHL teams in the United States. He was named to the Hockey Hall of Fame in November 2008. Fetisov played with the New Jersey Devils and the Detroit Red Wings. Named a UNESCO hero of sport in 2004, today he is the president of the Russian Federation's Agency for Sports, Physical Education, and Tourism.

nations considered all westerners to be suspect. The warm solidarity of which Bordeleau may have dreamed had always been impossible. For many years, going back to the era when the RCMP was responsible for counter-espionage, it routinely created a police file for every visiting westerner. A document from the 1970s that we examined shows that more than 9,500 "suspects" were already on the list. The old RCMP files have evocative names like "Canadians Visiting USSR," "End Racism Committee," "Campaign for Nuclear Disarmament," "Hockey Series Canada-USSR," and "The Moiseyev Dance Company."

We wanted to hear Michel Bordeleau's side of the story. But we scarcely had time to introduce ourselves on the telephone before he launched into a long monologue about his KGB interrogation. He set out to explain and perhaps justify his decisions.

"I collaborated with CSIS . . . I gave them information. . . . It's thanks to me that the Soviets were expelled from Canada, especially Vladimir Dorofeyev, a translator at the International Civil Aviation Organization . . ."

Bordeleau also insisted that "a number of Canadian diplomats" had been expelled from Moscow for sexual indiscretions while he was there. Finally he agreed to an in-person meeting.

We checked out his statement about Dorofeyev. There is no evidence that he was ever expelled. A confidential source in Canada assured us that he was one of the "cleanest" people in the Soviet delegation.

Our second conversation with Bordeleau ended abruptly when we let it be understood that we had heard a different version of the story he'd told us. After that he didn't return our calls.

Today, Tretiak is a deputy in the Douma, representing Vladimir Putin's nationalist party, United Russia. He is also president of the Russian Hockey Federation, and he still spends his summers in Toronto teaching at the Vladislav Tretiak Elite School of Goaltending.

We sent Tretiak a series of eleven questions concerning his career, hoping the answers would clarify the position he had played on what we like to call the "Gauntlet and Shield" team. We'd have been equally happy with a statement that he had never played for this particular outfit at all. Here are four of the questions he was asked:

"In 1980, Michel Bordeleau told a newspaper that he had experienced some difficulties with the KGB in Moscow. He underwent a long interrogation but never explained why it occurred. . . . Did you help him in any way to smooth things out with the KGB? Do you know why he was questioned?"

"How did you react to the fall of the Berlin Wall, to glasnost, and to Mikhail Gorbachev's perestroika? Did these events distress you? Astonish you?"

"Around that time CSIS would have identified you as working for the KGB. This would explain why the Canadian government refused to issue you a work permit for Canada. Were you afraid this would hurt your image in North America? Or did you know (or accept) that this was all in the past and that you were going to turn the page? How involved were you?"

"You have embarked on a political career under the banner of Vladimir Putin's United Russia Party. Why did you choose this party? How would you describe Vladimir Putin?"

Tretiak replied by stating, first, that he would not answer any of our questions. This was primarily because our book was concerned with the Cold War era, though he also had other reservations.

We persisted in asking that he comment on the issues and offered him every opportunity to deny any connection with the KGB. Once again he refused.

"How can you imagine Monsieur Tretiak would ever answer those questions, given his present position?" asked Mr. Tretiak's personal assistant.

CHAPTER 002

Paul William Hampel: The Spy Who Loved Canada

(Spying is not a saint's meditation.)
—Maloy Krishna Dahr, assistant director of the
Intelligence Bureau (India)

A good spy must have many qualities. These include discretion, charm, the ability to create loyalty among others while concealing the truth about oneself, a chameleon-like ability to blend into the environment, dexterity with a camera, and a good cover story to deflect suspicion while travelling.

All of these things Paul William Hampel possessed, but they did not save him from the ignominious fate of being forced to board a jet to Moscow on Christmas Day, 2006. His most compelling quality was perhaps his charm, which he possessed so abundantly that he might have stepped out of a John le Carré story. As for blending into the environment, no chameleon of Russian birth ever spoken English quite so well. His French wasn't bad, either.

But was he really the Russian spy he was accused of being? Was he in truth the protagonist of the extravagant story that plunged

Canada into a crisis worthy of the Cold War—even though the Cold War was by that time long over?

To his lawyer, Stephane Handfield, Hampel was just an illegal immigrant, one of the unfortunate ones who'd been accused of spying by overly hasty Canadian authorities. To Russia's ambassador in Ottawa, Georgiy Mamedov, Hampel was a drug dealer and a dangerous arm of the Russian Mafia, but not a spy.

"We're no longer on a 'war path,'" declared Mamedov with aplomb, some hours after his arrest, to a waiting media scrum. "That's why I don't see what kind of secrets might motivate any country to send an agent to Montreal."

To the Canadian government and its secret services, "Paul Hampel," as such, didn't even exist. After a long investigation they concluded that this was nothing but a borrowed name. Behind the name was an elite agent of Russia's external information services, the Sluzhba Vneshney Razvedki, or SVR.

The SVR came into existence in December 1991. It was a hasty birth, just four months after the KGB, under director Vladimir Krioutchkov, had tried to overthrow Mikhail Gorbachev's government. Once Krioutchkov's *coup d'état* was suppressed, Gorbachev abolished the KGB. But he still needed a foreign spy service. That is how the KGB's old foreign information branch (called the First Directory) became a new organization: the SVR.*

Of course there were new senior officers and a new name. But the government carefully neglected to give the SVR an "official" mission. As if a spy service is created for anything but spying!

In a document submitted in 2006 to the Federal Court after Hampel's arrest, CSIS has this to say about the SVR:

---

* The First General Directory had twenty departments, which together covered all countries. One of them focused on the United States and Canada.

> When speaking to a Russian audience, the SVR does
> not conceal the fact that it practises intensive and
> high level espionage. [It] frequently boasts of stealing
> Western financial and industrial information in order
> to compensate for weaknesses in the Russian economy.
> However, when speaking to an international audience
> the SVR prefers to talk about cooperation with the
> United States, Canada and other countries in the battle
> against terrorism, organized crime and the traffic in
> nuclear materials.[15]

CSIS goes on to argue, citing a Jane's Intelligence Digest (JID) report from 2002, that the Russian Federation has considerably beefed up its ability to spy on Europe and North America.* A year later, in the fall of 2007, Russian president Vladimir Putin himself ordered new SVR chief Mikhail Fradkov to improve the service's clandestine information-gathering ability—particularly with respect to economic information. This, Putin stated, was to protect Russian interests.

Since then the Russian secret services have extended their operations in the Canadian cities where most Russian emigrants live: Toronto, Montreal, Calgary, and Vancouver.

Also in 2007, the website for Jane's Intelligence Digest detailed the dreadful story of Lieutenant-Colonel Alexander Litvinenko, a former Russian spy officer who was poisoned in London in late 2006. Radioactive materials had been planted in his food, leading to an agonizing death. Nobody knew better than Litvinenko the methods used by his ex-employer, including this one. He had

---

* JID is a private British organization that collects information on security and data gathering from open sources. It also does consulting work.

previously revealed that the SVR, during the Cold War, routinely blackmailed Russian emigrants in western countries into becoming collaborators.

At that time the blackmail consisted of threats to members of the emigrant's family still living in Russia. China still uses this method, but Russia has since developed an easier one. Nowadays it approaches the emigrant directly and threatens to fabricate a fully documented criminal record for him in Russia. If the target continues to resist, the Russian government simply requests his extradition.[16]

But bullying expatriates this way risks a backlash. The Kremlin is, after all, trying to intimidate ex-Russians who have developed loyalties to a new country and who may react with anger rather than fear. For that reason the extradition threat is usually deployed only when other approaches fail. Instead, for the first approach, Moscow uses a method known by the acronym MISE (which will be discussed in a later chapter).

In the jargon of the trade, Hampel was an "illegal" ("non-legal" in Russian) of Line N, the branch that recruits all the illegals working in foreign countries. These persons are under the operational control of the SVR's Directory S in Moscow, which trains and finances them. Other countries have similar "sleeper" agents: China picturesquely calls them "the fish of the great deeps."* The United States, which has to deal with them, rather prosaically calls them "NOC"s ("No Official Cover") since they lack diplomatic immunity.

They are the crème de la crème. Unlike "official" spies with the protective cover of a journalist or diplomat, these are the shape-shifters who blend invisibly into the place where they are sent. They

---

* Also known as "bottom-feeders."

adopt a name that is commonly used in their new country, as well as an entirely bogus personal history that they smilingly share with their new neighbours and friends.* One can imagine the hard work and documentation involved in creating even one such agent—not to mention the agent's labour in mastering a new culture. Illegals are a long-term investment by the homeland, the human equivalent of an investor's patient money. They sit quietly for many years doing nothing at all. They are waiting for their mission.

Throughout the Cold War, the Soviet Union loved to parachute these illegals into Canada. By the 1960s there were so many that they were pretty much tripping over each other.

Before leaving Moscow, these fish-of-the-deep swore an oath to die rather than betray their secrets. They promised never "to abandon to the adversary any elements that might harm the political interests of the state" before concluding that "with every heartbeat, with every passing day, I swear to serve the Party, the Motherland, and the Soviet people."[17]

Quite often Canada was, for them, nothing but a short stopover during which they would erase their old identities before moving on to the real target, the United States. But there was always one left on Canadian soil, waiting to be activated in the event of war between East and West.

The "illegal" is to espionage what the "sleeper" is to terrorism. He or she lives as discreetly as possible, leading a dull everyday existence designed to attract as little attention as possible from the authorities.

---

* Their new identity is usually borrowed from a deceased person. This was the case with the false spouses Ian Mackenzie and Laurie Brodie Lambert, alias Dmitri Olshevski and Elena Olshevskaya, arrested on May 22, 1996, in Toronto and deported the following June 10 to Russia.

A less well-known side to this story, but one that makes perfect sense in the context of official bilingualism, is that Canada also
served as a nursery for Russian spies who were to be sent on to
France. In Canada they could become fluent in both French and
English. Once in France, their task—like that of their confreres
elsewhere—was to be ready for action when a crisis arose. In the
annals of French counter-espionage the stories of the "Petitclercs"
and the "Bordiers," pseudo-Canadians who emigrated to France,
are well known. Canada, France, and Switzerland shared the special
privilege of incubating Soviet spies.

In 1992, ex-KGB colonel Vasili Mitrokhine escaped to the West
with briefcases full of confidential notes and documents. Eventually
he collaborated with the writer Christopher Andrew on a well-
documented book that dwells on the colourful—if often futile—
adventures of illegal Soviets in Canada. Though these schemes
often ended badly, the KGB (later the SVR) never lost its faith in
"deep cover."

Mitrokhine recounts, for example, the convoluted case of
"Albert" and his Romanian wife "Gera." These so-called Belgian
emigrants arrived in Canada at the beginning of the 1960s with
their young son. The puppet masters in Moscow had an elaborate
plan in which Albert would become a mining entrepreneur, with
a scheme that involved selling land to mining companies. It was a
fiasco, and the company went bankrupt. Albert then decided to set
up a car dealership, but that didn't work either. He was eventually
called back to Moscow.

Luckily for the KGB, it also had "Douglas" and his wife "Gerda."
They were supposedly a couple with mismatched politics who had
fled from what was then called East Germany. Arriving in Montreal,
they continued on to Toronto, where they purchased a restaurant
not far from CBC headquarters. Douglas (alias Rudi Herrmann,

and actually named Dalibar Valouchek) then swapped his chef's hat for a director's beret and put together a promotional film for the Liberal Party of Canada. His name still appears in the credits.

Douglas would eventually abandon Canada for the United States, in 1968. But before doing so he became the controller of Hugh Hambleton, a professor of economic science at Laval University. Hambleton also held a position with NATO from 1956 to 1961, during which time he sent almost eighty confidential documents to the KGB.*

Unhappily for Hambleton, Douglas was picked up by the FBI in New York in 1977. He squealed like a squeeze toy, giving up every detail about his illicit activities, including the existence of Hambleton, who had been recruited ages earlier, in Paris in the early 1950s. Nearly two years later, when the FBI finally passed on the information to the RCMP, Hambleton was picked up and confined in a series of hotel rooms in Montreal and Quebec City. There he was grilled by the Mounties and then by the French secret service.

Unpleasant as this experience might have been, Hambleton knew that he had nothing to worry about.

Then there was the case of "Paul," who had sworn to his masters in Moscow that he would find a way to use the Front de libération du Québec (FLQ) to carry out terrorist attacks on American soil. Not that this plan was ever seriously put into practice. In fact, the KGB eventually withdrew him from Quebec altogether, but not before spreading a rumour that the FLQ was involved with the machinations of the Central Intelligence Agency. This bizarre tale made the front page of a Montreal newspaper in 1971 and was cited for years after-

---

* Professor Hambleton was arrested in London in June 1982 and sentenced to ten years imprisonment for espionage. He returned to Canada four years later.

ward as evidence of American perfidy. However, according to Vasili Mitrokhine, it was never anything more than a made-in-Moscow fantasy.

The SVR still exists today. Its headquarters in Yasenovo, a southern suburb of Moscow, is called The Centre. It broadcasts orders, in blocks of five coded numbers, all night long to its overseas illegals. The codes are then changed during the day.

The illegals are managed by Line N officers located in Russia's overseas diplomatic missions, whether the embassy itself or a consulate. These officers' responsibilities include the provision of money and logistical support to the agents, including the use of the famous "dead-letter box" of popular spy fiction. These handlers justify their presence in Canada by pretending to be official diplomats.

The agent rarely, if ever, meets his or her managing officer in person. Russia's secret services are well aware that their fake diplomats are monitored by the intelligence agencies of the host country, which are rarely fooled and always looking for the least excuse to expel them. Any meeting of controller and illegal risks exposing the illegal as well. This, from the SVR point of view, is unthinkable, because the illegal has no diplomatic immunity and will certainly be imprisoned, a major international embarrassment.

Line N is the SVR's most deeply concealed operation. It's not surprising that only the *rezident* knows the identity of the illegal in his sector. In extreme cases he doesn't even need to know his real identity in order to communicate with him. That's why, at the time of the arrest of Paul Hampel, Russian ambassador Georgiy Mamedov was perhaps telling the truth when he claimed to have no idea who Hampel was.

CSIS also had no idea who Hampel was. Nobody knew, apart from his lawyer, Stephane Handfield. And Handfield knew it only because the Russian had whispered his true birth date to him during a meeting in a small office attached to the waiting room of the Federal Court in Montreal. This occurred on December 4, 2006, the day when Hampel gave up the fight. He knew he couldn't prove in a court of law that he was a Canadian citizen born in Toronto.

Nonetheless, when the matter came to court Hampel demanded that Judge Pierre Blais suppress his true identity.* He did not admit to being a spy, and he loudly continued to deny it even as he was being bundled into an airplane bound for Russia. He later claimed to have done this in order to protect himself and his family, which did not really make much sense. His identity was no secret to the people back home, and why should he care what Canadians thought?

At the same time—and this is the most revealing thing—he also spoke of his desire to leave Canada as quickly as possible. "You can't imagine what a gift he's giving you," the judge observed pointedly to the four government lawyers.

FROM MONTREAL TO BELGRADE

It's not easy to assemble an accurate record of Paul Hampel's adventures in Canada. In his guise as a businessman he boasted a network of commercial contacts extending from France to Turkey, and from Serbia to England. He seemed to be everywhere, and yet nowhere at all.

The earliest evidence of Hampel's presence in Canada goes back to 1995. On May 8 of that year he showed up at the passport office in Montreal with a birth certificate delivered in Toronto on May 3, 1971. He wanted a passport.

---

* Pierre Blais was the solicitor general of Canada in 1989.

The forms he filled out at the time state that he was born on December 11, 1965, in Toronto, that he was 1.9 metres tall and weighed 78 kilograms, with brown hair and blue eyes. His occupation is given as "rescue worker," without further details. His guarantor, whose identity is still confidential, claimed to have known him for two years. That would mean that the latest date Hampel could have arrived in Canada would have been 1993. If that's the case, then he could not have been connected with the Lamberts, who, like Hampel, were also cut loose by the SVR, which claimed that they were nothing but leftover vestiges of the Cold War.

In November 1999, Hampel got a driver's licence through the Societé de l'Assurance Automobile Québec (SAAQ, the public agency responsible for car insurance in the province). The following May he received a second passport. Then, moving ahead to mid-April 2002, we find that he requested yet another passport, this time on the grounds that his earlier passport had been seized. Since his new application indicated that he would need to travel only seven days later, it's not surprising that he also requested the speedy return of his earlier document.

His trail turns up again in Dublin, Ireland. There, at the end of June 1997, he registered a company called Emerging Markets Research and Consulting (EMRC). After seven years of inactivity the company—evidently a shell—was dissolved in 2004. People in Dublin whose names appeared on the documents of EMRC assert that they never met Hampel and do not know who he is. But the phantom business held $2 million in assets nonetheless.

Such a company could be an extremely useful "umbrella," and that has nothing to do with Ireland's generous tax laws. Oleg Gordievski, a defector who had been a senior KGB officer, explained in an interview with the Irish media that their country was an obligatory stopover for spies on their way to Great Britain or North

America.[18] Hard to believe that Hampel's presence in Ireland was just another coincidence.

From the CSIS annual report for 1996:

> In the West the sudden end of the Cold War gave birth to hopes that have been disappointed. Intelligence services in most Western democracies began to draw down staff and reorganize themselves at about the same time that traditionally adversarial intelligence services were ordered to ramp up activities in the interest of their respective governments. While traditional espionage did not stop, these services were assigned new objectives. The long-term effect of this reorientation is not yet clear.
>
> After a period of drifting, the Russian intelligence services became active again after President Yeltsin ratified a new law on overseas information gathering in July, 1992. We have since noted numerous cases of traditional espionage in which Russians have been involved.[19]

One of Paul Hampel's few known addresses in Canada is a three-storey, yellowish brick apartment building on Rue Saint-Jacques Ouest in Notre-Dame-de-Grâce. Nearby is the great behemoth of the Turcot freeway exchange, beneath which a steady shower of decayed concrete patters down, as if to protest the din of unending traffic. A forest of satellite antennas on the balconies of the forty or so units in Hampel's building suggest a refuge for penniless immigrants rather than the stylish residence of a businessman.

The former owner, Monsieur A.V., suffered a convenient memory loss when his former tenant's notoriety landed him on the front page of Montreal's newspapers. He told journalists that he had "only the vaguest" memory of Hampel, although the man had lived in the building for five or six years.[20] Monsieur V. is not especially talkative these days either, as we discovered. Perhaps being stung by the man he had companionably called "Paul" still hurts. "Call the police if you need to know anything," were his first and last words before the door slammed. His son is now listed as the building's owner.

According to a reliable source, Hampel lived in the building on Saint-Jacques right up to the year before the police seized him. But "lived" isn't exactly right, because he was only a part-time tenant. When he first moved in, at the beginning of the 1990s, he specified that he had to be on the top floor. A second requirement was that, before signing, he required an hour by himself in his new home in order to be sure it was right. By that, he explained, he meant "quiet." An hour later he emerged, satisfied, and signed the lease. Then he lived there, but only for a few months.

His name was still listed at that address in the 1994–95 telephone directory. But he had adopted the odd habit, whenever he expected to be in Montreal between business trips, of phoning ahead to rent a furnished apartment somewhere else. When he found one, he would arrive in a rental car carrying nothing but his suitcase and laptop. He never stayed more than a few weeks. Nobody visited him. And if a furnished flat wasn't available, he would stay in a rundown motel instead. Failing that, he might elect to stay with his landlord, the memory-challenged Monsieur A.V., three kilometres away near the Concordia-Loyola campus (though still within the boundaries of Notre-Dame-de-Grâce). A.V.'s elegant home also served as the registered business address of Emerging Markets Research and Consulting (EMRC) and of its website.

At the end of the 1990s a certain "P. Hampel" also lodged in a ten-storey building on Cavendish Boulevard, about 1.5 kilometres from his place in the Rue Saint-Jacques. This location completed a vast quadrilateral on the west side of the Decarie Autoroute, with all of Hampel's various addresses located inside of it. Now this may be nothing but a coincidence, but it happens that a gigantic transmission tower is also inside the area, about 500 metres from his Saint-Jacques apartment.

People who knew Hampel speak of a tallish fellow, a little heavy-set but otherwise elegant and stylish. He was well-spoken, intelligent, and unfailingly courteous. He was always forthcoming when asked to describe what he did for a living, though he rarely gave the same answer twice. Some thought he had a computer programming job nearby, though an acquaintance identified as M.V. believed he was a student at Concordia University. When applying for a passport Hampel claimed that he worked in emergency services, or else as a travel consult. When he later published a book, *My Beautiful Balkans*, its flyleaf and accompanying website described him as an analyst specializing in emerging markets. His career path, then, was hard to follow. It still is.

Hampel was an inveterate traveller. "He went to Toronto a lot," recalls a Montrealer who chatted with him from time to time. "At least, that's what he said." Wherever he was going, his image showed up frequently on the surveillance cameras at Pierre Elliott Trudeau Airport. This was during the time that the RCMP began to monitor the cameras, several months before his arrest.

Hampel appeared to be a disorganized businessman, rarely looking in on his Irish company. But we shouldn't judge hastily. Could it be that the soul of an artist slept fitfully in the heart of the spy, finally awakening, finally insisting on its right to flourish?

Perhaps that is why, about 1995, Hampel began to make soulful peregrinations to the Balkan mountains. He wandered from place to place with a shiny new camera swinging from a stylish bandolier. At one time or another he was in Albania, Croatia, Bosnia,

Serbia, Montenegro, Macedonia (he had a temporary resident visa for Macedonia when he was arrested), Greece, and Romania. By a remarkable coincidence, wanderlust often seized him at just about the time that war broke out in this or that Balkan neighbourhood. These local disturbances were very worrisome for Russia.

Hampel took pictures. Hundreds of them. Thousands. Pastures and steeples and statues and storks' nests and milkmaids—the panorama of lusty Balkan life. And the more images he made, the more he revealed an assured aesthetic competence, remarkable for a man who insisted he was only an amateur photographer.

This is not to suggest that he was a giant of photography. He was a little too exuberant with the coloured filters, in our view. But by the turn of the millennium he was apparently ready to produce his master work. He moved into a Belgrade hotel for several months of exhausting but passionate labour. At the end of it he brought forth a book of photographs, which he then published at his own expense.

My Beautiful Balkans contains eighty-four pages and displays fifty supposed landscape photographs. It appeared in the bookstores of Belgrade in 2003, with an introduction in which Hampel describes himself as an "analyst and admirer of the Balkans." He also expresses his affection for the rocky, knotted countryside and for its people. "Without my camera," he confesses, displaying the wobbly lyricism of an amateur photographer, "it would take an eternity for me to find the words to perfectly express all that I feel for the Balkans—their past, their present, and their future."

Whoever reads the book soon discovers that it is not just an artist's quest for the perfect image. It's also a cry from the heart, an act of political faith. "Those who live in the Balkans understand that the great beauty of the land is their best inspiration to seek reconciliation among themselves and to enjoy the fruits of peace."

The book ends with another message from the author, this time hoping that the reader will enjoy his website, soon to be posted. It is accompanied by a self-portrait of the spy standing in the narrow corridor of a train, casual in a short-sleeved shirt, his face illuminated by a provocative, almost mocking smile.

Several months later, true to his word, Hampel went online in Belgrade with his website, mybeautifulbalkans.com.* It featured more extensive photo galleries and a more personal commentary. The title page was stripped down, elegant, designed. There one might read: "I believe that harmony and contrast are the great elements of beauty, and the Balkans are the best expression of this beauty."**

The author also included information on how to order extra copies of the book. The potential buyer was encouraged to write to certain bookstores in the Balkans or in Austria. But there was also a party in Montreal, a certain A.M.F., who would be delighted to help. His e-mail address was included.

The address, however, changed, and the name of A.M.F. was replaced by a pseudonym: ciaopicasso2004. Could this have been an affectionate farewell to the artist-spy, delivered with a wink and a nod?

THINGS COME UNDONE

Hampel's Montreal saga came to an end on the afternoon of November 14, 2006.

A large but discreet congregation of agents from CSIS, the

---

* The address associated with his domain name is located in a comfortable semi-detached house on Sommerfeld Street in the west end of Montreal.
** His obsessive interest in the Balkans is odd. There is no logical or artistic explanation for it. And Russian spies are not usually authorized to spend this kind of time on this kind of hobby. It is likely that it was, instead, part of a cover story justifying his lengthy missions in foreign countries—missions that ended with his arrest.

Royal Canadian Mounted Police, and the Canada Border Services Agency follows Paul Hampel onto the departure level at Pierre Elliott Trudeau Airport in Montreal. The trap is closing quietly, almost meditatively.

Briefcase in hand, the Russian is preparing to board a flight to Europe. He is carrying the apparently cumbersome, but essential, gear of the perfect secret agent who never leaves Canada without taking along every scrap of paper that might leave a record of his presence here: his false Ontario birth certificate is in a slender travel pouch hidden under his shirt, together with his true/false Canadian passport, five password-protected telephone Smart Cards, and about fifteen bank cards. Always practical, he is also carrying the equivalent of $7,800 in cash, three cellphones, two digital cameras, memory cards containing more than a thousand photos, and a shortwave radio.

Seven days earlier, Stockwell Day and Monte Solberg initialled a security certificate bearing Hampel's name. The signature of the minister of Public Safety and the minister of Citizenship and Immigration mean that Hampel has now been named under Article 77 of the Immigration and Refugee Protection Act and can be arrested at any time. After that he would be held until expelled, and never permitted to set foot in the country again. The still-wet ministerial signatures declare in effect that he is a menace to national security. A vast RCMP investigation, already underway, might or might not clear him in time. Even Prime Minister Harper, through a classified briefing note, is now au courant of Hampel's existence and privy to every detail of his ongoing neutralization.

Hampel approaches the airline counter. He wearily sets down two suitcases which have to be checked in. Then he placidly shuffles off to the security checkpoint in the departure zone. There he might have noticed, had he been more alert, the strange intensity of the security staff's greetings. It is a bit of official theatre that has been carefully rehearsed since the authorities learned of his travel plans. Mounties in civilian clothes—but with concealed weapons—stand discreetly beside each and every Canadian Air Transport and Security Authority employee, ready to intervene should it be necessary.

Does Hampel suspect anything? His trackers wait for him to empty his pockets, put his bag on the conveyor belt leading to the X-ray machine, and pass through the security gate. Their patience is doubly rewarded: now they know that he isn't carrying a gun, and that he is safely separated from his computer and can't delete anything from it.

Swiftly, before he or the stupefied passengers behind him can react, Hampel is seized and hustled downstairs to one of the holding cells in the airport's basement. These are usually filled with suspected illegal immigrants. The spy is still stunned by the sudden stripping away of the mask he has worn so long. His face wears a look that is almost penitent. He is being taken away to his first interrogation.

Hampel's questioning took place at his new temporary address, the protected wing of the detention centre in Rivières-des-Prairies. Shortly afterward he was moved along to the special detention unit at the Saint-Anne-des-Plaines federal penitentiary. Here the Canadian government united him with what it considered to be his peer group—fifty of the most dangerous criminals in the country.

Instead of admiring photographic groupies, Hampel's neighbours now included the baby-faced killer Maurice "Mom" Boucher, formerly of the Nomads, now chief of the Quebec chapter of the Hells Angels. "Mom" had television privileges, and he loved to tell his new friend what everybody was saying about him on TV. The little community inside the walls was thrilled to have a "Russian James Bond" to brighten their days. For the demobilized chief of the Nomads, now serving a life sentence, teasing a spy was poor entertainment compared with his former adventures, but it beat the usual tedium of prison life.

Paul Hampel began to send out an urgent stream of appeals for a lawyer. No joy, alas. Lawyers are not fond of the words "security certificate," which lead them into a Kafkaesque and not very profitable maze of procedural motions. They avoided Hampel. By mid-November, knowing he had no choice, Hampel applied for legal aid. His file was handed over to a lawyer named Claude Whalen. But Whalen, who lacked experience with security cases, soon discovered that there were all kinds of official obstacles standing between himself and his new client.

Through an odd coincidence, that very week in Moscow new Canadian ambassador Ralph James Lysyshyn was presenting his letters of credence in a gorgeously panelled Kremlin receiving room. Seven other new ambassadors were doing likewise. Their host was President Putin.

Obviously there was no mention of the awkward Hampel business that day. This was the time for greetings and champagne and small talk and little cakes. Putin was also spreading some icing on the freshly confected ambassadors, singing the praises of the wonderful relations between their countries and Russia. Turning to Lysyshyn, he said, "We give great value to deepening our close co-operation with Canada. Canada is our arctic neighbour and we have successful contacts in international affairs and with respect to ensuring global security. We also have sound prospects for strengthening our partnership relations."

These "partnership relations" were a bit of a poisoned chalice, as the ambassador would shortly learn when he attended another reception, this one celebrating Canada-Russia hockey collaboration. There he would meet Vladislav Tretiak. A journalist approached with some questions about the Hampel affair. The ambassador politely declined to comment.

Shortly afterward, the embassy secretary sent an e-mail to the Division for Europe East of the Balkans of the Ministry of Foreign Affairs in Ottawa. It set out the incident at the hockey reception and asked for "the media line" to be sent as quickly as possible, in case the ambassador had to deal with the matter again. It's not every day, after all, that a Russian spy is unmasked in Canada.

A laconic reply arrived in Moscow later that night: "'No comment' is the best response at the moment."

Meanwhile, it took two days of hard work for Whalen just to arrange a brief first meeting with Hampel. By that time he had begun to understand the situation, and he found that he didn't much care for it. He begged his colleague Stephane Handfield to take over the sticky situation. Handfield was delighted. Unlike Whalen, he saw the possibilities. For one thing, he had experience with the media. And, as a former immigration official, he was familiar with the work of undercover agents. During the 1990s he had studied the files of the major actors in what would soon be called the "Islamic network" in Montreal, including Ahmed Ressam. He knew his way around the shadow world.

During his first prison meeting with Hampel, on November 19, Handfield was charmed by a handcuffed giant who was "very courteous" and seemed perfectly sure of himself. However, the man acknowledged in a carefully controlled voice that he was somewhat overwhelmed by events. Obviously, he said, he was not a spy; his name was indeed Paul William Hampel; and, yes, he was a Canadian citizen born in Toronto in 1965.

But Hampel's self-control was strained to its limit by the heavy security detail that accompanied him everywhere, especially when he appeared in Federal Court. As Handfield complained to a judge: "There were nearly a dozen RCMP agents in bulletproof vests in the courtroom, each of them heavily armed. It was ridiculous. My client found the whole thing a bit much."

In his cell at Sainte-Anne-des-Plaines, waiting out the time between two Montreal court appearances, Hampel was under surveillance, his movements closely monitored. Like the other hard cases, he was kept in solitary confinement for twenty-three hours per day. Even then, nothing was left to chance. He was forbidden to flush the toilet until a guard had checked to see that no compromising object had been excreted there. And he had to make a written request to the distant authorities in Ottawa before he could so much as phone his lawyer.

Shortly after meeting Handfield (with whom he quickly developed a strong bond, based on their mutual passion for photography), Hampel told a judge of his desire "to settle this business as quickly as possible." But a few days later, on November 28, he was taken once more before a tribunal.

Two witnesses testified that day. The first was a CSIS agent named "Antony." Antony (false name) was tight-lipped when asked to explain the precise nature of Hampel's supposed activities in Canada. Instead the CSIS agent dwelt on the nature of Russia's SVR and its "illegal" agents, always speaking in general terms.

At the same time, however, all of the details about Hampel that he was not allowed to discuss were laid out in detail in a red file folder called the "Secret Proof," which was sitting on the desk in front of Judge Blais. But the judge, in turn, could not ask questions based on his knowledge of the Secret Proof, because that information was strictly concealed from the accused and his lawyer and therefore not to be discussed in open court. All that the judge was at liberty to discuss was the information in another file folder, this time a green one, which was also sitting on the table in front of him. But it contained only the pitiable amount of information that was already public.

The other witness was an investigator from Ontario's Office of the Registrar General. This official had, he said, searched the registry of children born in the province for any trace of a person named Paul William Hampel. He had found nothing, which meant that the birth certificate in Hampel's possession had to be a forgery. The investigator admitted that its registration number was authentic, but claimed that the number was attached to somebody else's birth certificate. However, he couldn't state the name of that person.

"Hampel doesn't exist," he concluded emphatically.

The Russian spy looked on placidly. But he couldn't help laughing when Judge Blais suggested that his parents come to court in order to prove he was the Canadian citizen he claimed to be!

Seven days later, however, Hampel realized that he had run out of room. It was time to drop the charade. That afternoon he took Stephane Handfield aside during a court recess and admitted that he was a Russian and revealed his real name and date of birth (October 21, 1961).

But he still claimed that he was not a spy, and this led to a classic standoff.

At first it seemed that everything was going to go smoothly. Handfield brought out his cellphone and called his colleagues at the Ministry of Justice. He reached them in a famous old bar in downtown Montreal, where they were amiably seated around a tableful of foaming draft beers. Soon they were hightailing it back to the Federal Court building.

The Russian's fate was sealed. Casually dressed in jeans and a blue shirt, his tiny glasses perched at the end of his nose, he smiled at the journalists. Then he renounced his right to a trial and insisted on speedy repatriation to his homeland.

Judge Blais, who hadn't dared hope for such a convenient outcome, immediately ordered Hampel's return to Russia. And Hampel went back to his cell, there to await the Russian consular authorities who would bring him a temporary travel permit.

But now, explicably, the process ground to a halt. Two weeks passed before a pair of Russian diplomats, including vice-consul Evgeny Katkin accompanied by Handfield, arrived in his cell. The Russians were withdrawn and impersonal; they did not seem to recognize him. Hampel, fearing that he was about to be abandoned, sank into a state of nervous exhaustion.

Three days passed. Finally the Russians agreed that, yes, he could be repatriated. But now they were left twiddling their thumbs. The rules said that the host country should contact them to organize the details of Hampel's return to Russia. But the phone was silent. Days went by.[21]

They weren't the only ones annoyed. "Canada washed its hands of him," fumes Handfield today. "It left the man to rot in prison."

But, where espionage is in play, there is a reason for everything. In this case it was that CSIS wanted a few days alone with Hampel to pump him for information. Stephane Handfield learned this one day when, arriving at the penitentiary to visit his client, he was told by a prison official told him that two men were waiting to speak with him in an antechamber.

"We'd like to meet with your client," was the substance of the first man's request.

"Who are you?" replied Handfield.

The men responded with their first names, as they had been trained to do.

"Then do you have business cards?" asked Handfield.

One of them flashed a CSIS card, allowing Handfield to see the characteristic colours but concealing his name with his finger.

Handfield said no. The two men walked out the door without further ado.

THE DISCREET DEPARTURE OF MR. HAMPEL

The day of departure drew near. But Handfield wanted to know exactly when it was going to arrive, so as to assist his client with the final details. Hampel, for his part, said that he simply had to have the memory cards from his computer. They contained his precious travel photography, and surely his lawyer, his only friend, knew how important that was to him.

Christmas arrived. So far as Handfield knew, he was still part of the game. But, on the evening of December 25, Ms. Toby Hoffman (the government's lawyer) called him and delivered the unexpected news that his client had just left the country. Hampel's fare had been paid by the Russian consulate. It took a few seconds before Handfield realized that he had been gulled, and then he was furious.

The spy on the payroll of the SVR had been escorted on board a Transaero flight to Moscow a short time earlier. His entourage was made up of Canadian officials in charge of returning lost parcels, as it were. Once inside, they removed his handcuffs and waited until departure was announced before leaving the aircraft. Hampel was left alone with his fellow passengers, mainly tourists. Were Canadian or Russian agents concealed among them? It's very likely. Before allowing him to board, Canada Border Service agents confiscated the bank cards that Hampel had insisted on bringing with him. This was done on the pretext that he had obtained the cards using his "borrowed" name.

The singular aspect of his departure was the absence of force.

This very much distinguished it from the way the affair had been managed since his arrest six weeks earlier. When the moment came for him to go, Moscow filed no official protest. Nor had it engaged in the diplomatic reprisals that are customary whenever one of its spies has been exposed. The business had all the earmarks of a prior arrangement, where both sides have agreed to save face.

But the Ottawa-Moscow ceasefire, if there was one, didn't last long. During the months after Hampel's return to his homeland, Russia's spy services turned on him. They questioned him angrily, as if he were concealing something. Hampel must have been surprised, but there was good reason for the change of tone. Part of the SVR's mandate in debriefing any agent who had been exposed and forcibly repatriated was to find out what damage had been done. This could only be a disagreeable process. The luckless party would be asked a number of pointed questions: How had he been unmasked? Who betrayed him? Had his network of contacts been exposed? Had his informants been identified? Any hesitation in answering would lead to a different kind of unpleasantness.

Back in Hampel's old Montreal apartment there remained a box of personal effects he had left behind. It included his shaving kit and various papers he had consigned to the garbage pail. But during their sweep CSIS agents had overlooked at least two copies of *My Beautiful Balkans* lying abandoned on a bookshelf. It was a surprising lapse because either might have contained microfilm or another variety of concealed document (in the opinion of an expert).

CSIS did find three short sets of notes about Canadian history. Now it was time to find out what purpose they had served. All of them were fully annotated, as if the agent were cramming for a test. But Hampel had already been living in Canada for fifteen years. With a purloined birth certificate in his wallet, he certainly wasn't going to be taking a citizenship exam. Was it possible that he kept them by way of boning up on the details of Canadian history, in case he got caught in a social conversation where everybody else knew what the Battle of Batoche was and he didn't?

The first of the three history cheat-sheets covered the period from the arrival of Jacques Cartier in 1534 to the resignation of Quebec Premier Louis-Alexandre Taschereau in 1936. The next, which consisted of a few jotted notes, covered the years in office and political allegiance of Canada's prime ministers from Mackenzie King in 1926 to Stephen Harper in 2006. The date of Harper's election victory was incorrect by a month. All the names were outlined, excepting those of Harper and of Paul Martin. Martin's name alone was not accompanied by the dates of his government, though elsewhere on the card Hampel had scribbled the date of the Meech Lake Accord.

The third card was much more detailed. It recapitulated the high points of Quebec history from 1899 to Jacques Parizeau's accession to office in 1994. Hampel had also made a sketch of the Quebec flag, noted the postwar baby boom and the decline of religion, written a few lines on the October Crisis of 1970, remembered the assassination of Pierre Laporte and the invocation of the War Measures Act, and recapitulated the first sovereignty referendum. In his mania for detail, the Russian had also recorded Jean Lesage's 1962 election slogan ("Masters in Our Own House"), the inauguration of the Mirabel Airport, the creation of the CSN (Confédération des syndicats nationaux, which represented all of the province's major trade unions), as well as the first appearance of the phrase "Je me souviens" on the licence plates of Quebec.

What happened afterward to the almost-Canadian who was now merely Hampel the Spy? He and his lawyer corresponded for several months after his expulsion. The lawyer's notes record that

Hampel offered updates on his debriefing, New Year's wishes, and repeated requests for his photo memory cards (which he needed for a second illustrated book). He also wanted the lawyer to locate his cameras, credit cards, and suitcases. By autumn of 2008 he was threatening to sue the government of Canada to get them back.

Throughout this period there was a nagging question in the back of the lawyer's head: if Hampel had been in Canada during 1995 and 1996, had he known Ian Mackenzie Lambert and Laurie Catherine Mary Lambert (alias Dimitri Olshevksy and Elena Borisovna Olshevskaya)? The SVR couple, who had appropriated the names of two dead Canadian infants, had been banished from Canada in early June of 1996. Like Hampel, they had been arrested on a security certificate. The investigation that finally caught them was called Operation Stanley Cup.[22]

The Lamberts are still the only deeply concealed illegals whose existence Russia has acknowledged. They lived in Toronto, a city Hampel visited regularly over a period of six years. Ian Lambert had, moreover, lived on the Rue de la Gauchetière in Montreal after arriving from Russia in the late 1980s, and later in Vancouver. He worked in a photo lab, while Laurie had a job with an insurance company.

In principle, Hampel should not even have known who they were, much less visited them. The illegals were not allowed to know whether colleagues from the homeland had been infiltrated into the same country as themselves. It was a wise precaution which ensured that, if captured, they could not betray their comrades.

Did Hampel and the Lamberts come out of the same group of trainee spies? Handfield asked this very question during a Federal Court hearing. The other side objected to the question on grounds of national security. Handfield was also unable to find out what illegal activities Hampel had supposedly been involved in.

Was Hampel a recruiter? Was he the manager of a mole working inside a Canadian agency or company? Or was Canada itself nothing more than a cover story that protected his identity during his missions to the Balkans?

The latter is the likeliest explanation, given what we know about SVR methods, and considering a certain coincidence that may shed more light on Hampel. We have learned that on November 9, 2006, shortly before his arrest, Hampel returned to Montreal aboard a flight from London, England. This was eight days after November 1, the day that Alexander Litvinenko was poisoned with Polonium-210 in the bar of the Millennium Hotel by men suspected of being Russian agents. We also know that London was crawling with Russian agents at that time. A number of them fled in the days following the Litvinenko assassination.

But the CSIS case analysis daintily avoids raising these questions. Is this because the agency in fact didn't know what Hampel was up to? It certainly wants us to think that, since one of its agents (identified only as "Antony") sturdily maintained in court that it had no definite information as to what he was doing in Canada.

There is, however, good reason to doubt Antony and to suspect that CSIS did know what Hampel was doing. A former CIA agent who was working in Canada during the months before Hampel's arrest told the Russian newspaper *Kommersant* that Hampel was an important player. "Very tolerant guys work in the Canadian intelligence," he said. "If they arrested him, it means that they spotted something serious. They don't take anybody into custody until they have enough charges." (Note in passing the kind of reputation our spy service has outside the country).

This is not the only occasion on which CSIS has pretended to know less than it really does. We can compare it with the very similar case of the so-called "Jesus Suares," another SVR illegal. Planted in Madrid with a business cover, "Suares"—who was actually Russian—managed to cause plenty of trouble for the United States, the European Union, and even NATO itself, while also becoming a thorn in the side of numerous foreign secret services.

Suares was finally identified in 2007 by western secret agents after he tried to corrupt an Estonian bureaucrat. The bureaucrat denounced him, and Suares was placed under tight surveillance, his every movement recorded until his shadowers had enough evidence to arrest him.

It was normal procedure to take a number of photographs of Suares while he was being shadowed. These photos would include people he met with and spoke with, and those images of course were carefully studied to see who these people were. In one of them the analysts spotted a sixtyish fellow with grey hair and blue eyes. They already knew this man, and seeing him in the company of a suspected spy set off alarms.

His name was Herman Simm and he was a high official of the Estonian Ministry of Defence. For at least ten years Simm had been senior enough to be able to read secret documents about European Union countries and their espionage operations. Even worse, Estonia had joined NATO in 2004. That meant that during the two years before the photo was taken, Simm had access to secret information about military plans directed against Russia and its allies. Among these were crucial specifications for the first western cyber-defence installation, which was located in Estonia itself.

This solved at least one mystery. For some time before Simm was identified, it was suspected that Russia's spy agencies had a source of highly classified information. They had known in advance about plans for the wars in Afghanistan and Kosovo, the proposed anti-missile shield to be installed near Russia's borders, NATO encryption codes, western attitudes toward the attack on Georgia in the summer of 2008, and western defences against cyber-attack. It was believed that an as-yet-unidentified mole, who likely possessed a diplomatic passport, had been funnelling this information to Jesus, his controller, using an old shortwave radio equipped to make use of illegal frequencies. This cozy little operation was still perking along when Simm and his wife were arrested by Estonian police in September 2008.

Under interrogation, Simm confessed that he had been blackmailed into collaborating with the SVR. He claimed that the SVR knew that he had worked for its predecessor, the KGB, and had threatened to reveal that. But the people who questioned him were skeptical. They thought that Simm had done it for money—in fact, that he had been paid colossal sums to betray NATO information. There was also a secondary motive, revenge, since Simm had been fired from his job on Estonia's police board in 1995 and was bitter about it.

The sums of money he received for his treasonous activity were enormous. He and his wife Heete owned a string of sumptuous properties, certainly enough to salve Simm's hurt feelings about losing his top cop job.

In other words, money and ego: the old story that never gets old! And there's more: as a master of the impostor's art, Simm was very likely a double agent for the German secret service as well.

THE (EX?) SPY WHO WANTED TO COME IN FROM THE COLD

The Lambert story returned to the headlines at about the same time that Hampel was arrested. At the end of November 2006, forty-three-year-old Laurie Lambert lost the last round of her lengthy judicial struggle against the Canadian government.

Back in December of 1996, the expelled Russian agent Laurie Lambert had officially become "Elena Miller" after marrying a British-born Canadian dentist named Peter Miller. Their marriage took place in Moscow. But even after it became known in Canada that she had previously been a spy, Lambert demonstrated a remarkably brazen attitude. She decided that she wanted to come back and live in Canada long after her right of residency, for obvious reasons, had been revoked. As we like to say in Montreal, quel culot! (What nerve!)

At this point Lambert, now Elena Miller, had already been back in Russia for ten years. But the United States still wanted to know what she had been up to, and so did Canada. The Russian authorities of course would have known that western governments were still interested in her, if only because they had attempted to recruit her before she left Canada. As one former CSIS operative told us, CSIS very much wanted "some money and an investigator competent to interrogate her." The belief was that Miller/Lambert possessed information on SVR training methods, not to mention a list of contacts, and perhaps even that ultimate prize in the undercover world, the identity of the moles burrowing away inside the Canadian government. It didn't seem to matter that, given the time that had passed, all of this information would likely be somewhat musty.

Elena ("Laurie") met her future dentist husband during the time she was an SVR agent. While still undercover in Canada, she had broken up with her spy-husband Ian Lambert ("Dimitri") after learning in autumn of 1994 that he was carrying on an affair with his SVR colleague Anita K.* In the weeks leading up to their separation CSIS agents had listened in on many a violent conjugal shouting match, thanks to up-to-date electronic listening systems. The listeners were impressed to discover that Ian and Laurie, who were

---

* In his book, Andrew Mitrovika describes how Dimitri and Anita were married on January 16, 1999, in the Russian city of Pskov, while Elena and Peter Miller looked on tenderly.

first-class illegals right down to their fingernails, remembered to carry on their fights in English even when they were completely enraged with each other. What professionals!

If one can believe her testimony, Elena resigned from the SVR shortly after her forced return to Russia. In a letter to public security minister Anne McLellan, postmarked August 2004, she wrote:

> On 11 June 1996 I informed the SVR of my resignation and subsequently went through weeks of debriefing. I have provided CIC [Citizenship and Immigration Canada] with all the evidence I possess verifying the fact that I did leave the SVR on 21 October 1996 at my own wish.
>
> I have no ties with the former employer, the SVR, whatsoever. I swore to that fact in front of a Canadian Consul in Russia. And I have a very clear idea of what it means to be under oath.[23]

The Millers began their quest to have Elena immigrate to Canada in the last month of 1998. On December 11 of that year Peter Miller asked to become his wife's sponsor so that the family could be reunited. It was the beginning of a bitter battle with Canadian officials who were adamantly opposed to the beautiful spy's reunion with her husband in Canada.

Nearly eight years later the battle continued. By this time the Canada Border Services Agency (CBSA) had become quite fierce in the tone it took toward the one-time spy. This is from a CBSA memo dated August 16, 2004 to Anne McLellan:

> Although Ms. Miller has reportedly resigned from the SVR, she nonetheless posed as a Canadian citizen for

a period of six years while working as an illegal for
the SVR in order to conduct espionage activities. She
refuses to discuss the nature of her activities while in
Canada, which is disturbing.

We are of the opinion that Ms. Miller has not demonstrated any positive contribution to Canadian society
nor has she demonstrated that her presence in Canada
would not be detrimental to the national interest.

By March 8, 2005, the Ministry of Public Safety Canada,
unsurprisingly, came down on the side of the Border Services
Agency. It would not revoke the order barring Elena Miller from
Canadian soil under Article 34(1) of the Immigration and Refugee
Protection Act.

A month later the Canadian embassy in Moscow informed
the Millers that their application had been rejected. They reacted
angrily, believing themselves unjustly treated and even harmed by
the immigration department's "excessive delay" in processing their
application. Once again they decided to go to the courts to obtain
damages and interest. In an affidavit in support of their request,
Peter Miller awkwardly reveals his inner turmoil:

8. It is my belief that, from the beginning, immigration officials who were involved in examining Elena's
request for legitimization and her request for ministerial dispensation had no intention of allowing her to
come to Canada and live here with me. Mme. Coulter's
first conclusion, to the effect that our marriage was not
authentic, appears to me to be a pretext for rejecting the
request and a means of preventing the Ministry from
seeing my wife's request for dispensation. We have given

her a quantity of items concerning our relationship, in particular our efforts to remain in contact with each other—records of telephone conversations, passport stamps attesting to my visits to Russia, photographs, as well as declarations from both our families testifying to the strength of our relationship. . . .

10. The officials involved in the administration of my wife's request have not shown themselves to be honest in their dealings with us. They have led both Elena and myself to believe that a decision would be made within the length of time specified by law, and have not respected this undertaking. They gave us hope while having no intention of responding to that hope. . . .

Not once before we received the unfavourable decision in May 2004 which denied us any right of reply did these immigration officials inform us that they had irrevocably adopted the position that the Ministry should not grant dispensation to my wife. It is much worse when one follows a process which seems to offer fair treatment, but which is later revealed to be a charade. It would have been better had the officials told us honestly that my wife had no chance whatever of obtaining a ministerial dispensation. In that case, with the truth in hand, we could at least have decided how to continue our marriage and where we should live. Instead we waited, and then waited some more; we hoped, and then we hoped some more, for a favourable outcome to our request.[24]

These arguments were rejected by Justice James K. Hugessen, who, in his decision on November 30, 2006, wrote the following:

> The proof produced in the present petition fails to
> establish that the officials in question had any obliga-
> tion other than to the people of Canada, which is to say
> that they were obliged to examine as impartially as pos-
> sible the request for dispensation and special treatment
> presented by an admitted Russian spy who has scandal-
> ously abused the hospitality of this country.

After so many reversals, the Millers appear to have abandoned
their quest and resigned themselves to living in Switzerland. Their
Toronto lawyer, Barbara Jackman, who was contacted during the
preparation of this book, said that her clients were not interested in
answering any more questions from journalists.

CHAPTER 003

Even Our Friends Are Spying on Us

Nations do not have friends, they have interests.
—Lord Palmerston, British statesman, 1784–1865

Canada has a rich history of espionage, which was particularly distinguished during the two world wars. One of the master spies who rose to the challenge during those conflicts was the celebrated Sir William Samuel Stephenson. A physically small man who grew up in Winnipeg, he carried on his trade during both world wars under the code name "Intrepid." In 1940 he was dispatched to the United States as the personal representative of British Prime Minister Winston Churchill to U.S. President Franklin D. Roosevelt. Stephenson was also authorized to make himself available to the American secret services, which needed reorganizing under an expert's supervision. It was his idea to create what would become the Office of Strategic Services (OSS) and he suggested his personal friend William J. "Wild Bill" Donovan lead the new organization. The OSS later became the Central Intelligence Agency.

From his base in New York, Intrepid directed all the clandestine operations of the British secret services in Canada, the United

States, and most of the African and South American countries. He also dispatched a number of undercover agents to Europe.

Stephenson was the driving force behind the building of a secret Allied training camp in Whitby, Ontario. "Camp X," as it was called, trained more than two thousand spies, largely but not exclusively Canadian, American, and British, and then sent them off to Asia and Europe as well as to North American postings. There is more than a bit of Intrepid in the fictional character James Bond, as confirmed by his creator, Ian Fleming. In a 1962 interview he specifically said that his character was modelled on Sir William Stephenson.[25]

Also worthy of note is the fact that many historians believe the Cold War itself to have begun in Canada, in the city of Ottawa. On a September evening in 1945, Igor Gouzenko, a KGB operative in charge of secret communications in the Soviet embassy, silently quit his job. He walked out the door carrying a briefcase containing 109 documents concerning the Russian spy system. Through these papers the world learned for the first time about "sleeper agents."

Gouzenko's decision to defect was not made lightly. He had gone so far as to discuss it with his wife, and they had agreed that they would never return to the Soviet Union. At the time, the USSR was devastated in the aftermath of its terrible struggle in the Second World War, and it was increasingly ravaged by government paranoia, which had led to the deaths of countless officials, most of them guilty of nothing. Understanding the finality of his decision, Gouzenko made sure to bring with him sufficient documents not only to reveal the scale of Soviet espionage, but also to lay bare the names of those making up the KGB network. So thorough was his preparation that he was able to prove that many countries that had fallen under Russian control during the war were already sending moles to live in North America.

Gouzenko's revelations were stunning, all the more so because western security services at that time had very little idea what the Communists were up to. Gouzenko's documents proved that not only were the Soviet networks extensive, they had also infiltrated an impressive number of western governments, the upper echelons of those countries' armed forces, and their major defence industries. Though Ottawa itself was a sleepy relic of the old British Empire, on that day it became the epicentre of a political earthquake the aftershocks of which would be felt for fifty years.

Until the collapse of the Soviet system, the East and West blocs were like the two stone walls of an archway. Where they lean in at the top to press against each other, they are held apart by the adroitly placed keystone. Canada was that keystone. And that was an uncomfortable position to be in. Our territory was located between the opposing blocs. In the event of nuclear conflict, American and Soviet missiles would literally whiz past each other in the skies high above the Canadian Arctic.

With the Cuban missile crisis in October 1962, the long-feared nuclear war very nearly came about. Thanks to a new generation of spy planes, the United States learned that Russia was building short- and medium-range missile launching ramps in Cuba. These were an immediate threat to the United States, since anything launched from Cuba would strike with virtually no warning. As political tensions skyrocketed, America resolved that the only solution was an invasion of Cuba.

Had this invasion occurred, the Soviet Union would have been obliged to enter the fight. But President John F. Kennedy stepped back from that precipice and bought time by imposing a naval blockade around the Caribbean nation. The USSR responded with an aggressive but finely judged move to break the blockade by sending a fleet of merchant ships to Cuba.

The moment of truth was fast approaching, and both sides put their armies and air forces on a war footing. For the United States this could be effective only if their planes and missiles had full liberty to move through Canadian air space on their way to attacking the Soviet Union.

America's need was so urgent that the first Canadians to hear of it, according to a retired Air Canada flight attendant, were the crews of civil aircraft flying between Canadian cities. In her case, she was working onboard a flight between Montreal and Vancouver when she learned that the U.S. armed forces had ordered all flights in Canadian airspace—including hers—to turn and fly directly north, as far as they could. This was to allow an unobstructed north-south flyway for nuclear-armed bombers and missiles heading for the Soviet Union. Fortunately the alert was quickly countermanded and civil aircraft were able to return to their scheduled routes before the passengers noticed that anything was wrong.

If this little-known episode demonstrates the importance of Canada's territory for American self-defence (an idea that returned with a vengeance after the terrorist attacks of September 11, 2001), the same could be said for Canada's importance to the Red Army. That is why Canada, however unwillingly, has been host to a significant number of KGB and GRU spies.*

With the rise of the New Russia under President Vladimir Putin, himself a former KGB officer, many experts have come to believe that there is now a resurgence of Cold War tensions (these specialists, if pressured, may admit that they also don't think the Cold War ever ended). CSIS has already noted the rapid growth of Russian-sponsored espionage in Canada. Observant members of the public have

---

* GRU (Glavnoje Razvedyvatel'noje Upravlenije): The Soviet Army Department for Offensive Intelligence, a branch that is still operational today.

also noticed how frequently Ottawa has ordered Russian diplomats to return home because of "activities incompatible with their official responsibilities."

CANADIAN PEACENIKS

With the dramatic dissolution of the Soviet bloc after 1989, Canadian politicians competed with each other to cut back on the amount of money spent on national security. Some leaders babbled about "peace dividends" and seriously contemplated abolishing counter-espionage altogether. CSIS's budgets and staff were reduced by nearly half, at a time when hostile governments were already rebuilding their espionage networks.

This raises questions about the Canadian political system. Why do we produce so few leaders capable of dealing seriously with these issues? There is in this country a persistent belief that espionage is somebody else's problem. Do we really believe that Ronald Reagan's "evil empire" has simply faded away? If so, who is sending all these freshly minted and highly motivated spies to Canada? Do we have something that they want? Why do China, Israel, France, Pakistan, and many other countries also do us the honour of sending legions of spies to take up a Canadian address?

"MORE THAN YESTERDAY, LESS THAN TOMORROW"

We can't really analyze the problem without first asking how many different kinds of espionage networks presently operate in our country. These are the principal areas of activity:

- Economic and industrial
- Surveillance and suppression of dissidents
- Manipulation of foreign political systems

- Military espionage
- Research into the proliferation of weapons of mass destruction.*

Many countries are involved in espionage, and their tangled activities are perhaps best compared to the Argentine tango. They are locked together in a tight and hostile series of manoeuvres where boundaries mean little, whether territorial, legal, emotional, or ethical. Nothing is respected, and the end always justifies the means. To put it simply, spies operate outside of all legal frameworks. The local loyalties that most of us feel have no importance on this chessboard, where all moves are strategic and the players treat people and places as mere pawns, to be played according to the needs of the game.

This is the dynamic that determines Canada's role in the great scheme of things. It is not, perhaps, an inspiring one. At worst, chance has dealt us the role of victim; at best, we are a happenstance pawn in a deadly game much bigger than ourselves.

ECONOMIC AND INDUSTRIAL ESPIONAGE

All the varieties of contemporary espionage have the same goal—to steal information and obtain an economic advantage it wouldn't otherwise possess—but the actors are always different. To put the whole thing in its simplest terms, there are two approaches:

- Economic espionage: state versus state (which may involve attacks on somebody else's corporate sector)
- Industrial espionage: corporation versus corporation

---

* Counter-espionage activity also includes research into a hostile country's acquisition of weapons or of technology necessary to the development of weapons of mass destruction.

Economic Espionage

Some countries structure their spy services specifically for the purpose of stealing industrial secrets or economic information. Many specialists believe that the end of the Cold War meant only that efforts previously devoted to gaining military superiority were now shifted to economic theft. The object is still, as it always was, the domination of various markets, but warlike methods have been replaced by aggressive national marketing strategies.

This means that a rivalry once frankly military in nature has morphed into something more difficult to pin down. Today we have nations aggressively positioning themselves to monopolize strategic markets. Where the traditional laws of the marketplace don't offer a winning outcome, certain countries have found that aggressive espionage can give them the advantage they need. Here there are no rules: spying, corruption, technology theft, and even assassination of the other party's key researchers are part of the vicious new game. And nations will likewise "defend" their economies by tracking and brutally eliminating spies.

Once the logic of the game is accepted, the "Napoleonic defence" is easy to justify.*

After the collapse of the Soviet Union, leaders of the G8 countries committed themselves to economic espionage. They made no secret of it. The stakes had changed, and it was time to become proactive. Canada, however, did not make this commitment. Our governments were aware of economic espionage, of course, but never did more than timidly advise the intelligence services to keep a watching brief on the matter. This was hardly the same thing as adopting the decisive and ruthless policies that our supposed allies were already employing.

---

* "The best defence is a good offence," a popular adage usually attributed to Napoleon.

In 1993, President Bill Clinton, addressing the Central
Intelligence Agency, listed the following U.S. priorities: environmental security, economic espionage, and democratization. The
following year, in a speech directed to America's undercover agencies, he reminded them that a spy's first loyalty is to his elected leaders. Undercover agents were directed to help in the formation of
new national policies by keeping leaders abreast of developments in
parts of the world where America had strategic interests.

Warming to his subject, Clinton also made it clear that he would
not be satisfied with mere summaries of publicly available information. When America negotiated commercial arrangements with
other countries, it needed to have their classified information at its
disposal. On top of that, it was intolerable that American companies should be harassed by foreign intelligence agencies. They were
also entitled to know what their foreign competitors were up to.

The upshot of all this speechifying was the 1996 Economic
Espionage Act. It has since been the subject of more than two hundred court challenges and lawsuits.

There is nothing surprising in this. It was the logical outcome
of a slowly dawning realization among the great powers that they
had to "defend themselves" against economic sabotage by other
countries. The United States in particular set out to develop a legal
framework that would legitimize its activities not only at home, but
also abroad. Here are the countries that adopted such legislation:

- 1992: Russian president Boris Yeltsin ratifies the *Law on the
Collection of Information Abroad.*
- 1992: France modifies its Penal Code in order to legitimize the
law concerning espionage. This new legislation is intended
not only to protect "national defence interests" but also the
"fundamental interests of the nation."

- 1994: Great Britain ratifies the Intelligence Services Act, which for the first time makes public the responsibilities of the various British secret services. It also reveals that Britain has created an organization analogous to America's National Security Administration. It is to be called the Government Communication Headquarters.
- 1996: America adopts the Economic Espionage Act.

And what about Canada? There was no reaction to our allies' dramatic moves until 2002, a lapse of six years. And when legislation finally emerged, it did not seriously touch on the subject of espionage within Canada. It was, instead, an obligatory response to the horrific events of September 11, 2001. The federal government, under Jean Chrétien, brought forth Bill C-36 (usually referred to as the Anti-Terrorism Law), a piece of omnibus legislation that dealt with a number of issues. These included an updating of the obsolete Official Secrets Act as well as several provisions to the Act on Protection of Personal Information.

C-36 was, in effect, a kind of "hobo stew" with a lot of ingredients. Almost lost among them were two tiny clauses about espionage in general, and economic espionage in particular, which government lawyers were able to insert. Neither has ever been used. It was a sad and ineffective response to a problem that was, by that time, acknowledged as urgent and global by our allies.

THE GOOD, THE BAD, AND THE UGLY

When the time came to identify the major players in this new melodrama, the usual suspects (in their usual roles) came onstage to take a bow. They "owned" these parts, which they naturally expected would continue to be the leading roles. These players were Russia, China, Iran, Syria, and Iraq. In Iraq, Saddam Hussein was hard at work locating key technologies necessary to the production of weapons of mass destruction. All of these countries had previously operated in Canada.

But there was a new and disquieting development. Nations traditionally friendly to Canada were now setting up intelligence-gathering operations within our borders. Among them were nations that had regained freedom after the collapse of the Soviet bloc. Operating independently once again, they quickly terminated previous information-sharing agreements. They became suspicious of each other.

At this time, CSIS possessed a reasonably exhaustive list of the countries involved in economic espionage against Canada. By the mid-1990s the list included the following:

Economic Espionage		
Argentina	Iran	Philippines
Brazil	Iraq	Russia
China	Israel	South Korea
Cuba	Italy	Spain
Egypt	Japan	Taiwan
France	North Korea	United States
		Vietnam

The KGB and similar organizations had always frankly aimed at stealing western technology, whether military or not. The West used to look down its nose at that sort of thing. But now many countries had come to appreciate that it is easier to steal than to invent.

What did this mean? Less-developed countries came to feel that the best way to catch up was to obtain from others the information they hadn't developed for themselves. Where the technology in question was military, there was also the strategic benefit of maintaining a balance of force by neutralizing the other party's technological advantages.

If the technology was commercial, stealing it not only saved the money that the originating country or corporation had spent on development, it also allowed the thief to put the product on the market faster and cheaper than its inventor could.

During the 1980s, France's Direction Générale de la Sécurité Extérieure (DGSE), responsible for espionage outside France, managed to infiltrate both IBM and Texas Instruments. Its network was eventually shut down by a combined FBI-CIA operation, leading the DGSE to suspect that an American mole was at work inside its own headquarters.

This skirmish created quite a lot of ill feeling between the two security services. The Americans were bitter enough to make public some embarrassing French documents—evidently stolen—that dated back to 1988 and came from France's minister of Science, Technology, and Exports. These constituted a kind of shopping list of forty-nine companies and twenty-four public institutions in Canada, England, and the United States that were to be targets of French espionage. The object was to find out what weaponry America intended to purchase abroad, its plans for satellite systems, its negotiating strategy for commercial treaties, and to secure as well "professional" information on high-ranking American officials.

Pierre Marion, at that time director of the DGSE, had earlier declared that French agents would assist French companies in competing with foreign corporations, but piously added that they would never stoop to stealing military and political information from their allies. But it seems he was defining those words very loosely, because the documents revealed by the American spooks clearly showed that France was trying to steal British Aerospace's drawings for the combat systems of the Tornado jet fighter, the Advanced Short Range Air to Air Missile (ASRAAM), and the marketing plan of the Advanced Medium Range Air to Air Missile (ADRAAM).

Also included in the French shopping list was information on the British Navy's deal to help Germany and Italy build warships for NATO use, as well as Britain's Rapier air defence program. That might seem odd, given that France itself is a member of NATO, but until 2009 its representatives declined to be part of NATO's high command. This unhelpful attitude was not always in France's interest, but General De Gaulle's lifelong dislike of the Anglo-Saxon countries made it worthwhile to stick a finger in an English eye for the intrinsic pleasure of doing so. Anglo-French relations have never completely recovered.

In 1991, six French operatives were deported by the FBI after they tried to appropriate America's stealth technology for radar camouflage of ships and aircraft. But the French-American game has never stopped. The French government responded by expelling five Americans accused of being CIA agents (the Paris station chief and four pseudo-diplomats). These apparently had infiltrated the government of Prime Minister Édouard Balladur while François Mitterrand while still president.

There was also the business of the secret microphones said to be stitched into Air France's well-padded business-class seats. Although Air France categorically denied any connection to espionage, if the DGSE was curious about the plans of a foreign business delegation, it reportedly would simply ascertain which Air France flight it was on, call the airline's head office, and make sure the gentlemen in question were seated in those particular seats. The tape recording of their conversation during the flight would then be passed back to the security agency.

Industrial Espionage

Very recently a scandal broke out in Canada when WestJet and Air Canada accused each other of stealing commercial information. WestJet believed that Air Canada had hired private detectives to rummage through the domestic garbage pail of a WestJet executive. Air Canada in turn accused WestJet of hiring a former Air Canada employee in order to get hold of his access codes and thereby ransack Air Canada's computer database. In the end, it was WestJet that acknowledged "unethical and unacceptable" conduct and paid for it with a legal settlement.

This kind of behaviour isn't nearly as unusual as most Canadians may think. The problem is that the average company doesn't want its customers and shareholders to know that its security system failed, and so it covers up. At the same time the Canadian government refuses to take the problem seriously. One must fall back on American and French statistics to get an idea of what is really going on in Canada.

In 2002 the American Society for Industrial Security (ASIS) and PricewaterhouseCoopers estimated that industrial espionage had cost Fortune 1000 companies more than $59 billion in lost revenue during the year 2001 alone. The corresponding French figure for the same year was 1.5 billion Euros, according to French intelligence.

So far as we know, the only Canadian study of the problem dates back to 1995. Prepared by CSIS, it shows that the average annual loss to Canadian business from espionage was between $10 and $12 billion. This startling figure, which amounts to a billion dollars a month, includes intellectual theft, loss of market share, and loss of contracts as well. It's a steep price in terms of a reduced ability to compete, loss of employment, and diminished prestige and credibility on the international stage. For every hundred million dollars lost, it is said that one thousand jobs vanish.

The spies don't always come from away. As much as 85 percent of industrial spying is carried out by people on the payroll of the company affected. Consider Ottawa-based Mitel, a developer of business communication networks. In 1998 Mitel had the courage to reveal that some of its employees had stolen proprietary information. The case, which ended up in court, is instructive.

It began when, one morning, a young Asian woman arrived at Mitel's front desk and handed a brown envelope to a security agent. She then turned on her heels and left. The envelope contained information about a certain To Van Tran, who had been working for Mitel for sixteen years. It revealed that Tran had stolen Mitel's newest product in the cutting-edge telephone technology called Private Branch Exchange, or PBX.

Mitel learned that three years earlier Tran had begun a business relationship with people in his homeland, Vietnam. One day he had simply slipped a PBX unit under his arm and flown back to Vietnam, where he sold it to that country's armed forces. Less than a month later copies of the unit flooded into the international marketplace at a price that Mitel could not hope to match.

The company's security chief later told authorities that Mitel had lost six years of research, $45 million U.S. in research and development, and somewhere between $200 million and $1 billion U.S. in market share. Mitel took its grievance to Canada's security agencies, but they were not able to help. Tran was then arrested by the Ontario Provincial Police and charged with fraud and possession of stolen property. He paid a $25,000 fine and received a six-month suspended sentence.

Tran's punishment was ludicrous when compared with the damage he had done, but it came as no surprise to the security industry, which sees similar cases almost every day. Even when the evidence is overwhelming and the court actually convicts the perpetrator (a near-miracle in our justice system), the penalty meted out has no deterrent effect.

In a word, our laws are useless and our investigators have their hands tied.

If the police and the counter-espionage services are impotent, does that mean that the battle is already lost? Perhaps not, but it's hard to see a silver lining in the situation. At present the security burden is carried entirely by corporate management. There are few preventive measures they can take, though, since they have little access to data that might help them understand the problem. There is also a culture of shame and silence that cloaks the subject, where those who have been victimized hide the fact rather than sharing what they have learned.

It's harder still to detect and measure the quantity of clandestine information theft carried out by so-called "front companies." While appearing to be legitimate and properly incorporated private businesses, these are owned and controlled by a foreign government. They have no bottom line to worry about. Their sole purpose is to steal intellectual property or merchandise designated as "controlled."*

In Canada these companies enjoy a tremendous legal advantage that prevents our counter-espionage people from collaring the spies

---

* The Canadian government each year releases a list of goods and services designated as "controlled," which are generally of a military or military/civilian nature. The control is intended principally to prevent weapons proliferation.

they conceal. This is how it works. Front or "umbrella" companies, as stand-alone commercial entities, are committing what the law calls "industrial espionage." But CSIS management decided long ago that federal agents may not investigate industrial espionage. They are permitted only to chase after economic espionage. To their sorrow, CSIS officers have come to understand that this distinction is absolute. Any espionage practised by an incorporated company is considered to be industrial in nature. Only the police or private security agencies can investigate these offences. This bureaucratic leg shackle has tripped up CSIS agents again and again, while the industrial spies jog happily on down the road. The cost to our economy is very large.

And You Thought You Were Safe in Canada: The Immigrant's Dilemma
Together with the losses caused by economic spying comes the scourge that we call "foreign interference." This means the surveillance and intimidation of our cultural communities by agents sent from their homelands. It's nearly as big a security problem as the economic theft of products and ideas.

Canada has become a refuge for any number of individuals and communities that have been persecuted in their country of origin. Enjoying their newfound freedom of speech, they turn eagerly on the homeland regimes that abused them and continue to abuse those left behind. They publicly proclaim the illegitimacy of governments that are, to put it mildly, unaccustomed to criticism. These regimes strike back. Many send agents to Canada to report on the behaviour of their emigrant community. Some instruct the agents to track and occasionally to silence dissident voices. We have seen cases that run the gamut of undercover activity from the recruiting of local informants to the importing of double agents, with considerable intimidation, harassment, and physical assault along the way. There have been assassinations.

Clandestine Foreign Interference		
Algeria	India	Romania
Saudi Arabia	Iran	Russia
Armenia	Israel	Taiwan
China	Malaysia	Tunisia
Cuba	Morocco	Ukraine
North Korea	Mexico	Vietnam
South Korea		

Canada has a responsibility to protect people who have chosen to live here from this kind of reprehensible behaviour. And
CSIS does in fact have a mandate to report such espionage to the
Canadian government. But these are long, complicated, and expensive investigations. It can take literally decades before the Canadian
government feels it has the evidence in hand to put an end to the
bullying.

We will return to this subject for detailed analysis in a subse-
quent chapter, but just to underline the stakes for those affected,
we want to dwell for a moment on the role played by India's police
authorities in the Air India affair. This is a case in which there is
troubling evidence of that country's undercover agents infiltrating
Canada's Sikh community and being in contact with the principal
suspects in the crime. The agents operated secretly out of India's
embassy in Ottawa. We might also mention Iranian agents based
in Canada who systematically intimidate Iranian emigrants living

here. Many have become Canadian citizens but find that that offers little protection.

Canadians would be shocked if they understood the climate of fear in which many of their fellow citizens must live, for no reason other than the happenstance that they were born abroad and chose to come to Canada. Many immigrant communities are, in effect, taken hostage by agents of their homeland government. These governments have few or no democratic scruples. When the victims approach Canadian authorities for help they are met with avoidance and moral equivocation. After being repeatedly rebuffed, they lose hope. After all, the Canadian government is now the only government they have. If it chooses to ignore them, there is nowhere else to go.

Those who are exceptionally determined will persist until they have put together incontrovertible proof of bullying and harassment by non-Canadians who are holed up in one embassy or another under diplomatic cover. Their message reaches the Ministry of Foreign Affairs. It reaches Industry Canada. And there the functionaries consider the range of reprisals that they are legally mandated to exercise. These include official complaints to the foreign government, expulsion of diplomats who have abused their privileges, or summoning the country's ambassador for a private audience with the minister concerned. They consider these things, and then they put them back in the drawer and have a cup of coffee. Oh my, they think. What if this country expels our ambassador? What if a Canadian company loses its contract with them?

Canada has become a country where trade and commerce are far more valuable than the security of the citizen. Law enforcement agencies reluctantly accept that most Canadians and their representatives don't really understand the issue. Agencies will issue releases and call press conferences, but they expect little response.

At the same time, those in the security business must share the blame. They have not effectively educated the public (and the government). Nor do they like to share information. Many journalists have complained about the brick wall they encounter in trying to obtain information from CSIS, our major counter-espionage authority. And when it comes to explaining its mission to the public, CSIS is as guilty as the lamest bureaucrat of muffling the message in platitudes and jargon.

Many CSIS employees have questioned a media strategy that consists of little more than a brisk "No comment." For many years the working agents have lobbied for a policy of transparency. They reason that it's better for the public to know what's involved in defending its interests against espionage, state interference, or outright terrorism. They also know, as working agents, that their own safety depends on concealing some information. But this is not actually very difficult to do, in spite of claims to the contrary from the authorities. Reasonable precaution can be part of a policy of greater openness.

Still, CSIS's senior officials, together with successive governments, have turned a deaf ear. This is the major cause of the media's endless sniping at CSIS. This, unfortunately, plays into the hands of those who have the most reason to fear a strong and effective CSIS.

Political Espionage and Foreign Interference: The Vulnerability of Elected Representatives

It's perfectly legitimate for foreign diplomats to meet with Canadian political representatives, and later on to socialize with them, and even invite them to their homelands as part of a healthy exchange of experience and ideas. All of this, in the long run, serves Canada's interests. But it can also be a screen for less admirable activities. For some foreign representatives here, Job One is finding ways to influence politicians, and their methods go well beyond sightseeing, chit-chat, and charm. They may instead be carefully studying an elected official's personal activities, or the vulnerabilities created by his or her political position. These things are hard to conceal, and they make it relatively easy to compromise the person in question.

The compromised victim might be an elected leader or government official. The snares they fall into include not only the familiar tactic of sexual entrapment but also situations that most people would take to be innocent, or at least unlikely to involve foreign spies. A business person or diplomat, for example, is used to signing complicated deals or accepting a goodwill gift. Just one example among many: For quite some time it was the custom for Canadian diplomats in Hong Kong to receive "red envelopes" from wealthy entrepreneurs and, occasionally, from criminals associated with Chinese gangs. The several hundred dollars in the envelope were accompanied by suggestions that they enjoy activities considered innocuous in Hong Kong, such as betting at horse races. Obviously the idea was to make it easier for the giver to ask for an occasional favour, such as a visa for a family member or business associate. The practice might seem harmless if it involved only an occasional undesirable arriving in Canada, but CSIS and RCMP records show that Chinese agents and criminals who benefited from these informal gestures on the part of naive Canadians now number in the hundreds.

From time to time, and with the best of motives, a Canadian diplomat will make a poorly reasoned decision or become an advocate for a cause he doesn't really understand. Others do it for monetary gain. Yet others are sexually compromised, or caught in a conflict of interest. These gullible Canadians soon find themselves in the shadowy underworld of intimidation and blackmail.

CSIS puts a lot of effort into educating our representatives abroad about the risks, particularly of doing things that the host country considers illegal. They also tell people who should not need telling that it's a good idea to shun any sexual opportunity that looks too good to be true. Generally the warnings fall on deaf ears. Then, in due course, the inevitable happens and security people deliver the bad news to the Prime Minister's Office. The PM bounces the guilty party into another job and figures the matter is done with. Not a single Canadian official has yet been charged for collaboration with foreign agents. Meanwhile, incidents of collaboration become ever more frequent.

Military Spying and Weapons of Mass Destruction

In the area of weapons proliferation and military technology, Canada has more to offer than most of us realize. Militarily speaking, despite a habit of underestimating our prowess—or apologizing for having any—our country is an important player on the international scene. We have a place at the NATO and NORAD tables.* Weapons of mass destruction (WMD) research, from nuclear to chemical to bacteriological, is carried out in our universities. That's why our weaponry and operational plans are of great interest to foreign powers. They are also aware that our allies share desirable information with us, and that hundreds of foreign military officers

---

* North Atlantic Treaty Organization and North American Aerospace Defense Command.

are posted to our army, navy, and air force bases. It's up to us to see to it that these individuals are not approached, threatened, or harmed by the agents of unfriendly countries.

International trafficking in Canadian-made weaponry is another poorly understood subject. We are an unusually open society and, for the time being at least, we enjoy a reputation for integrity. International arms traffickers take advantage of the situation. They steal weapon prototypes or use Canada as a convenient transit route for international arms shipments. Spies from Iran and China—and even from allied nations such as Israel and France—come to Canada in order to recruit collaborators. They approach private business people or officials in certain government ministries who may, for a fee, be persuaded to serve as go-betweens in the sale of technology categorized as "dual purpose."

"Dual purpose" technologies are those originally developed for civilian products but which can also be used to improve weapons; sometimes they appear on the frontier between bio-weapon research and legitimate medical research. They are subject to high security, but foreign agents exploit the lapses that occur in transferring them between private sector and military use.

A good example is a large shipment of sophisticated ceramic pipes that was intercepted in the port of Vancouver some years ago. An Iranian diplomat in Ottawa had persuaded a Canadian company to lend itself to this lucrative arrangement. The pipes, designed to resist high pressure and able to transport corrosive and toxic chemical products, were supposedly to be shipped to Asia and used in the manufacture of agricultural equipment. But the real destination was Iran.

The shipping manifest, of course, mentioned neither Iran nor the true nature of the cargo. Iran was on the list of countries prohibited from purchasing this product, for the very good reason that it could be used in its controversial nuclear program. But it is now among the technologies successfully acquired by this Islamic republic.

Though the file remains confidential to this day, we can safely say that Canada was not the only country targeted by Iran. Similar incidents have occurred in Great Britain and the United States. Germany recently lost a valuable informant who had worked as a double agent for more than ten years. This person was Iranian-Canadian and was known to have supplied Germany with sensitive information about Iran's nuclear program. He was a businessman with interests in Germany and Canada.

HOW IT IS DONE

Most spies in Canada are working under protection of diplomatic immunity. It's the best possible cover because it allows the "diplomat" to socialize with Canadians from all levels of society. He or she will meet with city councillors, journalists, captains of industry, and even writers and artists. But this strategy shows its true value when things go wrong and the foreign agent posing as a diplomat demands her rights under the Geneva Conventions, which set out the rules for diplomatic immunity. If this "diplomat" commits a crime, whether espionage-related or a regular Criminal Code offence, he or she cannot be tried before a Canadian judge, only sent home as a *persona non grata*.*

---

* We recall the case of Catherine MacLean, who died, and of Catherine Dore, who was seriously injured after being struck by the vehicle of Russian diplomat Andrei Knyazev on 27 January 2001. After a day of ice-fishing and heavy drinking, Knyazev was at the wheel of his own car. Since Russia refused to withdraw his diplomatic immunity he could not be tried in Canada. Once he was back in Russia, however, Canada brought diplomatic pressure to bear and Knyazev was tried and convicted of manslaughter by a Russian court.

There are sometimes good reasons for a spy to eschew diplomatic status, especially where a civilian identity gives him better access to restricted information. That's why we find spies posing as university students, researchers, and sometimes even tenured professors. They may also be engineers on a temporary overseas posting, foreign correspondents, or even an artist looking for inspiration in an exotic setting.

The Art of Collecting Information

Within the trade we recognize three different forms of information, identified by these acronyms:

- HUMINT is Human Intelligence, meaning information gathered from informants.
- SIGINT is Signals Intelligence, gathered by intercepting all forms of electronic communication.
- OSINT is Open Source Intelligence, or information that might be published in newspapers or broadcast publicly.

All three are used by agents planted in Canada, but the recruiting of informants is by far the most popular. As a rule this involves a series of carefully planned encounters with the target person, meetings that are made to appear coincidental, or at least predictable within the target's lifestyle (a journalist meeting a journalist, for example). Eventually, if everything works out, a collaboration is agreed on. The agent-spy will have spent time weighing the pros and cons of different approaches and identifying the one most likely to work with a given target.

There are four main approaches, corresponding to the most reliable human weaknesses: Money, Ideology, Sex, and Ego. Agents sum it up with the acronym MISE (the French acronym, AISE, is easier to remember, since it stands for Argent, Idéologie, Sexe, et Ego, and *aisé* also means "easy").

An appeal to one of the "four weaknesses" is remarkably effective, even though few believe it would work on them. That is perhaps what makes it "easy."

AND WHAT ARE WE DOING ABOUT IT?

In spite of CSIS's best efforts, Canada's leaders do not take the problem of espionage seriously. That isn't because they don't know about it, but it can fairly be said that they don't appreciate the extent of it. If we reflect on the kind of espionage story that makes the headlines, it's usually a case in which a well-meaning government minister or CEO becomes aware of a particular outrage and denounces the country that committed it. It's usually something that threatens that individual. To the average Canadian, this adds up to a series of piecemeal and unconnected events. There is really nobody outside intelligence agencies who knows how all these various crises fit together, and so there is nobody who can rally public support behind an effective solution.

And yet solutions are possible where the political will exists. That will happen when Canadians collectively decide that this situation is no longer to be tolerated.

CHAPTER 004

Chinese Espionage: The Greatest Threat

*In this way the true strategist manipulates the
enemy while concealing his intentions.*
—Sun Tzu, *The Art of War* (c. 509 BCE)

The Canadian executives could not believe their eyes.

They had spent three weeks in China at the invitation of
their Chinese counterpart, an important civil and military
vehicle manufacturer. And from the moment they'd arrived to
their final farewell handshake, the Canadian business delegation had been the object of persistent and intrusive surveillance.
Everywhere they went, whether for work or relaxation, in hotel
rooms or boardrooms, they all but tripped over the electronic
listening devices. It was so obvious that it was almost insulting.
But while it had the appearance of slapdash, last-minute work,
some of the Canadian delegates wondered if they weren't meant
to notice it.

During the flight home, the head of the Canadian delegation
called ahead to his chief of security and ordered him to prepare for
a meeting as soon as they landed.

The delegates had, for the most part, found the experience
stressful. But this was not because the company's chief of security
had not warned them beforehand of the risk they ran in accepting the Chinese invitation. "China, and above all the Chinese
Intelligence Service*, practises economic espionage," they had been
warned. "Be aware that you will always be under visual and audi-
tory surveillance."

Before the trip, the Canadians had gone so far as to invite a
CSIS officer to come and brief the management team about what
to expect. But, as often happens, the executives were not receptive.
They could see that the CSIS man was experienced, yes. The problem was that the details he was laying out were so preposterous—
or seemed to be—that some of the executives looked forward to
recounting them as dinner party entertainment. "They see spooks
in the spiderwebs," or repartee to that effect, was, for the most
part, what they took away from the meeting.

A familiar scenario: people in the business mainstream, including the worldly and capable winners of many a corporate power
struggle, do not take the espionage issue seriously. And it's true,
of course, that in a trade built on deceit and trickery, the security
expert can't be right all the time. What the executives forget is that
people who know nothing about the field are likely to be wrong all
of the time. All the more so when they are blinded by lucrative business opportunities in totalitarian countries.

In China, any important business enterprise is controlled by
the state. Since the Chinese Communist Party is a highly centralized
and authoritarian government, it's not surprising that the Chinese
Intelligence Service is expected to make use of these enterprises for

---

* The Chinese Intelligence Service is composed of many branches and departments, the most important of which is the Ministry of State Security (MSS), also
known as Guoanbu.

operational purposes. Add to that the fact that China has, for some years now, enjoyed unprecedented economic growth and the whole planet has been beating a path to its factory doors. Most foreign corporations, however, haven't done their homework and don't know what they're getting into. In particular, they are unaware that, for the Chinese, commerce is merely a continuation of war by other means. Resources, means, and strategy must converge and produce a "victory." Sun Tzu, prescient as always, predicted that places where money accumulates will offer great opportunities to the strategist: "He who would tempt the enemy to expose himself need only dangle a tempting opportunity in order to be assured of victory." And businesses are all about "dangling opportunities" in front of other people.

A common failing of Canadian business is a lack of curiosity about its opposite numbers in other countries and cultures. And yet it's a commonplace in schools of management that you should learn everything you can about the entity you're signing a contract with. How else can you hope to do well? This lesson is lost on the numerous Canadian businesses that show little interest in the countries and cultures with whom, as a trading nation, we must do business.

Canada has many companies that have great expertise and cutting-edge technologies. This makes it an obvious partner for so many foreign companies that would like to get their hands on that knowledge. One company in particular is one of China's foremost transportation companies. But you'd think, in this day and age, that any business would do a simple Internet search on the foreign company it proposes doing business with. A search of this particular Chinese company would show right away that it has been involved in any number of cases of economic spying; it is even suspected of stealing blueprints of foreign technology. In 2002 it came out with an all-terrain vehicle that was an obvious copy of the American Hummer. The fact that it was called the Zhanshen (meaning "God of War") was just a bit of historico-Chinese flummery that a child would see through. Well, all right, we'll admit that the Zhanshen was in one respect very different from the Hummer: it sold for one-third the price.

Why would anybody want to do business with this company?

In the Canadian company's defence, we must say that it's not the only big western company to do business with this Chinese company. We could even argue that to stay competitive, they must do business in China. American and European giants have been selling various components and building factories in the home province of that Chinese "partner."

But did the Canadian company ever stop to reflect on the fact that their Chinese counterparts have been given a mandate to build the next generation of stealth aircraft for the Chinese air force? Time will tell.

This brings to mind the case of Xiaodong Sheldon Meng. A forty-four-year-old man who had grown up in China and who held Canadian citizenship, Meng was sentenced in July 2008 in California to two years' imprisonment after he was caught trying to sell U.S. fighter training software to the Chinese navy.* That same year, three other Chinese nationals were charged with espionage in the United States:

• Fei Ye, an American citizen of Chinese origin, and Ming Zhong, a Chinese citizen with permanent resident status in the United States, pleaded guilty to charges of stealing microprocessor blueprints.

---

* Meng was charged under the 1996 Economic Espionage Act.

- Lan Lee and Yuefei Ge were charged with stealing microprocessor blueprints for the purpose of manufacturing them
with venture capital provided by China.
- Dongfan "Greg" Chung, a Chinese-American engineer
employed by Boeing and space shuttle manufacturer Rockwell
International, was charged with attempting to sell shuttle
technology to China, as well as information about military
transport and next-generation rocket propulsion. And
remember that Boeing continues to do business with
SAC.

Of all the countries that happily dance across the Canadian
border to shoplift our technology, China is far and away the busi-
est and the most aggressive. Chinese agents exploit a certain liberal Canadian sympathy toward their country that dates back to
the 1960s. They don't even much bother to disguise what they're
doing as they operate out of their Ottawa embassy and their three
consulates in Vancouver, Calgary, and Toronto. Meanwhile, the
Canadian government—including, unfortunately, CSIS itself—is
so befuddled that it hasn't begun to understand how serious the
problem is.

In the United States, Great Britain, and Australia there is an
average of one trial per month of Chinese agents charged with economic or industrial espionage. One per month. In Canada, Chinese
spies have never been brought to court, even though Canada is
at least as rich a target as those other countries. Is it possible that
Beijing's State Intelligence Service has overlooked us? Do we sup-
pose they've run short of spies? Perhaps we don't have enough
secrets worth stealing! Or could it be that we're spineless?

Mockery aside, there really is a dramatic disconnect between
Canada's indifference and our allies' active concern. Some reasons

for the disconnect suggest themselves. The obvious one is a lack of understanding of the Chinese culture. This is a failing that extends from CSIS right up to the Privy Council and the Ministry of Foreign Affairs. Habitually, these agencies look no further than the operational methods of the CIS's many branches. Here they learn that it is, like the intelligence services of other advanced nations, professionally active on many fronts. But if they looked into CIS more seriously, they would discover its cultural unique-ness: China's agency plans its operations on a timeline that can extend to decades.

China also has the strategic finesse to put its political goals into alignment with its industrial goals, thereby creating a single, uni-fied vision of its future (which Canada has never attempted to do). Its chief mechanism for achieving this goal is the strategic plan-ning process that takes place in the Communist Party's Central Committee. Supported by their ability to "charm" government offi-cials, industry leaders and politicians, the Central Committee has the capability to neutralize any criticism or attempt to block their "takeover" strategy.

Another reason for Canadian indifference is that, while we have the ability to take on the CIS, we lack the will. Instead we are blinded by what we mistakenly see as the opportunities pre-sented by trade with China. And if this is true of the employees in Ottawa's Commerce and Foreign Affairs ministries, as well as the MPs and government ministers who court the Chinese-Canadian vote, just imagine the temptation China presents to Canada's pri-vate sector executives. The money to be made is so enormous that our largest companies and business associations actively lobby for CSIS to reduce its efforts. They even, rather disgracefully, ask that exposed Chinese agents not be deported.

This leaves China's spies in full control of the situation. They are not much impressed by the occasional timid peep of protest from Ottawa. When everything is taken into consideration, we have to say that our leaders have done more damage by enabling CIS than CIS could ever have done on its own.

CHINA'S OFFICIAL GLOBAL STRATEGY

China spends, according to the best estimates, over $25 billion per year on security. This includes the cost of spying on its own citizens as well as operations abroad. It doesn't include the $65 to $90 billion that goes to military expenditures.

All of these efforts, taken together, support a highly coordinated strategic plan that is based on four key concepts:

- Conquer as much territory as possible.
- Acquire as much influence as possible.
- Plan for the very long term, which can extend over generations.
- Combine the mass collection of information with precise and highly targeted operations.

Territorial Conquest

China requires an extraordinary quantity of natural resources and energy. To house, feed, and employ 1.2 billion people is no small undertaking. To put it in perspective, the United States has ten times more people than Canada. Now imagine a country with a population forty times greater than our own. This enormous demographic means that China's international relations must be based on alliances with other countries, and above all on gaining access to their natural resources.

Although China is capable of innovation, the underpinnings of its culture and society are heavily connected to tradition. There are two particularly useful tools for understanding what kind of tradition this is: Sun Tzu's book *The Art of War* and the ancient board game called Go.

For some, comparing the Chinese strategy to a board game might seem strange. Be assured that there is nothing fanciful in the choice. The game of Go, with its underpinnings of philosophy and strategic thought, has been learned and played as a discipline by China's emperors, ministers of state, warlords, and imperial officers since the fourth century BCE. Used for centuries as a way for the Chinese to shape strategy, the game is based on an initial division of power between the realm of outright control and the realm of influence. The player seeks to move his pieces on the board in such a way as, first, to encircle and conquer territory outright, and second, to encircle and thereby influence whatever can't be conquered. Whoever possesses the most territory at the end wins.

Sun Tzu's life predates even the popularity of Go. He was a general in the sixth century BCE His small book, which has thirteen chapters, covers military strategy generally but concentrates on the mechanics of leading successful campaigns and of carrying on clandestine operations within enemy territory. It is part of today's compulsory curriculum for the Chinese officer corps and, of course, for aspiring SIS agents. The book's final chapter looks exclusively at the kind of undercover information-gathering that must take place before the troops are mobilized. It should be kept in mind whenever one thinks about the CIS's operational strategy.

Obviously, our intention here is not to teach anybody how to play Go, or to write a long dissertation on Sun Tzu. But it's important to have some understanding of the ideas behind these two pillars of Chinese culture.

How Influence Leads to Control

An adroit player of Go wants to maximize influence by placing his stones (the game is traditionally played with black and white stones) in strategic locations on the playing surface. To do this, he has to create a network of relationships and understand the tensions among them.

Chinese strategists have long understood that influence is more important than control. This is because influence, wisely deployed, will ultimately lead to control. That's why the Go player will rarely launch a frontal assault. Almost always he begins by moving his players to locations where the enemy finds them to be unthreatening and even useful.

Imagine an army that wants to take possession of a territory. The military option will force it to spend time and energy pulling together a vast stock of food, clothing, and weapons behind the lines. And that's only the beginning. Once the battle is won, the enemy's territory must be occupied. That means more soldiers, more supplies, more weapons—and the additional task of pacifying an angry population by bribing spies to turn in potential rebels or troublemakers. After spending the money necessary to amass all these logistical resources, you still don't get a moment to relax. Remember, you're living in a place where you are not wanted.

Making friends and influencing people, the principle that made Dale Carnegie a wealthy man, is much easier and far more profitable than making enemies. When a nation sets out to make friends, the first "soldiers" into the battle are honey-tongued emissaries who really do hope for good relations with your country. If you'll be our special friend, they say, we'll buy what we need from you alone. And when we sell, well, talk about getting it wholesale! You won't believe the deals!

Soon you'll have a number of admirers in your newly opened market. Some will become fond of Chinese books and music and talk them up at dinner parties. Others will be filling their pockets by selling your wonderful products to their compatriots. A few will require an outright bribe, but that's all right. A few will need to be caught in flagrante doing something or other, and that's all right too. All's fair!

You'll also want to invest in the economy of your new ally. You'll buy real estate, to show your commitment. And of course you'll donate generously to each and every political party.

Eventually you'll have quite a few friends in this particular country. When these reach a critical mass, it will be time to take the next step, and you will be able to choose the time and place to take it.

Patience, Perseverance, and People—Lots of People

Placing your stones (that is, agents) for maximum influence and ultimate conquest of the desired territory requires patience and perseverance. In this manoeuvre, Chinese undercover specialists once again come out on top because of their strategic thinking. They have patience, yes; but in a sense they also have millions of agents working for them.

The Security and Intelligence Service of China plans its operations in generational rather than calendar-year intervals. This kind of long-term planning, all by itself and without further cleverness, is enough to baffle the fast-food mentality of western intelligence agencies. These take as their mantra the dubious slogan "Time is money." Meanwhile, their Chinese counterparts sit back and relax. Given the time-obsession of the enemy, it's only a question of waiting for him to grow tired and inattentive. When the other side drops his guard, that's the moment to activate one's sources. Also, if you flood the enemy with an overwhelming number of agents, some might be caught but several will succeed.

We have already mentioned the Chinese term "bottomfeeder." The practice (and there is good evidence of it) is to recruit agents while they are still at university, train them, and then send them to western countries before they're out of their twenties. Ten, fifteen, twenty years pass. During this time the sleeper agent has not had a single contact with the home base. Then, one day, he or she receives the signal that means "activate."

What was going on during all those years the agents were out of contact with the homeland? They were steadily climbing the career ladder of their chosen Canadian company or their government ministry. In either case, they're now at the executive level and they have received security clearance. To the employer they are long-term, very loyal employees, and giving them a high-level clearance was the easy and obvious thing to do.

Remember that these agents are looking for a plausible cover story. It's taken a long time, but they have one, and it's the best one imaginable. Who is going to suspect them after an adult lifetime spent obeying Canadian rules? They would have to make an egregious blunder in order to give themselves away (something that, from our point of view, is more a vain hope than a likelihood). And now, by way of recalling that it is useful to be curious about the workings of Chinese culture, remember that in China there are countless thousands of young people who aspire to become exactly such sleeper agents for their homeland.

Combining Two Tactics: "Mass Collection Process" and Specific Targeting

What is most distinctive about the CIS is its blending of two different approaches. This is the method that evolved in response to the catastrophe of Mao Zedong's "Great Leap Forward," which ruined the social and technological advantage China had accumulated between the revolution of 1949 and the beginning of the 1960s.

Western intelligence agencies, as a matter of course, prefer to train and employ professionals. The Chinese, on the other hand, are happy to make use of anybody who has a round-trip airline ticket to a foreign country. This is the key to what security people call "mass collection process." The Chinese national who goes abroad is pressured into returning home with whatever information he or she can find. No matter that a lot of it will be set aside as irrelevant—a little useful information is all that is required. And the naive informant may also have met sympathetic foreigners who can be helpful to the CIS.

Contrast this with the method widely employed in the West, and used as well by the Soviet Union and its satellites during the Cold War. Western intelligence services have come up with a kind of fable in order to highlight this difference between the Soviet and the Chinese approach.

Imagine that each of the countless grains of sand on a beach contains useful and interesting information. The Russian spy slips off the deck of a submarine and swims steadily toward the beach, navigating by the light of the full moon. A shovel and a pail are strapped to his body, and his plan is to get as much sand as possible back to the submarine by daybreak.

Meanwhile the Chinese have awarded a thousand loyal citizens a free holiday in Canada. They've all slipped swimsuits on and gone down to the beach. They lay down a beach blanket and work on their tans. Back in the hotel, they shake the sand out of their towels. But they all do the shaking in the same place. The resulting sandpile is quite impressive. It could fill a couple of submarines.

As parables go, this one is straightforward enough. It makes its point, which is that the CIS strategy is to gather any and all kinds of information. As a totalitarian country, China has the additional advantage of knowing that its citizens will do exactly what they're told. To refuse is unthinkable. If you hesitate, your family will be told that you are a "traitor" to the nation. The punishment for your ambivalence will be meted out to those you hold nearest and dearest.

Let's return to the Chinese sunbathers. They are, in prosaic and everday reality, students doing Master's degrees at Canadian universities, or engineers who have come here to take specialized training. Perhaps they are technicians on a professional exchange trip, or experts invited to work in a research facility. Or they may be travelling artists. They are simple citizens, usually Chinese but sometimes sympathizers of other nationalities who love China and see considerable advantage in currying favour with high-ranking Chinese officials. Through force of numbers they make "mass collection" into a massively effective tactic.

Information collected this way will be something of a jumble. If the Chinese traveller is signed up for a training course or a personnel exchange with a western company, the CIS back home will expect to receive a report on the company's products, including sourcing and manufacturing specifications where possible, together with the names of any people the traveller encountered who seemed interested in China—or hostile to it. All of this goes into the database, because much of what is produced through mass information collection isn't immediately useful. Some of it won't be specific enough. Some of it has no relevance right now, but might in the future.

This is where the other information collection method, "specific targeting," comes into play. It is the domain of agents, otherwise known as "talent spotters," who are specially trained to spot people who might be recruitable.

The former Ontario Hydro utility was a victim some years ago of a variety of the specific targeting method called the "training swindle." While checking messages faxed from their nuclear power station in Pickering, Ontario Hydro's security department noticed that a document that tied up the fax machine for more than ninety minutes had been transmitted to China. While it was not possible to identify the contents of the document, the recipient was located in a hotel next to the headquarters of China's Ministry of State Security (MSS)Intelligence Service and known to be used by its agents. The investigation also showed that the fax had been sent during a period of time when the power plant was hosting a visit by Chinese trainees. The trainees had left three months before the fax was identified.

At this point we should recall that the Chinese technique of mass collection process has a particular advantage in that it often turns up individuals who in all simplicity want to help their "new friends," often by sending information to them. Eventually, if the recruited individual is receptive enough—or needy enough—he can be led to furnish more and more information, including confidential and even secret files. The seduction of such a contact may be the hope of a contract, or the chance to work in China, or, frankly, it may be sexual, or even monetary.

The Chinese agent has skills of all sorts, as seen in the tale of two FBI agents, James J. Smith and Bill Cleveland. Both were arrested in 2003. Both had been to bed with a Chinese woman named Katrina Leung, who was supposedly an informer working on the FBI's behalf. She was an informer, all right: a professional spy working for China's Ministry of State Security (MSS). She picked the two agents clean, which was ironic, since both had received special training in Chinese counter-espionage. Imagine what Katrina Leung could have done with your average junior executive or Ottawa bureaucrat.

More than 80 percent of espionage is carried out not by the foreign agent but rather by his or her local contacts. The elaborate Hollywood-type masquerade that lets a foreign agent "infiltrate" a foreign government or corporation is not much used in the real world. The perpetrator is far likelier to be an exceedingly naive Canadian who is anxious to please a new Chinese "friend." The friend in question is often a diplomat who is grateful for any information that might help him to "do his job or come to a better understanding of Canada." From our perspective, the most amazing thing is the puppy-dog-like wagging of Canadian tails as we endeavour to be of service to our exotic new friends.

THE RANGE OF ACTIVITY IN CANADA

Chinese spies carry on an astounding range of activities in Canada, as elsewhere. Entirely apart from economic espionage, there is the matter of supervising and controlling dissident Chinese expatriates (see Chapter 006), together with the customary political and military spying.

Later in the book we will investigate cases and files involving Chinese agents who have been deported for illegal activities. In 2005, two Chinese diplomat/spies who defected, Chen Yonglin and Hao Fengjing, revealed that China had more than a thousand agents working in Canada. They repeated this allegation in 2007, after testifying before the U.S. Senate Select Committee on Intelligence. An RCMP-CSIS study in 1997 stated that China also has more than two hundred front companies in Canada whose purpose is to acquire restricted technology. The Mounties also allege that China's Security Intelligence Service collaborates with organized crime while gathering information in Canada.

Looking at the number of Chinese diplomats posted to Canada is useful. It's much more extensive than we see in embassies of similar size. Canada freely grants China the right to keep more than 120 diplomats on Canadian soil—twice the number that the United States has here. And remember that America is obviously our more important economic partner.

How can this bloated roster be justified? We have only to turn our attention to the worthy functionaries of the Ministries of Foreign Affairs and Commerce. These ladies and gentlemen sincerely believe that the best way to open the great Imperial gate to the riches of the Chinese market is . . . to do whatever China wants us to do.

CONFUCIUS AND THE COMMUNIST CADRES

To expand and to anchor its influence, China has developed a strategy similar to that of the Trojan horse. Confucius, the celebrated moral and political philosopher of ancient China, was far ahead of his time in understanding that peace and justice can thrive only where rulers are professional and scrupulously honest. He certainly had a vision of such a future world. But did he ever dream that, two thousand years after his death, a totalitarian Communist Party of China would cry his name from the rooftops in order to justify a gigantic campaign of lies and disinformation? That time has arrived. Today Confucius has become the patron saint of "soft power."*

This is the same Confucius whose writings were once banned by Mao Zedong because they emphasize respect for a hierarchy. This was thought to be "reactionary" and not compatible with Communist principles. But history has its own sense of irony, and today the honest humanist described by Confucius is seen as the saviour of the system, the good federalist who will ride to the rescue and revive China's pride and nationalism.

* A concept described by Harvard Professor Joseph S. Nye.

Some years ago, the Chinese Language Council International, which is financed by China's Ministry of Education, set up a system of Confucius Institutes in countries around the world. These were supposedly inspired by Germany's Goethe Institutes and France's Alliance Française, both of which have branches in most major countries, where they offer books, music series, and film programs promoting the culture of their respective countries. Likewise, any American or Bulgarian or Colombian may go to their local Confucius Institute and take courses in calligraphy or *putonghua* (the major Chinese language, often called Mandarin in the West). The teaching is impeccable, since the teachers are sent from the homeland and subsidized after they arrive. Any person hoping to do business in China will find a ready and well-informed staff officer to help them out.

"The Confucius Institutes are a window on the world for Chinese culture and a bridge which encourages mutual understanding between peoples," said Zhou Ji, the minister of education, in a speech in Beijing in December 2007. The occasion was the second conference of the Confucius Institutes.

The system dates back to 2004, when the first Institute was opened in Seoul, South Korea. They have since multiplied with astonishing speed and can now be found in more than eighty countries. They are ubiquitous in Africa, where China is working to establish a dominant presence. But there are numerous Institutes in Canada, the United States, and most South American countries, as well as in Europe and Asia. After only five years, in February 2009, there were 314 in operation in 81 countries, and the program is just getting underway. China expects to be operating a thousand of them by the year 2020.

But, as Confucius says, "Fine words and an insinuating appearance are seldom associated with true virtue." The hyperactivity
of the Confucius Institutes soon began to attract the attention
of various national intelligence services. Was it possible that this
charm initiative, apart from its evident intention to create Sino-
mania wherever it went, might also conceal a darker purpose? That
is what CSIS analysts asked themselves in 2006 when Canada's
first Confucius Institute popped up inside the British Columbia
Institute of Technology. In a report labelled "Secret," the introduction contains the following words: "The government of the
People's Republic of China is determined to increase its military
and economic power while augmenting soft power at the same
time. In other words, China wants the world to fall in love with
everything Chinese."[26]

As usual the Canadian government blacked out most of the
report before releasing a declassified copy. They wouldn't want
anything to become public that might pose a diplomatic problem
or reveal matters under investigation. But it means a great deal that
CSIS took the trouble to write a report on the Confucius Institutes in
the first place. All the more so if we remember that, just a few weeks
after the report was delivered, CSIS's director vividly denounced
China in a presentation to a Senate committee.

The agents who wrote the report found themselves asking the
same questions as their opposite numbers in other western capi-
tals. The big issue is this: are the partnership agreements that these
Institutes habitually sign with both a Chinese and (in this case)
Canadian university—and in many cases with Chinese high-tech
enterprises—not in fact a cover-up for a gigantic system of siphon-
ing and draining away of other people's scientific research? In other
words, are the Confucius Institutes a case of "soft power" in the
service of "soft spying"?

It's no surprise to learn that a good number of Chinese security people can be found on the Confucius network's management team. They come from the government's Department of United Front Work, which manages important dossiers concerning foreign countries. These include propaganda, the control of Chinese students abroad, the recruiting of agents among the Chinese diaspora (and among sympathetic foreigners), and long-term clandestine operations. In 2007, the Central Committee of the Chinese Communist Party increased this ministry's budget by $3 billion. Interestingly, the increase was allocated to the development of "soft power" and the burnishing of Chinese's image abroad.

How does the system work? To take a random example, the Confucius Institute in Poitiers, France, is connected with ZTE Technologies, a Chinese telecommunications firm, and Nanjing University. There is also a Confucius Institute in Dallas, Texas, which opened its doors in 2007 with a $100,000 (U.S.) grant from the Chinese government. One of its top officials is also vice-president of Huawei Technology Industries. Could this explain the Institute's interest in the University of Texas in Dallas, which prides itself on being located in the "telecom corridor" where many major multinationals are based?

Huawei Technology competes with giants like Cisco, Lucent, and Alcatel. It considers itself a world leader in the manufacture of next-generation telecommunications networks. Its vice-president is a one-time officer of the People's Liberation Army, though Huawei claims that he has no link with the current government or the Chinese military. But the Chinese software giant has been publicly criticized in India and Great Britain for trying to get software contracts with businesses that have security clearance. Today, Huawei has a joint venture with Canada's Nortel and, as of our publishing deadline, was still on the list of potential buyers of some Nortel operations. It went so far as to try to purchase British defence contractor Marconi, and it has been convicted of illegally copying a Cisco microprocessor. In each case, the government affected was warned about Huawei by its own secret service.

In the Cisco case, Huawei's defence suffered somewhat from the fact that its chip contained exactly the same bugs as Cisco's. There was also the awkward revelation that Huawei assembled its chip in the same factory used by Cisco's Chinese subsidiary. After the conviction, Huawei was banned from doing business in the United States for five years.

There are five Confucius Institutes currently operating in Canada:

- Edmonton (Alberta School for the Deaf)
- Waterloo (University of Waterloo), twinned with Nanjing University
- Moncton (Atlantic Education International)
- Montreal and Sherbrooke (Dawson College and the University of Sherbrooke), linked with the Beijing Normal University

Each of these Canadian institutions has been showered with thousands of books, DVDs, and other documents pertaining to China. These "gifts," accepted in good faith, adorn their libraries today.

Provincial governments have also opened their wallets. The Quebec Ministry of Education gave a non-renewable grant of $65,000 to help start up the Quebec Confucius Institute. By the spring of 2009, provincial officials still did not know how much the Chinese government was investing in the startup.

As for the Institute's board, where Chinese officials are represented, it has still not been finalized. When the Institute was announced back in September 2005, the rector of the University of Sherbrooke was pleased to announce that the university "has nationally and internationally recognized expertise in all the areas identified in the agreement, including aeronautics, biopharmaceuticals, biotechnology, engineering, environmental science, optics and laser research, as well as telecommunications and information technology."

CSIS NAPS, WHILE THE MOUNTIES ARE COMATOSE

CSIS does have investigators knowledgeable about China's Security Intelligence Service. But this team isn't supported by CSIS's top brass, and it doesn't study the cultural norms that underlie the work of CIS. Also, the CSIS team isn't allowed to set out operational timetables extending over ten or twenty years, which would allow it to track CIS operations of similar length, or analyze CIS's long-term techniques. The underlying problem is that the federal bureaucracy is not interested; if anything, the Privy Council and the Ministry of Foreign Affairs set out contradictory parameters. So it's not surprising that top CSIS people rarely pay attention to the issue—and even more rarely sound the alarm on Parliament Hill.

The Royal Canadian Mounted Police pay no attention whatsoever to China. This is, on one level, a bureaucratic snafu. The Mounties can investigate only where the law gives them authority, which in practice means that a conviction must at least be possible. But Bill C-36 (the Anti-Terrorism Act), despite the changes made to it in 2002, is legally unenforceable in any real way. It's a dead letter. Spy cases are also agonizingly slow. That's why they are left to CSIS. But CSIS is not, let us recall, a law-enforcement agency.

It's like a dog chasing its tail. And a Chinese spy, should he wish to watch a dog engaged in this entertaining activity, may do so at his leisure, knowing he will be arrested only when the dog finally catches it.

In spite of CSIS's habitual discretion, this situation so frustrated its director, Jim Judd, that the following exchange occurred between him and members of the Senate Standing Committee on Defence and National Security. It was the last day of April 2007, and it caused great consternation in diplomatic circles:

> Senator Zimmer: I'd like to ask you about your response to people who are sent to foreign countries in order to carry on clandestine activity. Do other countries do the same thing? I presume they do. People say that the Cold War is over, but I am not entirely convinced. Do other countries send these people to Canada? I presume they do. If this is indeed the case, do we know about it when these people come here? And do we know where they are at every moment they are on our territory? From what part of the globe do they come?
>
> Mr. Judd: Yes, such people do come here. And we hope to know, when they arrive here, where they are going and who they are. And we often do. One of my foreign colleagues said one day, concerning this matter, that we spend most of our time worrying about what we don't know. And that's certainly true of this particular case.
>
> Sometimes it's amazing to see how many hyperactive tourists come here, and what their countries of origin are. I don't want to be politically incorrect, so I won't single out any country in particular, but there are at any time perhaps fifteen countries we find interesting in

this respect. It comes and goes, depending on the files which are prominent at any particular time.

Senator Zimmer: Is it evenly spread around, or are there particular countries which send a lot of people here?

Mr. Judd: There does seem to be a certain concentration, yes.

The president of the committee: It surely can't be politically incorrect to mention public reports we have seen on the subject of the Chinese and what is thought to be an aggressive program which they carry on in our country. The government has spoken publicly on the subject.

Mr. Judd: That country would count among the fifteen.

The president: Is it high on the list?

Mr. Judd: Rather.

The president: Does this country occupy 50 percent of your time?

Mr. Judd: Just about.[27]

The man in charge of Canada's spies couldn't have spoken more clearly. We are entitled to ask why our federal government has taken no action on the matter. What explains the conspicuous absence of commentary, studies, and conferences that might increase public and above all corporate awareness of the problem? Is anybody in charge?

CHAPTER 005

Cyber-Surveillance: Virtual Espionage, Real Threats

"It's not personal, Sonny. It's strictly business."
—Michael Corleone, *The Godfather* (1972)

It all came out in August 2007. "Trojan horse" viruses had pillaged the computers of the German government—in particular, that of Chancellor Angela Merkel, as well as the ministries of Research, Economy, and Foreign Affairs. These slices of malicious code, concealed in PowerPoint files, had hijacked over 160 gigabytes of information.

Analysts soon learned that the attack had been skilfully launched from inside the Fourth Department of the People's Liberation Army. The Fourth Department is in charge of Chinese electronic intelligence.

In the following weeks, word leaked out that similar attacks had occurred in England and France. At the time, however, these three countries agreed to make no public accusations against China. France did mention—casually—that the virus trail had "passed through China." But even this timid observation, it was felt, might cause somebody to lose a bit of face, and so the general secretary of National Defence added a clarification: "When I say China, that does not mean the Chinese government. Nor do we have any evidence that the People's Liberation Army is involved."

Mum was also the word from Washington, where, in June of the same year, spies managed to access the computer system at the Pentagon and pay a virtual visit to the terminals in Secretary of Defense Robert Gates's office. Only unimportant stuff was stolen, said the Americans, waving it off as if some kids had egged the family car. In reality it was very serious, and the Pentagon computer whizzes spent a good part of the summer shutting down hundreds upon hundreds of terminals. A few were indiscreet enough to comment to the media, anonymously fingering the People's Liberation Army.* The Chinese responded with a quantity of tedious boilerplate about "dishonest accusations" and "Cold War mentality."

To be fair to China, though, nobody believes that it's the only country guilty of cyber-espionage. In the spy business we like to remind ourselves that you can never go wrong if you start by suspecting your "friends." A source in French counter-espionage puts it this way: Yes, China is a menace. It's aggressive and destructive. But it's not a patch on France's allies, the three guiltiest parties being England, America, and Germany.

At the beginning of 2009, Germany's BND intelligence agency was embarrassed by revelations that 2,500 of its software systems had been compromised, both domestically and abroad. But its boss, Ernst Uhrlau, had also been forced to admit earlier that the BND was spying on e-mail exchanged between a *Der Spiegel* correspondent in

---

* What made their testimony even tastier was a dash of hypocrisy. The sources admitted that America spies on China as well, but wished to draw a distinction between everyday U.S.-type spying, and Chinese spying, which they found to be unsportingly large-scale and just generally "not cricket."

Kabul and an Afghan ministry whose computer was infected with a Trojan horse virus.

That said, the scale of the Chinese operation is breathtaking. American authorities have named it "Titan Rain," and they believe it began in 2002. The attacks span a number of agencies, including the Department of Defense, but concentrate particularly on the Information Systems Engineering Command, the Defense Information Systems Agency, and the Space and Missile Defense Acquisition Center[28] Somewhere between 10,000 and 20,000 gigabytes of confidential information (enough to fill the shelves of the Library of Congress twice over) have transited through South Korea before landing in China. That's a lot of information, but the CIS has lots of people, and we can assume that every paragraph has been carefully studied.

Untypically, the U.S.-China Economic and Security Review Commission decided to speak out on the matter. In a November 2008 report to Congress, it accused China of deliberately attacking government and defence contractor computer systems. And remember: some of these U.S. companies have branch plants in Canada. One of the most disturbing points in the report is that North America's computer network is largely made of component parts, big and small, that are imported from China. Could these be compromised? Contemporary electronic manufacturing is sophisticated enough that, in principle, China's security services might conceal malicious code in these parts and then activate it at a later date. Astonishing, but not far-fetched.

Reflecting on this kind of trickery inevitably recalls the odd case of the software product called Promis. The Israeli security agency Mossad sold it to a number of police forces and security agencies around the world—including Canada—in the 1990s.[29] The programming turned out to include a "trap" or "back door." It was a dirty trick that allowed Mossad to follow the movements of Palestinians in Canada when they were under surveillance by our police. The information was used in Israel's bloody struggle with Yasser Arafat and the Palestinian Liberation Organization.

It didn't take long for Mossad to realize that Promis could also be used to spy on "competitor" agencies, thereby extracting useful information. Among those identified as being part of the scheme were the now-deceased press magnate Robert Maxwell, together with a colourful character named Ari Ben-Menashe (still very much alive and kicking). Ben-Menashe worked as a businessman in Montreal, but he was also a former senior Israeli spy and arms dealer. Nearly twenty years later, Ben-Menashe is still delighted to talk about the mysterious "improved version" of the Promis software. Smiling broadly, he explains how Promis was developed by Inslaw Inc., a company founded by a former NSA agent, with 570,000 lines of code. It could steal information anywhere, including from electric power, water, and telephone companies. It would then automatically collate the information to help identify terrorists, among other things. For years Promis surfaced in RCMP investigations and hearings. Ben-Menashe adds that the RCMP itself was sold infected software (the "Big Brother" virus) by American intelligence organizations.

The U.S.-China Economic and Security Review Commission also documented 250 pirate organizations in China whose actions are "tolerated" and finally "encouraged" by Chinese authorities. Hard evidence to justify this number, however, is difficult to come by.

The conclusion reached by the U.S. Senate is rather disconcerting. According to its report, China's cyber-espionage and cyber-attack techniques are so advanced—so "sophisticated," to use the language of the report—that the United States at present would be hard-pressed to detect them, much less to "thwart" them.

ATTACK ON "THE HILL"

Meanwhile, back in the frozen north, a Freedom of Information request in June 2008 forced the Ministry of Public Safety to release a report that it clearly didn't wish to make public. The document revealed that the massive cyber-attack of 2007 in the United States had also penetrated twenty Canadian government ministries, including that of then Public Safety Minister Stockwell Day. This intrusion was first spotted by the Canadian Cyber Incident Response Centre (CCIRC). Both the Mounties and CSIS labelled it part of "an international global menace" after a serious, if quick, investigation.

The Canadian government was nervous about accusing China in public. In confidential documents, though, it went so far as to state that allies such as the United States, Great Britain, Australia, and New Zealand strongly suspected that the pirating was done by hackers on the People's Liberation Army payroll, if not by the Chinese military itself. One of these documents was written in early December 2007 by two officials working for Public Safety Canada and sent to a deputy minister in that department. It contained the odd assertion that "the media has reported that the director general of Britain's security services has blamed China for the attacks."

What is remarkable here is that the ministry responsible for security in Canada finds it acceptable for expert staff to quote from the newspapers in a report labelled "Confidential." Why did they not go directly to our allies for the information? To cap it all off, the authors of the memo then wrote this: "In any case, it [Chinese spying] is a secondary consideration, with the primary focus being on protecting Canada's critical information infrastructure."

THE SNOOPING DRAGON

In the plush salons of Parliament Hill in Ottawa, there is much trepiditation if anyone whispers the word "China." But some researchers at the University of Toronto's Information Warfare Monitor group bravely spoke up in March 2009, revealing that they had uncovered a huge cyber-spying network that was operating out of that country. They hastened to add that they had no way of proving the Chinese government was behind it. Their idea was that "patriotic hackers" (such as the China Eagle Union) might be responsible. Or else organized crime. As we say: whatever.*

They baptized this newly discovered network "GhostNet," adding that its reach extended into 103 countries, having infected 1,295 known computers with malware. That wouldn't be a big deal, except that a third of the corrupted machines contained confidential information. The most prominent victim was the Dalai Lama (who commissioned the study), as well as several NGOs, dozens of Foreign Affairs ministries (Iran, Lithuania, the Philippines, and Barbados, among others), embassies (India, Germany, Pakistan, South Korea, Indonesia, Romania, Taiwan, etc.), NATO, some banks, and some media companies.

The researchers found that GhostNet operated by first infecting the target computer with a Trojan horse called "ghOst RAT," which arrived in an e-mail attachment carrying the address of somebody known to the target, or else lurked in a website to which the target was directed. All the booby-trapped messages came from a set of IP addresses in the same part of China, mostly Hainan Island, where the People's Liberation Army operates a SIGINT station. Once the target computer was under control, the GhostNet "conductors" could orchestrate some serious theft, playing on the e-mail server, downloading documents, making screen

---

* Deng Xiaoping is well known for referring to Chinese organized crime (Triads) in the past as "patriotic organizations." It is also well documented that the Chinese Intelligence Service has used Triads extensively for security operations, including the murder of a dissident journalist in the United States.

captures, and commandeering web cameras to spy on the room where the computer was located.

University of Cambridge researchers dug into the attacks on the Dalai Lama and the Tibetan government in exile. Their report, wittily called "The Snooping Dragon: Social-malware Surveillance of the Tibetan Movement" (March 2009), accuses the Chinese government of being the sponsor and instigator of the attacks.

These two studies reveal China's modus operandi in great detail, with technological evidence to support the allegations. A striking aspect of the "ghOst RAT" method is that it began by extracting the target's IP address from a social network that he or she belonged to. Sometimes this preliminary attack would be against a company the person worked for, which shows that the techniques in question probably originated in economic espionage work.

As usual, the release of these studies occasioned an official response from China that might best be described as a "hissy fit."

THE INTERNET AND ITS "ILLEGALS"

Cyber-espionage is not only about the theft of military and industrial information. It can also sabotage and even collapse communication, energy, and financial infrastructures, as well as government systems. This is obviously the kind of activity that has always been considered illegal.

You'd have to be very innocent to think that a totalitarian country like China, where the state seamlessly monitors the Internet, would find it hard to track down a few pimply kids in a back room in Chengdu or Xian who are busily launching gigantic cyber-attacks.

Back in 1999, when the Internet was young, two People's Liberation Army officers, Ziao Liang and Wang Xiangsui, realized that this new technology would soon become a fourth field of battle, joining the realms of air, sea, and land war. Their paper,

Unrestricted Warfare, sketches the broad outlines of a new kind of conflict. In their scenario, the instigators would no longer be a few criminals skilled in the art of sabotage (such as we describe in the chapter on Russia), but rather a committee of pirates comfortably installed in a computer room thousands of kilometres away from the "battlefield":

> If the attacking side secretly musters large capital reserves without the enemy nation being aware of it and launches a sneak attack against its financial markets, then it may engineer a financial crisis and bury a computer virus and hacker attachment in the opponent's computer system in advance, while at the same time carrying out a network attack against the enemy so that the civilian electricity network, traffic dispatching network, financial transaction network, telephone communications network, and mass media network are completely paralyzed. This will cause the enemy nation to fall into social panic, street riots, and a political crisis.[30]

Mei Ping, a former Chinese ambassador to Canada, didn't even blink when, having run into us by accident in the fall of 2008, we peppered him with questions about the cyber-attacks recently launched against Canada and other countries. Mei Ping assured us that China had nothing to do with it and doesn't even carry on espionage here. Nor would China ever dream of harassing its opponents. "There are no Chinese spies in Canada. That's just more lies, propaganda and fabrication . . . a CIA scheme to demonize China. They always need an enemy. It used to be the Soviets."

Kayum Masimov, a coordinator for the Uyghur Canadian Society, believes that he was also the victim of a Trojan horse virus.

The methods used strongly resemble those described by Information Warfare Monitor researchers. The Uyghur people, Muslims who inhabit the far west of China, are a target for Beijing's agents wherever they emigrate. Masimov, a young activist, recounts a number of very strange attacks on his computer—one in particular. It happened just as he was preparing for a conference his movement had organized in Germany. An e-mail from a close friend, written in the Uyghur language, appeared in his inbox. His "friend" wanted him to translate into English a Uyghur document in an attachment. Since Kayum had previously lost the entire contents of his laptop to a hostile attachment, he was on his guard. Wisely so.

"I was wary because his e-mail address wasn't the same one he usually used," says Masimov. "So I went to an Internet café, just to be sure. My fears were well-founded. The attachment was a virus."

For Lucy Zhou, a Falun Gong spokesperson in Canada, Masimov's story is a classic of its kind—one that is very familiar to her: "I've also had hackers steal the names of correspondents from my e-mail address book," she says. "Then they send viruses. Our Internet sites [www.falundafa.ca and www.minghui.ca] were also attacked in the summer of 1999 [shortly after the movement was banned in China]. The way we frustrate them now is to put up Internet mirror sites. The whole business is pretty unsettling. We've made a complaint about it to Canada's Foreign Affairs ministry."

At that time, the thread of the attack led back to the IP address of an organization called the Information Service Centre of XinAn Beijing. Its offices were in the very heart of the Public Security headquarters in Beijing. To add insult to injury, the software used in the attack also hijacked Falun Gong's computers; China then hinted to American authorities that these might have been the source of a number of attacks on U.S. government websites, especially the Department of Transport.

With the Chinese government using such underhanded tactics, it's not surprising that victimized dissident groups sometimes decide to hit back. That's how a group of dissidents called The Blonds of Hong Kong, who were exiled from China after the massacre at Tiananmen Square in 1989, retaliated when the PLA attacked their computers: the Blonds set out to mangle the PLA's computer system.

Blondie Wong, one of these young geniuses, was almost eliminated in 1999 by a team of Guoanbu assassins (Guoanbu is the security service of the Chinese government). The attackers were following up a rumour that Blondie was living in Canada under official protection. They travelled to France, and from there went to Vancouver and finally Toronto. But their target had already slipped out of Canada and is now in another country.[31]

It's now clear that the cyber-attacks aren't just to steal military/political secrets, launch disinformation campaigns, or keep opponents off balance: it's much more than that. The aim now is to accomplish a full-scale rehearsal of what would need to be done, in a future conflict, to electronically annihilate the enemy's strategic network and energy infrastructure. This same infrastructure, for better or worse, has by now become the essential platform for all of our economic activity. Individual Canadians would find it difficult to carry on daily activities without it.

The most effective technique for this kind of assault is Denial of Service (DOS) or Saturation (DDoS). These both work by inundating a server with millions of requests, generated by a large number of captive or "zombie" computers. The server then "cracks." The language is playful (as befits its origin in youthful hacker slang) but the reality it describes is very unpleasant. A cyber-thief takes control of a computer without the knowledge of its owner. The victim could be you, your next-door neighbour, or a large corporation. A team of hackers, working methodically, can easily create a network of hundreds of thousands of personal computers ("robots") to carry out massive attacks. Such a network, these days, is called a "botnet."

Russian hackers demonstrated their mastery of this new form of digital hunting in the spring of 2007. The tiny state of Estonia had dared to pull down a statue of heroic Soviet soldiers erected in the capital city, Tallinn, while the country was under occupation. Russia's revenge was a botnet attack that took down government, bank, and corporate servers. The little Baltic country was paralyzed for weeks.

The virtual trail led not to Grandmother's house (Russia) but rather to the offices of the wolf-in-chief, Russian President Vladimir Putin. The Estonians accused Russia of having very big teeth. The Russians replied that that was a terrible thing to say about your grandmother.

It's true that it is quite a challenge to follow a cyber-trail back to the mastermind who created it. These intrusions are usually carried out through a maze of servers, sometimes numbering thousands, so that the malware leaps from country to country with impunity. A September 2008 study by the American company SecureWorks estimates that at least 20.6 million cyber-attacks have been launched using computers physically located in the United States.* In China the figure is 7.7 million, while Canada has experienced 100,000 (putting us in tenth place).

The director of SecureWorks points out that, even where one is certain of the country behind the planned attack, it is useless

* These statistics should be treated with caution, since they represent only SecureWorks' clients.

to block incoming messages from computers located in that country. This is what was attempted by the Republic of Georgia, whose major governmental systems were shut down in July and August of 2008, just when the Russian army began its offensive in South Ossetia.* Georgia had strongly suspected that the attack was in the offing. To prevent it, Georgian authorities blocked all incoming transmissions from computers located in Russia. But the Russians simply redirected the attack through terminals located in Turkey and the United States.

CANADA LOSES GROUND

Canada has lagged behind in developing a serious cyber-attack defence system. It's true that we do have the Canadian Cyber Incident Response Centre (CCIRC). At the end of 2008, however, it counted a grand total of seven employees. This is unacceptable, since the threat has been under study for years, and numerous internal intelligence reports have warned of "state-based" hackers and vicious malware. There's a lot of talk about China right now, but other countries (not always big ones) are also after us. Philippine secret services, for example, have penetrated the research departments of two Canadian communications companies: they were looking for money embezzled by ex-President Ferdinand Marcos when he fled to Hawaii in 1989.

A reliable indicator of Canadian foot-dragging is the fact that, at the time of writing, CCIRC did not yet have its own web page. The only clue to its existence is on the website of the Ministry of Public Safety. Once again we can only deplore the rose-coloured

---

* Hackers even managed to post a photograph of the Georgian president in a Nazi costume on the welcome page of the Minister of Foreign Affairs, and standing beside Adolf Hitler on the presidential website.

complacency that makes it so hard for the public to find important information about when these attacks occur, and whether they have taken place here or overseas.

Following the cyber-attack in the summer of 2007, three months passed (up to November 21) before the CCIRC got around to informing twenty federal ministries and agencies about the situation. It helpfully offered some strategies they might use to minimize the after-effects of the attacks. The rest of the federal government, as well as the provinces and territories and the Canadian Telecommunications Cyber Protection working group, waited another eight days for their briefing.* The chartered banks heard about it on December 4, while the large oil and gas companies didn't hear about it until the end of December.

In recent years CSIS has twice focused its efforts on the danger of computer attacks. A first report, published in June of 2007 (coincidentally the very month that a coordinated attack was undermining Ottawa's computer systems), is called "The Electronic Aspect of National Conflict: Are We Prepared?" In this case, unfortunately, to ask is to answer.

In its second report, CSIS focused on the energy infrastructure's vulnerability to electronic attack. But there the interest was really in Al-Qaeda and the kind of information that computer pirates could place in its hands. Virtual espionage was not on the program.

While Canada napped, other countries moved the dossier forward. At the end of 2007 the director of England's MI-5 wrote to the leaders of his country's major corporations and banks to make certain they understood what they were up against. MI-5 specifically underlined the cyber-piracy of "Chinese state orga-

---

* The Cyber Protection working group was made up of federal officials and major players in the industry.

nizations." Companies doing business with China were given a detailed description of the People's Liberation Army and its Internet expertise.

Back in 2002, France had created its Central Directorate for Information Systems Security (CDISS) in the General Secretariat of the Defence ministry. This quickly evolved into an e-security system with an annual budget of more than $1 billion (U.S.). Its mandate is to armour all systems containing sensitive economic/ political information. It also made a priority of education and prevention by setting up a comprehensive Internet portal. A select list of economic and government actors now had a one-stop location for mutual communication, self-education, research, and receiving alerts on new problems.

Today, France has named cyber-spying and cyber-attack as the largest single threat to state security after terrorism. It makes no distinction among attacks by activists, criminals, or other nations. Official commitment to the policy was underlined in 2008 by President Nicolas Sarkozy, in a white paper called "Defence and National Security." He wrote that "moving from a strategy of defence to a strategy of full-spectrum action, combining systems protection, permanent [threat] surveillance, rapid reaction, and counter-attack, requires strong government action and a new way of thinking."

A year earlier, in 2007, the United States inaugurated what amounted to a new branch of the military dedicated to aggressive cyber-war. A sub rosa aspect of its mandate is to develop techniques for intercepting electronic information. The U.S. Cyber Command (AFCYBER), under the command of Air Force Major-General William T. Lord, has four divisions:

- 688th information operations wing
- 450th electronic warfare wing

- 689th cyber wing
- 67th network warfare wing

What's new in this military doctrine is the way it conceives of cyberspace, which is now looked on as a battlefield in the literal sense: turf has to be controlled as well as defended.[32] For this, you have to be able to move into the enemy's electronic systems and destroy them.

THE WOLF IN THE SHEEPFOLD

A nettlesome aspect of the problem that often gets swept under the carpet is this: Spies don't always come from somewhere else. Most are homegrown. Corporate and government employees are complicit, when they're not actually guilty, in 80 to 85 percent of electronic crime. Motives range from monetary gain to simple revenge for slights real or imagined. Methods range from the photocopier to extensive looting of databases. And perpetrators can appear anywhere in the organization, starting with the aspiring new employee who fills out an application form. It spreads anywhere there's a weakness or a large quantity of information—which is to say pretty much anywhere.

It's still corporate practice to spend heavily on technical protection. But not much is being done about upstream security checks. For example, the most propitious time to prevent a bad guy from getting near the database is on day one, when you meet him at the job interview. This is where the candidate has to submit to company procedures. It shouldn't need repeating, but the first procedure should be a criminal record check. We're not talking about the grilling and roasting that a CSIS job-seeker has to endure, just the candidate dropping into the local police station and getting a clean judicial bill of health, which she pays for out of her own pocket. Common sense says that a clean criminal record tells you only that the person hasn't been caught yet. But that's not a bad thing to know. The real point, after all, is to roadblock the person who has been caught.

Canadian authorities know what our allies are doing. Lately it has begun inviting experts to brief high-level bureaucrats. But there have been few approaches to the private sector, which is at least as important. Federal authorities haven't even tried to find out how big the problem is in corporate Canada. Instead, we see an occasional token "conference" on electronic security where there isn't a scrap of useful information to be had. Anything like that is stamped "SECRET" and locked up. For the average chief of corporate security, these talkshops are a pointless and stale exchange of technical information.

CHAPTER 006

Foreign Interference: From Manipulation to Assassination

To overshoot is as bad as to fall short.
—Confucius

The scene takes place in one of the salons of a five-star hotel in the heart of Montreal. It's October 21, 2008, one week after the election of Stephen Harper's Conservative Party. A short, heavy-set Asian man, his bald head conspicuously sporting a comb-over, stands at the lectern. Shaking with indignation, he unleashes an attack on Canada in general and its government in particular. But, pausing in mid-rant, he begs us not to see this as a criticism. Nothing of the sort! It's just the simple truth. There's been a "growing chill" and a "rupture of confidence" between Canada and his homeland. And it's all our fault.

The speaker is China's former ambassador to Canada, Mei Ping—a person of importance. He was, during the 1970s, an overseas student who took political science courses here. Since then he has represented his country in Malta, San Francisco, New York, and Ottawa. Since stepping down as ambassador to Canada in 2005 he

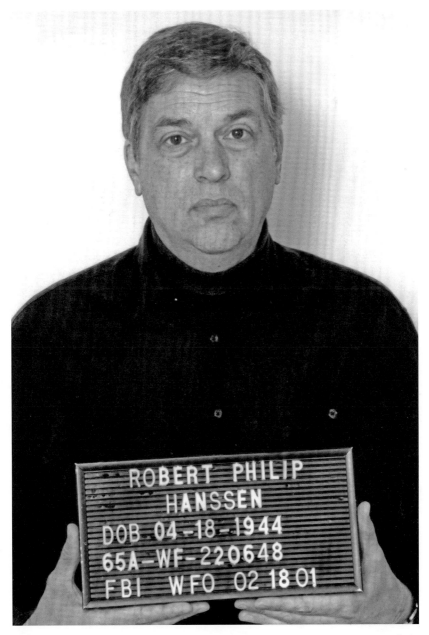

FBI counter-intelligence agent Robert Philip Hanssen was arrested in November 2001 and given a life sentence after being convicted as a Russian spy. For fifteen years, the man known by the code name "B" supplied the KGB and its successor organization, the SVR, with approximately six thousand pages of secret and top secret information. For these he was paid in diamonds and cash, the latter amounting to $600,000. (FBI photo)

Hanssen and his Russian contact communicated using the classic system of a marker on a utilities pole (the signal site) combined with a location in which to conceal notes for each other (the dead-letter box). A pre-established signal—a strip of adhesive tape, for example—on this electric utility pole meant that the dead-letter box had to emptied at a certain agreed-upon time. (FBI photo)

One of the hidden dead-letter boxes used by "B" and his Russian handler was under a wooden boardwalk at the Long Branch Nature Center in Arlington, Virginia. (FBI photo)

One of Aldrich Ames's notes to his Russian contact. Ames, a CIA officer, became a mole for the KGB in 1985 while working for the department in charge of Soviet counter-intelligence networks in eastern Europe. He was arrested in 1994 and sentenced to life imprisonment. (FBI photo)

Grid-type reference table for encrypting and decoding messages supplied to Ana Belen Montes, an analyst at the U.S. Defense Intelligence Agency (DIA), by her handler from Cuba's spy agency. Montes was arrested in September 2001 by the FBI in Washington, D.C. (FBI photo)

Vladislav Tretiak and the young Michel Bordeleau at the Quatre Glaces arena in Brossard, Quebec, during the 1980s. (Photo, Pablo Durant)

Defector Sergei Tretyakov wrote his contact information on the back of a CSIS business card while working in Ottawa during the 1990s. (Authors' archives)

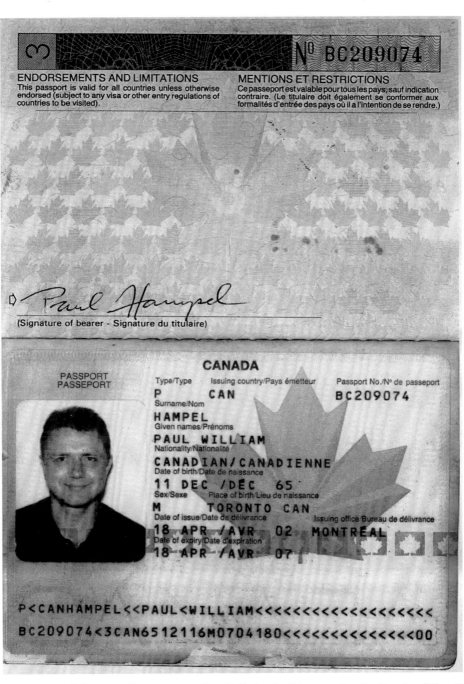

Photograph of the Canadian passport "legally" obtained in 2002 by the Russian "illegal" Paul William Hampel, using his pseudonym. (Authors' archives)

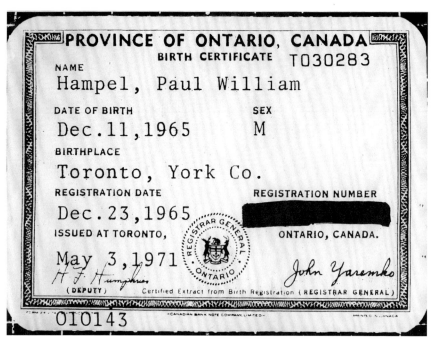

At the time of his arrest, spy Paul William Hampel was carrying a small folder under his shirt. Inside the folder, Canadian police investigators found this birth certificate in his fictitious name. (Authors' archives)

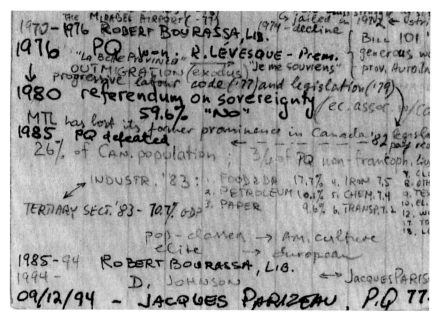

Careful to make his cover story as believable as possible, Paul William Hampel never let himself be separated from these notes, in which he briefly recorded the most significant dates in Canadian and Quebec history. (Authors' archives)

The fire in the Soviet Union's Montreal consulate on January 14, 1987, instigated a gigantic information-collecting operation on the part of CSIS. Defiant Soviet officials and consulate staff kept all outsiders—including the fire department—away from the blaze as long as they could. The consulate was a virtual fortress, as evidenced by new brick walls concealed behind window curtains. (© *Journal de Montreal*—Claude Rivest)

Alexandre S. Yereskovski, seen here in discussion with a Montreal police officer, was the consul general at the time of the fire. (© *Journal de Montreal*—Claude Rivest)

TRANSLATION
FROM THE
RUSSIAN LANGUAGE PRESS REVIEW
Telephone (613) 993-9042

TRADUCTION D'ARTICLES DE LA
REVUE DE LA PRESSE
DE LANGUE RUSSE
Téléphoner au (613) 993-9042

VOL. 1 NO. 21
VOL. 1 N° 21

From/tiré de : Pravda, 91-10-15, p. 4

OUR ASHES ARE NOT TO BE TRIFLED WITH
- AN ECHO FOUR YEARS AFTER THE FIRE

During the winter of 1987 there was a major fire at the USSR consulate-general in Montreal. Shortly after this incident, which, fortunately, only involved the loss of material, the Cuban consulate in Montreal burned down. Both accidents received a great deal of attention from the local press.

The memory of the fire faded in Montreal not long after the black smoke. Our rebuilt consulate-general has been punctually receiving visitors for a long time. Then suddenly, a day or two ago, the Canadian press once again returned to the bygone event. But there was now a totally unexpected twist.

Guy Chamberland, a 29 year-old former employee of the Canadian Security and Intelligence Service (CSIS), filed a $150,000 claim in the federal court against the federal government. The biochemist believes that he should be compensated this amount for damage to his health during his service with CSIS.

What does Guy Chamberland's chronic illness have to do with the fire in the USSR consulate-general in Montreal? As the "Southam News" agency and the Canadian newspapers confirm, these two seemingly totally unrelated facts are linked by ashes and charred embers; that is, by all that was left of the contents of our mission, which should have ended up in some garbage dump. Still hot on the heels of the fire, the Canadian press had reported that the Soviet ashes would be dealt with by the appropriate parties - that is, Canadian counter-intelligence. Within its walls, apparently, they were convinced that, coupled with their equipment, our ashes were priceless.

Due to the secret nature of the work which followed, it is difficult to say what kinds of "gems" of secret information were uncovered by the Canadian special service among our smouldering ruins. For now the public has only learned of one secret result of these investigations - Guy Chamberland, who, together with a group of colleagues has analyzed our remains, has fallen ill.

Poor Guy accuses his superiors of criminal actions in hiding the dangerous nature of the work from him, and in refusing to allow him to reveal the details of the work that he had been doing for the service to the doctor who was treating him, even after he began

2

to experience breathing difficulties and pains in his back and chest.

At least the victim is making claims against his own government and not ours. Not that we would able to help him anyway - we have no currency. Besides, we "supplied" the Canadians with some excellent ashes (perhaps even containing grains of some personal secrets), but they themselves made a mistake somewhere. Did they not store them properly? And, as a result, Guy Chamberland, as we are told by the press, is now insisting that the materials which were to be sifted through had "decomposed and become contaminated by fungi and bacteria" (Canadian, of course - V.Sh.) - hence the illnesses from which the experts working with the materials now suffer. Thus, we have an absolute alibi in this case.

Perhaps the people in the West who warn that the smoke from our motherland can cause a lot of trouble for them are right.

V. SHELKOV

On October 15, 1991, a correspondent for the Russian newspaper *Pravda* wrote a bitterly ironic account of the legal action launched by Guy Chamberland, a former CSIS employee, against the Canadian government. The suit concerned major health problems that Chamberland had developed, allegedly due to his work investigating objects recovered from the fire at the Soviet consulate. (Authors' archives)

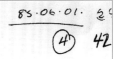

OU YYZKZAI
.BOMDOAI 010915
DO 14/5222
WE QUOTE BELOW THE TEXT OF LETTER RECEIVED FROM DCAS ADDRESSED
TO MD STP QUOTE
ASSESSMENT OF THORAT RECEIVED FROM INTELLIGENCE AGENCIES REVEAL
THE LIKELIHOOD OF SABOTAGE ATTEMPTS BEING UNDERTAKEN BY SIKH
EXTREMISTS BY PLACING TIME/DELAY DEVICES ETC. IN THE AIRCRAFT
OR REGISTERED BAGGAGE STP IT IS ALSO LEARNT THAT SIKH EXTREMISTS
ARE PLANNING TO SETUP SUICIDE SQUADS WHO MAY ATTEMPT TO BLOW UP
AN AIRCRAFT BY SMUGGLING IN OF EXPLOSIVES IN THE REGISTERED
OR CARRY DASH ON DASH BAGGAGE OR ANY OTHER MEANS STP THIS CALLS
FOR METICULOUS IMPLEMENTATION OF COUNTER SABOTAGE MEASURES FOR
FLIGHTS AT ALL AIPORTS STP BASIC RESPONSIBILITY FOR COUNTER
SABOTAGE MEASURES IS THAT OF AIRLINES STP
FOLLOWING STEPS SHOULD BE TAKEN TO PREVENT EXTREMISTS BY
CARRYING OUT THEIR DESIGNS
1/ PHYSICAL IDENTIFICATION OF REGISTERED BAGGAGE OF BY PASSENGERS
SHOULD BE ENSURED AT THE TIME OF CHECK-IN STP
2/ SUPERVISION OF REGISTERED BAGGAGE IN BAGGAGE MOKE UP AREA AND
ALSO TILL IT IS LOADED INTO THE AIRCRAFT CMA SHOULD BE STRENGTHENED STP
3/ PROPER SUPERVISION SHOULD ALSO BE EXERCISED IN THE LOADING OF
CATTERING/FOOD ARTICLES INTO THE AIRCRAFT STP
4/ ALL SERVICE PERSONNEL LIKE SWEEPERS AND OTHER EMPLOYEES
PERFORMING ANY JOB IN THE AIRCRAFT SHOULD BE THOROUGHLY CHECKED
AND THE RECORD OF THEIR MOVEMENTS SHOULD BE MAINTAINED STP
CLOSE SUPERVISION SHOULD BE EXERCISED BY RESPONSIBLE OFFICER OVER
THE PERSONNEL OF VARIOUS SERVICES PERFORMING THE DUTIES IN THE
AIRCRAFT STP
5/ EXPLOSIVE SNIFFERS AND BIO DASH SENSORS BRKT DOGS UNBRKT MAY BE
USED TO CHECK THE REGISTERED BAGGAGE IN VIEW OF THE THREAT
MENTIONED ABOVE STP ARRANGEMENTS SHOULD BE GET MADE TO CONDUCT
PHYSICAL RANDOM CHECK OF ALL REGISTERED BAGGAGE AT THE TIME
OF CHECK DASH IN ATLEAST TILL JUNE 30 CMA 1985 CMA PARTICULARLY
IN PLACES WHERE EXPLOSIVE SNIFFERS ARE NOT AVAILABLE STP
UNQTE
THIS IS FOR YOUR INFO AND NEC ACTION STP SUBRAMANIAN
;011006 0180

A Telex message sent by Air India's head of security to the company's offices around the world. It refers to information received from other intelligence agencies "which reveal the probability of acts of sabotage by Sikh extremists." The document was sent to the RCMP but not to CSIS. (Courtesy of the Air India Commission/John C. Major)

An "urgent" request written in October 1984 by an investigator in CSIS's British Columbia bureau to the organization's head office, seeking permission to place a wiretap on the telephone of Talwinder Singh Parmar as quickly as possible. Permission was granted five months later. (Courtesy of the Air India Commission/John C. Major)

A Level Four investigation, the highest level possible, against Parmar was authorized in October 1984 by top authorities at CSIS, as explained in this note. It was written on November 9, 1984, by CSIS investigator Ray Kobzey. (Courtesy of the Air India Commission/John C. Major)

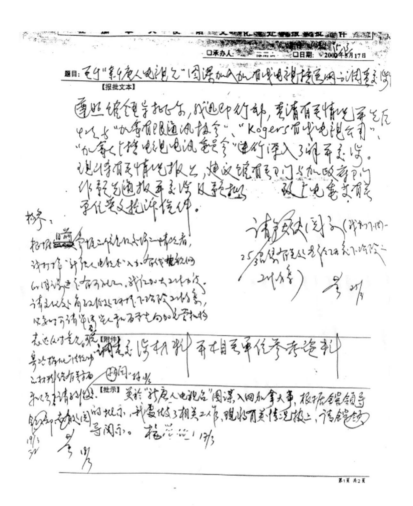

The wife of a Chinese diplomat in Ottawa defected in March 2007, carrying this note. She claimed it had been written by an official at the embassy and contained details of pressures Beijing agents applied to prevent a Falun Gong–backed television network from obtaining permission to broadcast in Canada. (Authors' archives)

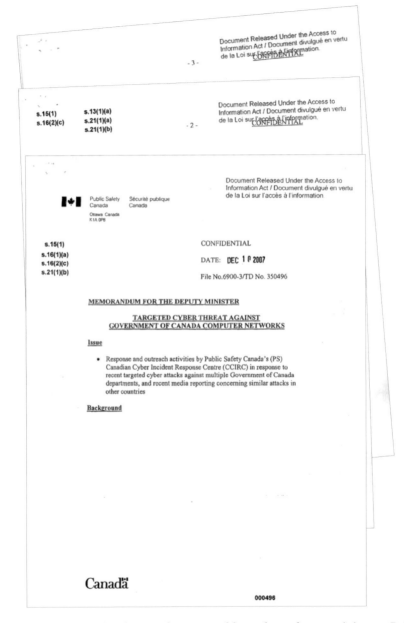

- 3 -

s.15(1)   s.13(1)(a)
s.16(2)(c) s.21(1)(a)
           s.21(1)(b)

- 2 -

Public Safety   Sécurité publique
Canada   Canada

Ottawa Canada
K1A 0P8

s.15(1)
s.16(1)(a)
s.16(2)(c)
s.21(1)(b)

CONFIDENTIAL

DATE: DEC 1 0 2007

File No.6900-3/TD No. 350496

MEMORANDUM FOR THE DEPUTY MINISTER

TARGETED CYBER THREAT AGAINST
GOVERNMENT OF CANADA COMPUTER NETWORKS

Issue

- Response and outreach activities by Public Safety Canada's (PS)
  Canadian Cyber Incident Response Centre (CCIRC) in response to
  recent targeted cyber attacks against multiple Government of Canada
  departments, and recent media reporting concerning similar attacks in
  other countries

Background

Canada

000496

In this memorandum dated December 2007, addressed to a deputy minister at Public Safety Canada shortly after an extensive cyber-attack against the government, two emergency management officials at the ministry of Public Safety explain, with some distaste, the methods employed by Chinese authorities. (Authors' archives)

- 2 -   SECRET

Liaowang, un certain professeur PANG de l'UNIVERSITÉ DE NANKAI soutient qu'il ne faut pas
mesurer à la même aune les puissances douces des États-Unis et de la Chine, mais que le concept
de la « puissance douce » lui-même a « une très grande valeur stratégique ». Le professeur PANG
affirme que « si elle est développée entièrement, la puissance douce peut suppléer à une insuffisance
en puissance brute. Ainsi, il suffit d'une politique étrangère correcte, d'un art de la diplomatie
exceptionnel, d'habiletés à la négociation

- 1 -   SECRET

RÉSUMÉ

Le gouvernement de la République populaire de Chine (RPC) est déterminé à accroître sa puissance
militaire et son pouvoir économique et à augmenter sa puissance douce en même temps. Autrement
dit, la Chine veut que le monde s'éprenne d'elle et de tout ce qui est chinois. Dans le cadre de cette
campagne, elle a implanté plus d'une centaine d'INSTITUTS CONFUCIUS (IC) un peu partout
dans le monde. Elle en a inauguré un au BRITISH COLUMBIA INSTITUTE OF TECHNOLOGY
(BCIT) de Vancouver

les IC occupent une
place plus importante dans la panoplie des efforts déployés par la Chine pour améliorer sa
réputation dans le monde lorsque les Jeux Olympiques 2008 de Beijing seront terminés; ces derniers
font l'objet d'une poussée chinoise en matière de puissance douce.

La campagne de la Chine pour accroître sa puissance douce

1. Joseph NYE, professeur à Harvard, a défini la puissance douce de la façon suivante : « la
capacité d'atteindre ses objectifs par la séduction et la persuasion, plutôt que par la coercition ou
l'argent. Elle découle de l'attrait qu'exercent la culture, les idéaux stratégiques et les politiques d'un
pays. » [traduction][1] La puissance douce augmente lorsque des choses sont considérées comme
légitimes par les autres. NYE est d'avis que la puissance douce a été cruciale pour remporter la
guerre froide et qu'elle est essentielle dans la lutte contre le terrorisme. MACHIAVEL estimait qu'il
était préférable d'être craint que d'être aimé, mais en politique internationale l'idéal c'est encore
d'avoir les deux émotions de son côté.

2. Pendant que les intellectuels débattent de l'importance relative de la puissance brute — les chars
d'assaut, les missiles, les fusils et autres articles du genre — par rapport à la puissance douce, le
gouvernement de la République populaire de Chine (RPC) considère le concept de la puissance
douce comme utile. Les autorités chinoises parlent de la quête de la puissance douce dans les
médias officiels.

Pour que la Chine atteigne ses objectifs, il faut que les gens en viennent à l'admirer dans une
certaine mesure. Dans le numéro de novembre 2005 du journal universitaire officiel du PCC,

---

[1] Voir Joseph S. NYE Jr., *Soft Power: The Means to Success in World Politics*, Public Affairs, 2004.

A CSIS report concerning the launch of a number of Confucius Institutes in Canada.
(Authors' archives)

CONFIDENTIEL

RÉSUMÉ

Nous pouvons maintenant nous attendre à ce que tout conflit politique ou diplomatique dans lequel un pays, une faction politique ou une autre entité est engagé comprenne un volet électronique ou en ligne.

Les dirigeants ou les ministères en vue ou encore les entités économiques ou commerciales comme les banques sont des cibles probables d'attaques électroniques lors de conflits diplomatiques.

Un examen des derniers conflits électroniques permet de constater que les attaques électroniques sont de plus en plus perfectionnées et utilisent   des variantes des attaques par saturation, la défiguration, l'envoi de pourriels et d'autres moyens offensifs.

Introduction

1. Le récent conflit diplomatique entre l'Estonie et la Russie a donné lieu à une campagne électronique concertée contre les sites Web gouvernementaux et commerciaux estoniens. Ces attaques électroniques   confirment l'idée qu'Internet jouera désormais sans doute un rôle important dans tout conflit politique ou diplomatique. Bon nombre des caractéristiques et des techniques généralement associées à un conflit électronique ont d'ailleurs été utilisées au cours de ce conflit qui constitue, comme les campagnes électroniques antérieures, un guide utile pour les gouvernements et les entreprises en matière de cyberdéfense et de reprise des activités.

Contexte

2. Les opérations d'information, autrefois appelées « guerre de l'information », ont beaucoup évolué depuis leurs débuts. De façon générale, chacun tient pour acquis que les gouvernements possèdent les ressources et l'infrastructure requises pour se doter d'une doctrine sur les opérations d'information et mener de telles opérations. Cette capacité et cette doctrine, qui voient généralement le jour au sein de l'infrastructure militaire, sont aujourd'hui normalisées et structurées. Elles comprennent non seulement les composantes traditionnelles comme les opérations de réseaux informatiques, les opérations psychologiques et la guerre électronique, mais également un important volet civil qui comprend les affaires publiques, les opérations civilo-militaires et le soutien à la diplomatie publique.

9. Les attaques se sont également perfectionnées au fil des années et pendant les campagnes électroniques. Les premiers conflits ne se traduisaient généralement que par la défiguration de sites Web et de simples attaques par DoS.

---

⁵ Les pirates adolescents ont recours à des techniques de piratage bien connues ou faciles à trouver pour exploiter les vulnérabilités d'un système et en comprennent bien souvent pas les conséquences de leurs activités ou ne s'en préoccupent pas.

A CSIS report concerning the threat of cyber-war and Canada's state of preparedness. (Authors' archives)

SUMMARY

In 2006, espionage reached a level of prominence in the public eye that has not been witnessed since the Cold War. Several cases of espionage capturing global media attention in 2006 including the poisoning death of former FEDERAL SECURITY SERVICE (FSB) officer Aleksandr LITVINENKO and the arrest and expulsion of four Russian military intelligence (GRU) officers from Georgia. The arrest in Montreal and eventual deportation of an SVR Illegal, identifying himself as Paul William HAMPEL,

In 2006 11, the Iranian government publicly accused the 13 - member Canadian diplomatic mission in Tehran of spying at the behest of the United States.

Media and public awareness of espionage reached new levels in 2006, as national security concerns have become increasingly prominent in policy - making and state - civil society dialogue.

Introduction

1. In 2006, espionage reached a level of prominence in the public eye that has not been witnessed since the Cold War.

12. The issue of PRC espionage, particularly science and technology (S&T) transfer and foreign-influenced activities, received prominent Canadian media coverage.

Additional reports surfaced relating to charges made by two PRC defectors to Australia in 2005 that the PRC maintains over 1,000 spies and informers in Canada.

One of the very few recent CSIS reports on the subject of espionage within Canada and around the world. (Authors' archives) has been the chairman of the China National Committee for Pacific Economic Cooperation (CNCPEC).

Today he and Ambassador Jiang Chengzong, secretary general of the CNCPEC, are here at the invitation of the Canadian International Council. The CIC describes itself as a "private and non-partisan Canadian organization which encourages greater dialogue and research on international questions." The evening's theme is "The Future of Canada-China Relations."

The audience is illustrious: prominent businessmen, students, important members of the Chinese community, and a famous "sinologist" who teaches in a Montreal university. This individual is known as a steadfast defender of the Chinese republic and a particular enemy of what he calls the "Tibetan theocracy," which he readily compares with the Taliban of Afghanistan. Intently listening in the front row is former Quebec premier Pierre-Marc Johnson, a board member of the CIC.

For the evening, the organization has invoked the Chatham House rules (associated with the well-known London think tank), which exclude the media in order that speakers may express themselves frankly, knowing they won't be quoted. This is the kind of setting in which Mei Ping feels at home. Of course, he would agree that self-criticism is central to the doctrine of Mao Zedong, as well as other Communist regimes. Just not now. Not here. Tonight he's more excited about that other Maoist doctrine: forced re-education.

His pedagogical efforts are aimed at Canada's newly proclaimed prime minister, Stephen Harper, who has pointedly failed to attend the opening ceremony of the Olympic Games in Beijing. Mei, claiming that he speaks as a private citizen, says that Canada greatly misunderstands the nature of the Chinese state. Moreover,

Canada has become a safe haven (his word is "paradise") for criminals sought by the Chinese government. Worse, only the year
before, Canada hosted the Dalai Lama, "a separatist political figure,"
with an official ceremony and declared him an honorary citizen.
Choking with indignation, Mei also points out that Canada has
welcomed more than one Taiwanese delegation, which suggests
that the practice is not accidental. Finally he moves on to the religious movement called Falun Gong, which has been outlawed in
China but is, in his view, unaccountably tolerated in Canada.

To Mei's left sits Jiang Chengzong, who leans sideways across
the table, supporting himself on one elbow and studying the
attendees with a fixed gaze. He has not said a word, apart from a
lively denunciation of the "ridiculous" and "totally false" charges
that his country has violated human rights in Tibet. In fact, things
are going swimmingly for the Tibetans since they came under the
protection of China and escaped the despotism of the Dalai Lama.
Did Canadians not know that their population had doubled? All of
this without blinking.

Jiang doesn't mention that Chinese Han immigrants to Tibet
now outnumber the native population by more than 2 million, and
that newcomers continue to throng toward Tibet's capital city, Lhasa,
with the kind of energy that Canadians can muster only when there
is a round of job offerings in the Alberta tar sands. Further masses
of Han colonists will arrive on the recently completed "railway to
the roof of the world" (sometimes described as the "railway of colo-
nization"), which was built with the help of Bombardier, Nortel,
and General Electric. Beijing spent $4.2 billion on the project.

Jiang would like Canadians to believe that the building of the
railway proceeded from affection for the people of Tibet, rather
than from its strategic proximity to India, not to mention the min-
eral wealth of the sprawling Himalayan country. This is a remark-

able assertion of selflessness in light of reports that Tibet contains the world's largest reserves of chrome and aluminum, together with not insignificant quantities of uranium and electric-car-powering lithium.

Today, former ambassador Mei sets aside diplomacy in favour of a straightforward plea for China. The propaganda is adroitly blended with economic blackmail. China, he says, is patiently waiting for Canada to come to its senses. How much longer can China maintain the current level of trade and commercial exchange if Canada keeps being so confrontational?

The audience easily gets the subtext. They are people of influence, and China requires them to use their influence to change Canada's foreign policy. Otherwise they will most certainly miss the diplomatic gravy train.

For a former ambassador to give such a speech, even to a select audience, comes very close to interference in the domestic affairs of another country. He also skirts Canada's laws on hate speech. But nobody minds, judging by the tidal wave of applause and the gracious words of gratitude from Pierre-Marc Johnson. As a board member of the Canadian International Council, Johnson has allowed Mei to abuse his diplomatic status, as well as the CIC's hospitality. He also let the ambassador, a past master at this kind of thing, manoeuvre the CIC into seeming to agree with policies odious to Canada.

This was also Mei's modus operandi during the seven years, beginning in 1998, when he occupied the post of Chinese ambassador to Canada. He worked steadily to marginalize and undermine the Falun Gong and the Tibetans, who are defined as "enemies" of the Chinese regime. He didn't hesitate to sign letters to politically influential people describing the followers of Falun Gong as "heretics" who were "mentally deranged" and whose activities had been declared illegal in

China. "I sincerely hope that, in your function as a Canadian legislator, you will understand and respect the position of our government and that you will contribute to friendly relations between China and Canada," he added in one of these missives, addressed to Rob Anders. An Alberta member of Parliament, Anders, well known for his frequent denouncements of the Chinese government, had spoken out against the persecution of the Falun Gong in China.

Only a year after arriving in Ottawa, Mei Ping dared to phone members of Parliament and the Senate, urging them to boycott a Reform Party breakfast in support of Falun Gong. Thugs and bullies emerged from his embassy and his consulates to harass legal demonstrations against human rights abuses in China. What was John Manley, then minister of Foreign Affairs, going to do about these "serious breaches of diplomatic protocol," asked Anders in a letter of January 3, 2002? The letter specifically criticized the behaviour of Chinese diplomats in Ottawa and asked for a public inquiry.

Well-wishers and photographers swarm Mei Ping as he steps down from the podium, camera strobe lights bouncing off his face and giving the event an Oscar-ish glow. Out in the corridor, in brief gaps between flipping petits fours into his mouth and tossing back red wine, a Canadian highly impressed by Mei's speech describes Falun Gong as a kind of monster created by the CIA that now menaces the well-meaning folk of our little northern dominion.

Mission accomplished. Over and out. And the faithful servant of the Chinese Communist Party can once again hit the road, confident that the good word will find welcoming ears across Canada.

A week later, Mei Ping was no doubt delighted to learn that Pierre-Marc Johnson—who did not at the time hold any elected office—had been asked by Quebec Premier Jean Charest to take his place in a party of provincial premiers who would be visiting China. Charest was too busy fighting an election to leave the country.

"Foreign interference" is a polite diplomatic term that masks a little-known aspect of international espionage. Setting aside for a moment the everyday theft of commercial and technological information, let's take a look at the extensive machinery that undermines Canadian government policy-making. It aims to intimidate the host government and suborn public and private organizations that can advance the foreign regime's interests.

At least twenty foreign countries have agents in Canada, tirelessly undermining the policy-making process. Obviously this is unacceptable to a democracy. But they won't be discouraged. Nor will they stop shadowing, subverting, harassing, intimidating, and coercing their diaspora communities here, especially the many political movements in exile.

Foreign interference now appears to be the most serious threat to Canada, at least so far as the scale of the operations is concerned.

More than 6 million Canadians, about one-fifth of the population, were born elsewhere. The great metropolises, especially Vancouver, Montreal, and Toronto, are now proudly multicultural communities. More than a few of these new Canadians are here because they had to flee for their lives, whether from tyranny or civil war. Others are seeking a better life. Whatever peace they might have expected, after putting thousands of kilometres between themselves and their homelands, often proves illusory. Multiculturalism has given birth to multi-espionage and multi-intimidation.

Who is affected? One would need to take a deep breath before reading the list aloud: Chinese who belong to Falun Gong, Tibetan resisters, members of the Uyghur people in Chinese Xinjiang (or eastern Turkestan), Kurds, Iranians, Sikhs from India, Tunisians,

Algerians, Moroccans, Libyans, Cubans . . . to name only the larger groups. They are relentlessly monitored by diplomats from their homeland, except when this work is subcontracted to the intelligence services of other countries.

THE BLACKLIST

It's one thing for a country to denounce emigrants who criticize the homeland. It's another to harass and intimidate them in their new country. These emigrants are now Canadians and no longer "belong" to the homeland. Why should they have to tolerate personal harassment or violence by agents sent from a country where they no longer live?

But today we do see harassment and outright violence carried out against dissidents living in Canada. Like other uncomfortable matters, this one has so far failed to arouse any particular concern among Canadians.

Cross-checking turns up a number of countries alleged to have harassed their expatriates in Canada. Their diplomats feign indignation, but for at least twenty years these are the names that persistently come up. It is, by the way, a "blacklist" that the Canadian government has tried to prevent being made public:

- South Africa
- Algeria
- Saudi Arabia
- Armenia
- China
- North Korea
- South Korea
- Cuba
- India
- Mexico
- Morocco
- Mozambique
- Pakistan
- Romania
- Russia
- Syria
- Sri Lanka
- Taiwan

- Iran
- Israel
- Malaysia

- Tunisia
- Turkey
- Ukraine

Some of these countries have the audacity to present Canadian authorities with a shopping list of their dissidents now in Canada. These are described as "dangerous criminals" or "terrorists," and our government is strongly encouraged to arrest them.

Unfortunately, since 9/11, we have a genuine terrorist threat. It is manna from heaven for these miscreant nations. It gives them a pretext for overstepping their authority and carrying on activity incompatible with Canadian laws—and certainly with Canadian values.

Without the limelight of the Beijing Summer Olympics in 2008, and the pressure brought to bear by pro-Tibet groups, and the persistence of influential associations such as Reporters Without Borders, it's a safe bet that few Canadians would much care what happened to Tibetans in the bloody street riots in Lhasa the summer before. The many protests by Falun Gong on Parliament Hill and outside China's consulates in Vancouver, Calgary, and Toronto would have taken place amid general indifference. Perhaps tourists in those cities would have found it picturesque. Even less can one imagine that the separatists of the Uyghur Muslim minority might attract sympathy. Who has even heard of them? Their only media coverage came when China accused them of a series of murders during the summer of 2008.

This is the same strategy used by small armed groups such as the Liberation Tigers of Tamil Eelam (LTTE) to extort millions of dollars from the Tamil-Canadian community.[33] They rely on the victims' fear of reprisals, but even more on the general indifference of Canadians.

In a 2006 report classified "Top Secret," the Canadian Security Intelligence Service (CSIS) wrote as follows:

> We are increasingly concerned with the question of foreign powers which carry out espionage in Canada in order to advance their political agenda or a cause linked to an internal conflict. They [these countries] have gathered information without authorization in order to advance their own interests in these conflicts. . . . [censored material] Regional conflicts which rage [censored] have inspired brazen operations to collect information in Canada, as well as campaigns of intimidation managed from outside the country.[34]

UNDER BEIJING'S WATCHFUL EYE

Since the late 1960s, the Chinese People's Republic has periodically (albeit timidly) been named as Suspect Number One by Canadian authorities. The first time this happened was in 1969, when Pierre Trudeau overrode the protests of the U.S. government and prepared to officially recognize Mao Zedong's China. W. L. Higgit, after a long career as a spy and spy hunter, warned from his new position as commissioner of the RCMP that there would be a surge of Chinese espionage in Canada the moment that country opened an embassy in Ottawa. Former prime minister John Diefenbaker grumbled that Canada would soon be "drowning in spies."[35]

Canada's first official visit to Communist China took place in

1973, when Trudeau and his wife, Margaret, stepped down from their airplane in Beijing, followed by a delegation of business people. In 1986, it was former solicitor general Robert Kaplan's turn to throw a rock into the stagnant pond of diplomacy. He declared that Canada had become a target of choice for foreign and particularly Chinese spies, and that these spies were under observation.

The activity of Chinese agents has sporadically caught the attention of the Canadian public, in particular after the bloody events of Tiananmen Square in 1989. Even before then, the media had reported on China's bullying of students who offended the authorities. Now it was the turn of overseas Chinese students at the University of British Columbia. They learned that unidentified parties had photographed and filmed their protests against the killing of students at Tiananmen. There was also physical harassment and attempts at blackmail. Some students received threatening phone calls. Others reported attacks on their families in China.

These practices continue today, with recent reports from Tibetan-Canadians of harassment by Chinese sympathizers dressed in matching red T-shirts. Colour-coordinated bullies have also assaulted Falun Gong demonstrators.

Back then, the major offender was the Chinese consulate-general in Vancouver, and in particular its education officer. Joe Clark, minister of Foreign Affairs at the time, took the matter seriously and recalled Canada's ambassador from Beijing. He also froze a number of commercial treaties between China and Canada.

Mr. Clark unfortunately declined to be interviewed for this book, perhaps because he now has a somewhat different view of China. He recently observed that Stephen Harper's Conservatives harmed our relationship with that country by harping too much on human rights. Clark, now a prominent professor at McGill

University, added that Canada made progress with China when it avoided obvious public attacks, and that this had become more important than ever, since China will soon rival the United States as an economic superpower.

Shortly after Mr. Clark's remarks, which were made early in 2007, CSIS director Jim Judd was uncharacteristically open in stating that China was the most dangerous of the top fifteen countries carrying out espionage in Canada. This was in front of a Senate committee, where he also uttered his now celebrated remark about "hyperactive tourists." The remark worth remembering, however, was that half of CSIS's counter-espionage agents were now busy monitoring Chinese activity in Canada.

That was the second time in less than a year that China was in Ottawa's cross-hairs. The previous April, Peter MacKay (then minister of Foreign Affairs) and the prime minister, Stephen Harper, accused China of having more than a thousand spies at work here stealing economic intelligence.

How many agents, one wonders, does Canada have in the field to do battle with this legion of infiltrators? CSIS, as we know too well, can answer only by saying, "We never comment on our operations and never give out this kind of information." But French investigative journalist Roger Faligot, who wrote an exhaustive study of the Chinese secret service, is certain that CSIS could not be fielding more than 85 agents against it.[36]

He added that 85 agents is not unimpressive when compared with the efforts of other western countries. But it is a very thin slice of the estimated 2,500 employees working for CSIS. The difficulty, as Faligot points out, is that no western agency can possibly match the "mass collection" resources possessed by China's counter-espionage service (the Ministry of State Security [MSS]) and the agency responsible for spying overseas (the Guoanbu).

Writes Faligot: "It's not realistic to think that we can fight them one on one. But there are other ways to go about it. CSIS' strategy, like that of some other Western services, is to identify a manageable three or four spy networks—whether inside or outside the embassy—and discover how they work."

That's all very well as far as it goes. But how far can that be, when we recall the tremendous mismatch of resources between CSIS and the overpopulated Chinese diplomatic corps in our country? Consider one fact: China has more people in Ottawa than the U.S. government does.

Obviously, CSIS has been asking questions about this for a long time. In 2008, for example, there were 120 accredited diplomats in the embassy's protocol department. That's a lot of people to make sure the ambassador is well supplied with hockey jokes and to remind him not to bow when he meets the governor general. There are dozens of consuls, and advisers by the bushel. Enough first, second, and third secretaries to shame a Ming emperor. And then you have to think about the hordes of journalists at the *People's Daily* and the flocks of professors perched in the Confucius Institutes.

Current investigations won't lead to the highly publicized deportations of spies seen in the Cold War era. But in Faligot's view, they have at least a kind of sad pedagogical usefulness. The lessons learned can be passed along to the beleaguered CEOs of Canadian corporations, many of which harbour spies. That's assuming the executives wish to listen. Many are extremely naive. We'll return to them later.

Meanwhile, it is true that the Harper government is for the moment being quite two-fisted about China, rhetorically at least. It remains to be seen whether the hard line will last into the medium and long term, given realpolitik and—above all—commercial pressures.

It's hard to catch professional spies red-handed, particularly since the good ones use go-betweens whenever possible. That said, it is still surprising that—with one possible exception—no Chinese diplomat, trained agent or not, has been expelled from Canada with loss of face and loud fracas in recent years. And yet we are beset with flagrant interference from that quarter. Looking at economic theft in particular, it seems that the greater the problem, the less we want to talk about it.

Given the situation, what can Chinese dissidents living in Canada expect? We know that the Chinese Communist Party has adopted a hard-line policy toward them. Today it seeks to locate, intimidate, and, in effect, take control of their lives. Considerable numbers of agents and large amounts of money are required, so that all participants in even a large demonstration can be confronted immediately afterward. Nobody escapes notice. Given how many Chinese democracy groups, community organizations, and student associations exist in Canada, the effort needed to infiltrate and manipulate all of them must be staggering.

Even were CSIS not continually calling attention to the problem, Canadian authorities must be aware of it. That they still prefer not to offend the "red giant" is disappointing, especially if one believes that Canada's greatest danger is not external interference, but rather internal interference!

"The audacity of the Chinese government!" is perhaps the phrase we heard most often during our research. And the only thing likely to discourage them would be the mass banishment of irksome diplomats under the glare of television cameras and a cortège of hulking, scowling Mounties.

"So long as this continues," observes Roger Faligot, "the Chinese

NEST OF SPIES   195

will simply raise the bar every day until they find where the breaking point is."*

There are a great number of examples, not only in Canada,
where petty politics and the eternal promise to get billions of dollars in contracts have succeeded in winning over national security.
Close business links often seem to get the upper hand over the con-
tinuous work of field intelligence officers. We just need to remind
ourselves of the concessions made in order to gain access to the
Chinese market by giants such as Yahoo, Google, Cisco, Skype and
Microsoft, to the detriment of basic human rights and the free flow
of information.[37]

Of course no business can afford to ignore the opportunities
presented by a powerful emerging economy. But in this case, western countries have agreed to a fool's bargain. Not only are we signing away our technological advantages, we are also shipping manufacturing jobs to a country that, in return, drowns us in gimcrack
goods and dollar store closet-stuffers.

"Sidewinder," an Embarrassing Friendship

The worst example of this kind of manipulation in Canada remains
"Operation Sidewinder." This was where we saw, for the first time,
the efforts China was prepared to make in order to steal economic
intelligence. RCMP and CSIS investigators who were put on the
job in May of 1996 proved that an elaborate three-way relationship
among China's secret police, its business community in Hong Kong,
and—ominously—the Triad mafias had been put in place to carry
out spying, in Canada in particular.

Their reports were greeted with skepticism in high places.

---

* According to some sources, the embassy of the People's Republic in Canada is
one of its largest operational espionage centres outside of China.

They were even described as the "conspiracy theory." As a result, the first "Sidewinder" report, called *Chinese Intelligence Services and Triad Financial Links in Canada*, was rejected out of hand when it was presented in 1997. CSIS went further, dismantling its Asia desk and transferring its analysts to other functions. Two years later the report was replaced with a softer and more consensual version. Given the code name "Echo," this report has been buried ever since.

The burying was done by the Security Intelligence Review Committee. SIRC is the watchdog organization that has been set over CSIS to make sure it obeys the law. In its 1999–2000 annual report it attacked the Sidewinder documentation using surprisingly hostile language. The SIRC report begins by stating that it "found no evidence of the alleged political interference." It continues:

> None of the documents and records reviewed, none of the interviews and observations collected,* lead us to believe that such interference, actual or presumed, ever took place. Project Sidewinder was not abandoned: it was delayed after its report was found unsatisfactory.
>
> As to the first draft of the Sidewinder report, we found it very faulty in almost all respects. It departed from standards of professionalism and lacked the most basic analysis. The measures taken by the Service to enhance the quality of its future work with the RCMP Sidewinder project were appropriate.[38]

Ironically, at just about the same time that Canadian authorities were suppressing the Sidewinder report, American authorities

---

* Taken from the official translation of the report.

published a study written by Christopher Cox that "echoed" most of its conclusions.

The Cox Report, hundreds of pages in length, details and denounces Chinese subversion in the United States. And, rather remarkably, the Chinese strategies that it describes sound very much like those listed in the Sidewinder report. The Cox Report speaks of false-front companies, pseudo "research institutes," joint ventures with North American corporations, and the calculated use of students, journalists, and official delegations in order to collect large quantities of publicly available information. (Later we will set out the strong similarities between that picture and what we encounter in Canada.)

Many specialists contacted in our research are familiar with the Sidewinder/Echo report and believe that it was suppressed by our government and its authors discredited. But nobody will name names, for fear of prosecution.

Other insiders take the more pragmatic (or perhaps cynical) view that the deed was done by mid-level bosses at CSIS, who would have understood right away that Sidewinder, if released, would be a career-ender for them.

It is, however, important to know why it was suppressed. Let's look back to 1997, when a Canadian, André Desmarais of the Power Corporation, was named to the board of CITIC Pacific (the China International Trust Investment Company). He has since been joined by two other Canadians. This is an example of a rare privilege for western-ers, and no doubt delighted Jean Chrétien's Liberal government, which had made trade with China the centrepiece of its economic strategy.

CITIC, one of China's massive business conglomerates, was created in late 1979 with the authority and benediction of Deng Xiaoping, secretary general of the Chinese Communist Party.* It

---

* A Canadian branch was set up in Vancouver in September 1986.

operates directly or indirectly in a number of industries, from commercial real estate to transport to telecommunications. It's also involved in weapons production through the China Poly Group, an arm of the People's Liberation Army (PLA).

A number of experts believe that CITIC also serves as a convenient base for undercover agents.

A Tougher Law?

According to the 2006 CSIS report mentioned earlier, Canada has committed itself to defending its cultural communities from outside threats. So the report says. And it goes on to say that these threats must be taken as seriously as the threat posed by conventional espionage.

Intimidation and harassment of minority Canadians has been ongoing for quite some time. But it rarely makes the headlines, even though it's generally agreed that there is as much of it as there is conventional political and military spying. A clue as to why Canadians don't hear more about foreign harassment of our citizens can be found in the recent phenomenon of international agreements to fight terrorism. These, as a rule, bind the domestic secret services of each signatory country to co-operate with the secret services of other nations party to the treaty. This includes nations usually considered to be hostile to each other. These unnatural alliances, if we may so term them, proliferated mightily during the run-up to the Beijing Olympic Games in 2008.

One such agreement accounts for the hundreds of Chinese police officers who have come to Canada since 2003 to take special training courses, the nature of which has not been made public. Chinese police are also trained in Germany, Australia, and England.[39]

A similar anti-terrorist partnership exists between Russia and China, two rival powers whose spies have rarely been known to be cozy with one another. The heads of Canada's investigative services have also met with their Chinese opposite numbers, just as they periodically encounter the bosses of the Russian SVR and FSB services.

Chinese authorities make use of these treaty-authorized encounters to present foreign secret services with lists of "criminals" in whom they are interested. These are almost invariably people with a record of opposition to the Chinese government. And finally, recalling what we said earlier about the audacity of the ruling party, Beijing even sought advice from Canada as to how it should control the movements of the thousands of foreign journalists who would attend the Olympic Games. Astonished Canadian authorities could only reply that they didn't have much experience in telling journalists what to do.

This kind of toothsome anecdote of course makes one wonder about the tone and reach of the co-operative accords that were signed with China at the time of the Olympics. Are we talking about agreements to protect the simple physical security of Canadian citizens and athletes who attended the games in 2008? Or did Canada, in a moment of wild assertiveness, think to use the leverage of its presence at the Olympics to pressure China into shutting down at least some of its hostile operations here?

Our attempts to coax CSIS into confirming or denying what transpired in these meetings met with the customary boilerplate reply. Here is the complete version:

> The Service is responsible for protecting Canada and Canadians, both at home and abroad.
>
> To fulfil its mandate, the Service maintains relations with law enforcement and investigative agencies both in Canada and abroad.

Within the framework of the 2008 Olympics in Beijing, the mandate of the Service is to support our many partners in law enforcement and investigation in order to ensure that the Games take place without incident.

It is important to remember that the Service has no role in law enforcement or protection.

The Service recognizes the importance of freedom of the press and the right of peaceful protest.

The Service does not discuss its relationships with other information services.

Raymond Nart, the retired head of French security services, confirms that China has also approached French authorities and requested inappropriately that dissidents living in France be seized and turned over to them. During the months after the Tiananmen suppression—ironically, at the same time that France celebrated the two hundredth anniversary of its revolution and its ringing declaration of the rights of mankind—a Chinese official approached Nart, who at the time was in charge of counterespionage operations. The official asked in all seriousness if Nart's agents would be kind enough to arrest Tiananmen protesters who had sought safety in France.

"There's quite a lot of them in your country, after all."

"Better with us than with you," replied Nart. "But don't worry, we'll take care of them."

"Obviously," adds Nart, "we did nothing at all."

At War with the Falun Gong

In late 2006, bad news arrived in the office of Wang Pengfei, the second secretary of Education in the Chinese embassy on St. Patrick

Street in Ottawa. Canada's Ministry of Foreign Affairs was refusing to renew his visa. He was, in effect, being shown the door.

Wang packed his bags, said goodbye to the Rideau Canal and the Byward Market, and left his pleasant Canadian life behind. By November his name was no longer in the protocol files.

According to revelations published at the time in a Falun Gong newsletter, Wang's specific duties were to persecute Falun Gong members in Canada.[40] Following the usual practice in these matters, China denied that Wang had been expelled or that he was in any way involved in illicit activities. His departure was part of a normal rotation of diplomats.

A person who knows better is Zhang Jiyan, the forty-eight-year-old wife of an auditor in the embassy. She is a follower of Falun Gong. For that reason she had been under surveillance for some time. She got into the habit of turning on the television and the kitchen range fan whenever she and her husband chatted at home. Their apartment, furnished by the Chinese government, had concealed microphones.

The Falun Gong has already figured prominently in this story.* Readers may well wonder why a religious group attracts such persecution in this day and age.

The Falun Gong (also called Falun Dafa) was founded—or perhaps "invented" is a better word—by Li Hongzhi in 1992. Its adepts practise a highly original mixture of non-violent Buddhist philosophy and Taoist gymnastics. At the beginning the movement was legal. But Falun Gong suffered a sudden reversal of fortune one night in April 1999. Thousands of its devotees from all corners of China converged without warning in Beijing. There they surrounded the head-

---

* Falun means "wheel of the law," and Gong is short for "quigon," an activity blending meditation and exercise.

quarters of the government and the Communist Party, where they stood in utter silence for several hours. Then they left the area in an orderly fashion, without making a sound.

The event was pacifist and brief, although certainly eccentric and unsettling. And all might have been well, except that the rally had fallen ten years after the infamous massacre of students in nearby Tiananmen Square. The authorities realized the connection, as they were meant to. But then they panicked. Apart from Falun Gong's boldness in protesting openly, it was humiliating to the apparatchiks that such a well-organized event had occurred without their spies hearing of it first. Lashing out reflexively, they banned Falun Gong and denounced it as a "heretic organization." Its followers were attacked and beaten wherever they were found. This quasi-hysterical frenzy has now passed beyond China's borders. Fengzhi Li, a former member of China's Guoanbu spy service, defected to the United States in 2004 and gave the inside story of this witch hunt while relating his own story, which culminated with his resignation from the Chinese Communist Party in the spring of 2009.

Today the movement's faithful still live in fear, and even paranoia. The entrance to their Chinatown headquarters on Clark Street in Montreal has an oversized poster on the wall with the address and phone number of the nearest police station.

In July 2004, two members of the consulate of the People's Republic of China in Calgary—we'll call them C.J. and W.J.—were the subject of an investigation by the Mounties and the Edmonton city police. They had been seen distributing "hate literature" the previous month in Edmonton during a conference of the American Family Foundation at the University of Alberta. The pamphlets in question were called "The Truth" and "Falun Gong Is a Diabolical Sect." They contained bloody images of immolations, crimes, and suicides, according to police reports that we obtained.

These two consulate employees were not completely protected by diplomatic immunity. At the conclusion of the investigation the police recommended that they be charged under article 319.2 of the Criminal Code.

Alberta's attorney general declined the suggestion, much to the frustration and discouragement of Falun Gong's Canadian activists, who asked for a judicial review of the decision. Again the answer was no. The matter is currently under appeal, but C.J. and W.J. have long since left the country. They were gone as soon as the initial police report was made public.

Even when there is a decision against denigrators of Falun Gong, it is another matter to see the decision enforced. This was the case in February of 2004, when Pan Xinchun, China's deputy consul-general in Toronto, was ordered to pay $11,000 in damages and costs for libelling a local businessman who practised Falun Gong. This was the first Falun Gong–related libel award anywhere against a Chinese official.

But Pan returned to China without paying. He appears to enjoy impunity in the matter.

When asked about the nature of Falun Gong, the group's Canadian spokesperson, Lucy Zhou, wants one thing understood: "We are ordinary people. Falun Gong is not a sect. Nobody is a 'member' of it. It's simply a way of life . . . that is beneficial for a person's health."

Such plain speaking is at the farthest remove from the highly imaginative views held by Chinese authorities. For them, the Falun Gong, the Tibetans, the Uyghurs of eastern Turkestan, and pro-independence Taiwanese, together with any and all democracy activists, are classified as the "Five Poisons." This is how the Chinese embassy in Ottawa describes Falun Gong on its website:

> Falun Gong is an anti-science, anti-humanity and anti-society evil cult which has been banned in China in accordance with law. It uses religion, Qigong or other things as camouflage to brainwash and control the practitioners. It preaches that humans can, through psychological meditation, from invisible magic wheels inside their bodies, cure their illness without medical treatment. It spreads Dooms Day theory, boasts that Li Hongzhi, founder of Falun Gong, is the most powerful God, claiming the sole power to foresee and avert the many unseen disasters that threaten the world. It also uses Falun Gong to amass dirty money, and commit economic crimes of tax evasion and money laundering.[41]

Wang Pengfei, the diplomat deported and declared *persona non grata*, enlisted and manipulated the twenty or so Chinese student associations in Canadian universities. Whether through naïveté, nationalist zealotry, or simple blackmail, the students jump to attention at the least whisper from the Chinese government.

The authorities lavish praise on them. The same Wang Pengfei, back in 2004, took time out to sing the praises of the head of the

Chinese student association at the Université du Québec à Montréal (UQAM). Writing in *Chinese Scholars Abroad* magazine, Wang admired the association's "propaganda activities . . . and its brave and ingenious campaign against the Falun Gong."*

The Mysterious "United Front Work Department"

The Chinese government relies on a couple of dozen front groups in Canada, ranging from student associations and community groups to professional organizations and journalists. At the top of this sinister pyramid is the United Front Work Department (UFWD) of the Chinese Communist Party's Central Committee.

In 2007 the UFWD, together with the Ministry of Foreign Affairs, was given the tidy sum of $3 billion to promote China's image worldwide in the run-up to the 2008 Olympic Games. This was on top of their regular budgets.

The UFWD's primary role, its real role, is espionage. A CSIS analyst has described its modus operandi as having solidarity with one's friends, the better to destroy one's enemies. In a report published on the agency's website, the analyst continues:

> As well as the organized recruiting of allies in key sectors of society and isolating its real enemies, the United Front's strategy is the Chinese equivalent of psychological warfare.
>
> In calling upon its diaspora to remember its duty to the mother country, China is requesting more than monetary donations and expressions of affection. The Front's object is equally one of compelling overseas Chinese to

---

* Among the exploits of Wang Pengfei was an attempt to block pro–Falun Gong demonstrators when Chinese Prime Minister Wen Jiabao visited Ottawa in 2003.

take part in economic and technical espionage, whether through patriotic appeals or simple threats.

The analysis advises caution in dealing with the Front:

> Since it relies on a divide-and-conquer strategy in carrying forward its program, Canada must respond with vigilance if the rights and freedoms of Chinese Canadians are not to be compromised.[42]

The coarse tactic of using students as an intermediary or front has been used by many totalitarian regimes apart from China. As a rule, nobody is deceived by the noisiness and false unanimity of these manipulated groups. But they're useful anyway, because they draw public attention away from the sinister activity of China's embassies and consulates.

At the same time, Chinese nationalism is a genuine and widespread phenomenon. Part of the Chinese overseas community is attracted to a radical strain called Huaqiao. These individuals—and some of course are students—need little persuasion to go after anyone named an "enemy" of the regime.

That said, the educational services of Chinese legations are always connected with its secret services. In a recent publication, Roger Faligot has described teams of so-called "cleaners" (some with diplomatic immunity) that went to China's embassies around the world shortly after the brutal Tiananmen Square repression. Their job was to bring overseas student associations into line. To do so, they used the familiar tool kit of threats, pressure, and blackmail.[43]

They did their job well. Some years later, in the winter of 2008, these same student associations poured into the streets (surrounded by embassy agents) to shout hateful slogans about Tibetans and their spiritual leader, the Dalai Lama. In Montreal they denounced the "lies" of the media and the "Taliban" behaviour of the Tibetan people. The Dalai Lama became a "liar and sadist" who had enslaved his people.

Falun Gong's Lucy Zhou recounts her experience when she followed a Falun Gong parade through the New York borough of Flushing in May 2008: "Hundreds of Chinese stood on the sidewalks and insulted us. They spat on us and threw bottles of water at us. At one point a bunch of them jumped over the barriers and started pushing us around. It was a lucky thing the police were there to get me out of harm's way."

This counter-demonstration was organized by the consulate-general in New York. One of its senior officials, Peng Kenyu, received a congratulatory telephone call for his clever work in having "discreetly encouraged" the interference with Falun Gong's parade. The phone call was recorded by a member of the World Organization to Investigate the Persecution of Falun Gong (WOIPFG).

During this call, Peng Kenyu worried out loud that he might be unmasked, in spite of the steps he had taken to disguise himself as a member of the crowd. His words, in a transcript that was sent to the media, were: "We have to be very careful with this kind of thing. Otherwise people are going to say that the Consulate-General of China is behind it."[44]

Peng described how he had "parked far from the location" of the demonstration, and how he had held himself well back in the crowd in order not to be spotted by the demonstrators. He then congratulated his troops for their good work and suggested story angles they might pass on to sympathetic media, especially the CCTV network.

As the opening of the Olympics approached, the Chinese government became steadily more concerned that groups like Falun Gong (which it had begun to suspect was a CIA puppet) might stage a new edition of its bizarrely effective silent vigil of 1999. Every possible resource was mobilized to prevent this happening.

By this time, however, a few students had stepped forward to speak out about the intimidation they had suffered both in Canada and after returning home. A young woman at the University of Ottawa, for example, received an e-mail back in 2005 from the local Chinese student association. She was warned that she was "under investigation" by other students and was accused of membership in Falun Gong. It ended with the words: "Watch Out."

In the archives of the Federal Court of Appeal, there is a case involving a student who was working toward a Master's degree at Concordia in Montreal that speaks eloquently of the challenges faced by Chinese nationals overseas. This student was a member of the Chinese Students and Scholars Association, a propaganda and patriotic association with branches in many countries and heavily subsidized by Beijing.

This young person, still a Chinese citizen, asked for permanent resident status in Canada in 1994. The process involved a number of meetings with the official who would decide whether to grant the request, as well as meetings with CSIS personnel (their report is still secret, for reasons of national security).

Four years went by. Finally, in mid-September of 1998, the official wrote to the student in question to say that his request had been refused:

> In the matter of your application for permanent residence
> in Canada, this is to confirm that I have determined that
> you do not meet with the requirements for immigration

to Canada. I originally advised you in person of this decision at your interview on September 17, 1998.

At your interview, I expressed to you my serious concerns that there were reasonable grounds to believe that
you had engaged in acts of espionage and subversion
against democratic governments, institutions or pro-
cesses as they are understood in Canada. I pointed out
that by your own admission during the interview, you
had engaged in a consistent pattern of reporting to the
Embassy of the People's Republic of China in Ottawa;
provided intelligence on the activities of individuals in a Canadian student organization known as the
Chinese Students and Scholars Association (CSSA); and
attempted to subvert this organization to meet the goals
and objectives of a foreign government. At that time, I
asked you to disabuse me of this concern, and advised
you that failure to disabuse me of my concern would
lead to the refusal of your application.

You responded by denying that you were an agent of a
foreign government, but readily admitted your numerous contacts with Chinese diplomats over a protracted
period when you were instrumental in "re-organizing"
the CSSA. You also admitted that you provided information to Chinese diplomats regarding individual members
of the CSSA and admitted further that you were in open
disagreement with pro-democracy students of this organization, that you had identified and reported on these
individuals to the Embassy, and that you had sought to
change the direction of the CSSA using funds provided
by the Embassy in support of certain activities, to make
it "sensitive to the Chinese Government and Chinese

officials." You argued that any congruence between the objectives and policies of the Chinese government and your activities was purely coincidental, and that you acted strictly out of personal conviction. I noted however, that your admitted activities were so clearly those of an agent that your argument lacked all credibility, and that I was obliged to treat your denial as self-serving. I noted that you were in receipt of one of only twenty tuition waivers awarded by the Embassy to Chinese students attending English-language institutions in the province of Quebec, and that the implications of a quid pro quo were too obvious for me to ignore.

It is my determination, therefore, that you have not disabused me of my concern, and that based on your own testimony, there are reasonable grounds for me to believe that you are a person who has engaged in hostile and subversive activities on behalf of a foreign government, directed toward gathering information used for intelligence purposes, that relate to the Charter Rights of individuals in Canada.

Accordingly, I have found that you come within the inadmissible class of persons described in subparagraph 19(1)(f)(i) of the Immigration Act....

This subparagraph reads as follows:

19. (1) No person shall be granted admission who is a member of any of the following classes:

[...]

f) persons who there are reasonable grounds to believe

[1] have engaged in acts of espionage or subversion

against democratic government, institutions or pro-
cesses, as they are understood in Canada, except persons who have satisfied the Minister that their admission would not be detrimental to the national interest.*

The student then appealed to a motions judge,** who overruled
the decision. This in spite of the fact that the judge agreed "with no
hesitation" that the Chinese national was indeed a spy and that he
had reported every possible detail about the activities of his young
comrades.

What then was the difficulty in upholding the immigration official's decision? Quite simply that the judge did not believe a student
association came under the definition of article 19 (1). In his words:

> . . . . the CSSA, which was a student organization at
> Concordia, targeted by the activities of the applicant,
> who reported on the members of the association to
> officials of the Chinese embassy in Ottawa, is not a
> "democratic institution" in the sense of the expression as
> intended in the pertinent document.

This judgment—in particular its interpretation of the phrase
"democratic institution" as limited to a strictly political sense—
caused quite a lot of difficulty in the court system, especially after
the Ministry of Citizenship and Immigration filed an appeal in
2001.[45] The three Court of Appeal judges found for the government
and sent the matter back to be dealt with by a new visa official.

---

* Translation taken from the website of the Federal Court of Appeals.
** Translation of "juge des requêtes."

In 2003 a journalist from the *People's Daily*, working in New York, was also barred from entering Canada. The CSIS investigation "allows us to believe" that Haiquan Yao was a member of a Chinese intelligence service, said the Federal Court decision. Like a number of pseudo-journalists parachuted into one country or another by the *People's Daily*, if not by the official press agency Xinhua ("New China"), Yao worked on behalf of Guoanbu, which is part of the Ministry for the Security of the State (MSS). The court described it as "an organization which gives itself over to, or is given over to, acts of espionage or subversion against democratic institutions, in the sense in which this expression is understood in Canada."[46]

The incorruptible journalist Haiquan Yao, having just finished his studies at the Institute of International Relations, was selected for the New York job because of his "loyalty." He acknowledged that his job in fact was to make sure Beijing received reports about Taiwan and the New York–area Chinese community.

The Secret Team in Ottawa

If Wang Pengfei's departure from Canada attracted no particular interest, the same can't be said for the spectacular defection of Zhang Jiyan on March 5, 2007.

Madame Zhang was the wife of a diplomat. Three weeks after her defection she made a public appearance on Parliament Hill, where she denounced certain clandestine activities carried on by the Chinese embassy in Ottawa. Undeniably dramatic-looking, with long ink-black hair and eyes concealed behind fashionable sunglasses, she also chose this moment to declare her loyalty to Falun Gong. Its precepts had, she said, "touched me to the heart."

She had first encountered the movement's ideas four years before it officially existed, through a chance meeting with founder

Li Hongzhi at the Chinese embassy in Paris. Li, who had not yet been banished by the Communist Party, had come to an embassy conference in order to speak about his ideas for spiritual renewal.

Now, after seeing Li's movement persecuted for eight years, Zhang had had enough. Reading from a prepared statement, she denounced the "systematic," "terrible," and "brutal" persecution of Falun Gong's devotees. And she wasn't just talking about those in China. Its gentle adherents in Canada and Australia were also suffering. Worse, the suffering was being meted out by a special team of about ten people implanted in the Ottawa embassy. Their job was to make sure Beijing knew where every practitioner of Falun Gong was located, as well as anybody else who might present a "menace" to the autocrats in the homeland.[47]

By now Zhang had made it clear to the Chinese government that, if "menaces" there were, she was one of them. She soon found those same agents following on her heels everywhere she went. They opened her mail for her, and solicitously monitored her every movement and gesture, perhaps for fear she might trip on the sidewalk. It must have been more diverting work than their usual routine of showing up at martial arts schools and taking down the names of the *taijiquan* (Tai Chi) and *qigong* students, just so there would already be a file in Beijing just in case they later joined Falun Gong. This was the same jolly squadron that organized a gigantic disinformation campaign in 2005 for the benefit of the Canadian Radio-television and Telecommunications Commission (CRTC).

Zhang asserted that she herself had seen hate literature about Falun Gong in the embassy. "The Chinese ambassador said . . . that he was going to send defamatory material about Falun Gong to members of Parliament, government officials, and also to the former governor general."

A chief purpose of the propaganda unit, according to an internal embassy document that she displayed to the media, was to use students and emigrants residing in Canada as part of a campaign to block a Chinese-language broadcasting licence from being awarded to New Tang Dynasty Television (NTDTV).[48]

New Tang had operated out of New York since 2001 and earned a reputation for being hostile toward the homeland regime. The network was also strongly affiliated with Falun Gong, and did not conceal the fact. One of Canada's major cable networks came under pressure not to pick up NTDTV's signal. The tactic was both detestable and, ultimately, futile since the New Tang network received its Canadian licence from the CRTC in November 2005.

At that time, the regulatory body acknowledged that "some Chinese community organizations opposed the application of NTDTV. . . . The majority of the opponents mentioned that NTDTV presented Falun Gong in a favourable light, some alleging that adepts of the movement were among the network's owners." The CRTC also went out of its way, a year later, to criticize China's official satellite TV network, CCTV-4, for "offensive" reporting on Falun Gong.

CCTV-4 had certainly demonstrated a visceral dislike of the movement and its founder, though it reserved the worst insult for the followers, who were described as "mentally ill." The CRTC wrote that:

> . . . these comments [by CCTV-4] are clearly abusive, in that they are expressions of extreme ill will against Falun Gong and its founder, Li Hongzhi. The derision, hostility and abuse encouraged by such comments could expose the targeted group or individual to hatred or contempt and, in the case of the first comment, the

statement could incite violence and threaten the physical security of Falun Gong practitioners.

. . . In the context of a news story, reporters, news
readers, and interviewees such as medical professionals, teachers and/or ordinary citizens characterize Falun
Gong as "anti-humanity, anti-science and anti-society"
and repeatedly describe it as an "evil cult" or "evil doctrine," or as having a criminal and homicidal nature, in
one case "extending its demon claw."

. . . These types of comments, made in the context of
reporting news, are likely to render the targeted group
more vulnerable to hatred or contempt.[49]

Of course, Falun Gong allegations must also be examined carefully. Their claims that numbers of followers have been sent to re-
education camps, psychiatric institutions or special hospitals where
their organs are harvested are very difficult to verify. But it is a well-
known fact that these are traditional methods of repression used in
the past by Chinese authorities.

However, the outrageous CCTV-4 commentaries cited by the
CRTC (and there are many others like them in its report) leave no
doubt about the hateful language employed by Chinese authorities. And that tends to reinforce accusations that it has authorized a
campaign of repression toward Falun Gong. When you call a group
"diabolical," you can hardly follow up by suggesting that it's not so
bad after all.

According to our sources, Zhang Jiyan has obtained refugee status in Canada. Her husband, an embassy auditor, was whisked back
to China.

Diplomatic Arm-Twisting Exposed

In the spring of 2008, Tourism Calgary and Travel Alberta suddenly cancelled their support for the global tour of the Divine Performing Arts Chinese Spectacular.[50] Although it paid tribute to China's traditional dance styles, the show also included certain tableaux depicting the suppression of Falun Gong. It was reported at the time that, according to tour organizers, the two tourist organizations had buckled under pressure from the Chinese consulate in Calgary. The producer of the show demanded that the diplomats responsible be deported. However, Travel Alberta denied there had been any economic threat from Chinese officials and said the affair arose from a misunderstanding at the agency about its permitted scope of sponsorships.

The Calgary episode was, says Falun Gong's Lucy Zhou, yet another example of the homeland's "strategy of constant harassment at every possible level." By way of supporting this observation, Zhou produced letters addressed by the Chinese embassy in Canada to a number of political personalities and journalists who might have thought of inviting the Falun Gong to speak, or betrayed curiosity about its philosophy, or been tempted to help it out or invite it to perform in their city.

Signed by the ambassador or by a consular official, the letters are remarkably similar. They exhibit a tone of betrayal and rage, and they describe the movement as "anti-humanity," "anti-society," and "anti-science." Several declare that "1,700 people are dead [in China] because they followed Falun Gong practices. Influenced by the cult's heretical ideas, a large proportion of these practitioners have suffered mental breakdowns."

Most of the letters conclude with a rather obvious and overbearing threat. It begins by recalling the close ties that Canada and China have developed in recent years, and then, in a tone of false regret, suggests that it would be a terrible shame to let the Falun Gong destroy such a good relationship.

Can such obvious manipulation, so clumsily laid on that it's hard to distinguish from schoolyard harassment, possibly work? It seems it does, sometimes, if Tourism Calgary is any guide. There is also the case of a Montreal city councillor, close to Mayor Gérald Tremblay, who backed down and would not sign a letter of support for Falun Gong practitioners. In this case, the business consideration at stake was the building of a cultural centre in Montreal's Chinatown.

In Toronto, back in 2005, some councillors also voted against giving Falun Gong a permit for a public demonstration. This must have pleased Madame Chen Xiaoling, the Chinese consul in Toronto, who had promised, in exchange for their "nay" votes, to see what she could do about getting a couple of panda bears for the Toronto Zoo.

Madame Chen, ever brisk and industrious, and also generous toward her friends, also thought to send a letter of warning to the forty-four municipal councillors concerning the visit of the Dalai Lama. Recalling that Tibet was, of course, an integral part of China, she urged the elected ladies and gentlemen to "neither authorize, nor facilitate" the spiritual leader's visit to the city—followed by the ritual mention of the wonderful cultural and economic relations between China and Toronto.[51]

In January 2002, Calgary MP Robert Anders sent yet another letter of complaint to Foreign Affairs Minister John Manley. It seems the Chinese authorities had been behaving in a manner rather more thuggish than usual, sending a team from the embassy to push him and insult him in the House of Commons corridor and let him know what they thought of him. Anders wrote: "I request that you study the possibility of withdrawing diplomatic privileges from this group which has shown disrespect for Canadian law and also that you threaten to remove the Canadian delegation from the Olympic Games in Beijing."

The Liberal government ignored the request.

"A foreign country can terrorize a community here and successive governments do nothing at all, on account of the lobbying,"
protested a former Canadian diplomat, Brian McAdam, who was
previously posted twice to Hong Kong and made great contri-
butions to the Sidewinder report. Today he is marginalized and
almost completely ignored in his own country. And yet he is often
asked to participate in conferences overseas.

McAdam's difficulties began early in the 1990s, when he was
the commissioner of immigration in Canada's Hong Kong High
Commission. Noticing that files had vanished from his computer, he
called the RCMP liaison officer at the high commission to help sort
it out. An investigation was launched by the RCMP, and the investigating officer unearthed a black market of Canadian visas organized
by a local employee of the high commission. It included a system of
bribes (called "red envelopes") involving several Canadian employees. The corrupted individuals were pocketing between $10,000 and
$20,000 from aspiring immigrants unlikely to get a visa any other
way, because they were affiliated with mainland Chinese security services or organized crime. Two investigations were launched and then
abandoned, supposedly for lack of proof.

Some people knowledgeable about the matter feel the investigation was quashed in order to maintain tranquil Sino-Canadian relations but mainly to preserve Canada from a big scandal that would
have created a rift between the RCMP and DFAIT. The problem was
that Brian McAdam didn't agree with this approach. In 1993, once
Ottawa understood that McAdam meant to see the affair examined in
full daylight, he was recalled to Canada. McAdam soon began to suffer from clinical depression, made worse by rumours that he had been
recalled for corrupt behaviour. In a particularly barefaced rewriting
of history, the anonymous character assassins spread the word that he

had set up the illegal trafficking of visas, apparently to buy a nice new house in Ottawa, where he would install his Chinese mistress.

By 1994 he'd had enough. After thirty years of loyal service McAdam retired. But then he shared everything he knew with the investigation team working on Project Sidewinder. McAdam, it turned out, was not at all inclined to drop the matter. He made a fresh complaint, and a third investigation was held in May 1995. It also went nowhere.

Here are some interesting excerpts from a decision handed down in November 2003 by the External Review Committee of the RCMP. The matter in question was a disciplinary appeal launched by Corporal Robert Reid, who had been in charge of the McAdam dossier. This officer agreed with McAdam's view of the Hong Kong matter, and didn't hesitate to tell the media that the RCMP was making light of it. Worse, the Mountie brass had complained to Reid's superior officer that he was "creating problems" at the inquiry. Reid was then forced to resign. That is, he was fired.

> In May 1996, the new officer in command of the immigration and passport section of the RCMP, Superintendant Jean Dubé, interrogated Mr. McAdam and came to the conclusion that the allegations were vague and unfounded and that Mr. McAdam, who disliked the way he had been treated, was motivated by the desire for retribution against his former colleagues. . . .
>
> Even if nothing proves that the Mounties had attempted to suppress the investigation, there are significant gaps in the investigative process followed by the RCMP since 1991. . . .
>
> The record reveals a whole series of disconcerting and suspicious activities which the Mounties failed to investigate in a timely and rigorous fashion. . . .

The investigation undertaken in 1999 has not succeeded in filling the gaps observed in the earlier investigations. It did constitute an exhaustive examination of
communication between ACE and the residents of Hong
Kong and revealed that the extent of the exchange of
presents, sums of money and other advantages was much
more extensive than DFAIT and CIC acknowledged to
the RCMP at the time. . . .

From the moment he became involved in this investigation, Superintendant Dubé has openly declared that,
in his view, Mr. McAdam's complaint was unfounded.
He still held to this view when the investigation was
reactivated at the end of the month of January 1999.
The result of the investigation was therefore decided in
advance. Superintendant Dubé did not seem to be prepared to conceive of an outcome which might find Mr.
McAdam to have been in the right . . . *

More than ten years after slamming the door of External Affairs
behind him, Brian McAdam has still not found peace. He claims to
have been followed and to have received death threats over the telephone. His mail has also been opened: neatly sliced with a cutting
tool rather than discreetly unglued and reglued, so that he could not
fail to get the message. These letters made their way to him sealed in
Canada Post plastic, in accord with the procedure employed when
a letter has been damaged. Was it a hoax? A form of intimidation?
If so, who was behind it?

"Whose secret service, ours or China's?" wonders Mr. McAdam.**

---

* In 2004, a diplomat from the Canadian embassy in Beijing was involved in
another case of corruption which permitted gangsters and spies to enter Canada.
** An investigation has been undertaken by the Crown corporation but with no
decision at the time of publication.

Central Bureau 610, "The Chinese Gestapo"

Thanks to Chen Yonglin, former first secretary and, since 2001, political officer at the Chinese consulate in Sydney, Australia, we now know a good deal about the work methods and dreadful efficiency of China's secret services when they set up shop in western countries. Including ours.

On May 26, 2005, Chen decided it was time that he (now thirty-eight), his wife, and their six-year-old daughter consider a new life. The thump of the door of his official apartment sounded louder than usual as it closed behind him for the last time. Left behind inside was a letter stating that he would never return to China.

Ever since, this former cog in the Communist machine has spent his time travelling from conference to conference around the world. His boyish and alert face has peered out from behind the podium of parliaments and congresses in a number of nations, and he is never short of useful information.

While in Ottawa and Montreal in June 2007, Chen confirmed that Canada was the "second priority" for China's undercover agents, after the United States.[52] These agents' major concern, as we have seen elsewhere, is industrial espionage. But Chen added the surprising observation that China's Enemy Number One, in its own view, is the Huaqiao, or the diaspora Chinese who become involved with the Falun Gong.

Earlier, in the summer of 2005, he appeared before a subcommittee of the U.S. House of Representatives. At the time Chen had only just defected. He spoke in great detail about the "systematic" campaign of "persecution" that was ongoing against members of Falun Gong in the Chinese communities of Australia, America, and Canada particularly.[53] The president of the subcommittee, Republican Christopher Smith of New Jersey, described Chen's testimony as "explosive."

Among the ex-diplomat's revelations was the existence of a mysterious Chinese undercover agency, which was created by that country's Central Committee of the Communist Party in June of 1999. It orchestrates the worldwide. campaign of repression. At first called the Office of the Falun Gong Issue, it later became the Department of External Security Affairs. Some dissidents are pleased to call it "the Chinese Gestapo." It is also known, less emotionally, as Central Bureau 610.

"The war against Falun Gong moved overseas in 2000," Chen recalls. "In every Chinese mission there had to be at least one official working on the Falun Gong dossier." In Sydney, Chen himself was that agent. Technically he was in charge of the "Five Poisons Working Group," but its work was in fact almost entirely about "surveilling and persecuting" Falun Gong.

According to this renegade, Chinese diplomatic missions are little more than false fronts for information theft and backroom political thuggery. In dealing with foreign governments and citizens, the full range of covert methods is employed. This begins with the classic methods of propaganda and disinformation, which are widely distributed in the host country to government officials, universities, the media, and anybody who walks through the doors of the consulate. Beyond that there is the extensive use of economic blackmail, directed at the government in power and delivered by methods overt or subtle, depending on the circumstances.

As we have already seen, these are the methods that have been identified by ongoing investigations in Canada. While our police and court systems continue to resist them, it should be understood that the pressure from Chinese agents is relentless. In the Australian state of New South Wales, the police department finally yielded to the pressure and began breaking up peaceful Falun Gong protests outside the local consulate.

According to Chen, this kind of influence is achieved by "cultivating close personal relationships" with Australian officials, who are invited to elaborate dinners, and eventually on all-expenses-paid trips to China. Juicy commercial contracts are dangled in front of susceptible business people.

Meanwhile, in Sydney, consulate staff were busily identifying and creating files on Falun Gong practitioners, who, like other overseas Chinese, are obliged from time to time to go to the consulate to renew a passport or sort out other documents. Like most idealistic undertakings, Falun Gong facilitates the task of identifying its members because its first principle is to never lie, even to one's enemies. And once the name is on the consulate list, that party will either be refused a visa, or offered one all too easily with the intention of arresting them once they set foot in the homeland.

Chen was also able to provide information that plugged some gaps in our understanding of events in North America. This included the reason why, for example, a European company suddenly decided not to renew its contract with New Tang Dynasty Television.

Before defecting, Chen had already co-operated with the Australian Security Intelligence Organization (ASIO), as he was to do later with the CIA. He believed that he would be offered political asylum in Australia when and if he did defect. The moment arrived, and he made an eloquent plea in an official request filed on May 25, 2005. In it he said that he feared the worst for himself and his family if the Chinese government ever learned where he was located. He spoke of his great affection for Australia, for its democracy and its human rights, and of his desire to make a contribution to what he hoped would be his new country.

The application was rejected less than twenty-four hours later.

A shocked Chen Yonglin then secretly approached Australia's

immigration authority, the Department of Immigration and Multicultural and Indigenous Affairs. This was on May 26, the day he learned his application of the previous day had been rejected. It's important to understand that, although he had not yet officially defected, Chen was severely compromised by the risks he had already taken. Not the least of them was this hasty meeting with the director of the immigration office, which was located very close to the Chinese mission. It was the beginning of a scandalous screw-up, which was later revealed in hearings of the Australian Senate.

The future defector was treated with contempt. Even as he was reduced to begging, one of the director's office staff made the inexplicable blunder of picking up the phone and calling the Chinese consulate to ask for proof that the gentleman in their office was indeed their second secretary.

Clearly Chen was past the point of no return. But that had not yet occurred to the Department of Foreign Affairs, whose officials showed up and spent the next few days pressuring him to go back to the consulate.

In terms of security practice there is a slender excuse for the Australian reaction, and that was the possibility of Chen being a double agent whom the Chinese were attempting to implant. But that theory doesn't stand up to scrutiny, especially in light of the far more compelling fact that Australia was just then in the middle of negotiating a free-trade treaty with China. And Australia was China's third-largest trading partner! Here, it would seem, was the reason why Chen's bid for freedom was terribly mistimed.

But the callous way he had been treated caused a huge uproar among the Australian public. And this in turn forced the government into an about-face. On July 8, less than six weeks after rejecting Chen, it granted him and his family a protective visa. The furious Chinese ambassador denounced what she described as Chen Yonglin's "greed" and warned the Australians that they would soon have other defectors on their hands.

Strangely enough (or perhaps not so strangely at all), the unfortunate Chen did not get a warm welcome when he visited Canada during his speaking tour in the summer of 2007. One meeting after another was cancelled. Even Colin Kenny, an ebullient Liberal senator famed for his sociability, begged off. This is the same Colin Kenny who is the president of the permanent Senate Committee on National Security and Defence and a dedicated terrorism fighter (one of his advisers is Barry Denofsky, the former CSIS boss who consigned the Sidewinder affair to the trash bin). Chen was also cold-shouldered by Conservative MP Jason Kenney, at the time the head of the Subcommittee on International Human Rights. Neither of these politicians responded to our request for an explanation of their behaviour.

A single, lonely CSIS investigator found the time to go and listen to what Chen had to say. And, as of the end of autumn 2008, we were still waiting to see whether the Senate on security committee would ever find time to actually have a meeting. They don't seem to think that espionage is much of a problem.

The consistent inability of officialdom to understand Chen's situation recalls a similar episode, which occurred around the same time. It concerned a certain Han Guangsheng, another ex-member of Bureau 610. At the time of writing, however, his fate was still uncertain.

Han, a former high-ranking party official, had been chief of Public Security. This position included responsibility for supervising four forced-labour camps and two prisons located in China's north-east. There, according to reports, hundreds of Falun Gong practitioners have been imprisoned and tortured. According to his testimony, which we have corroborated in conversations with members of Falun Gong, Han was a kind of Chinese Oskar Schindler (the German industrialist who saved hundreds of Jews from the Nazi death camps). Han also arranged to free a number of imprisoned Falun Gong, and went so far as to fire an officer involved in the torture of a teenager.

In 2001 Han was part of an official visit to Toronto. There he vanished into thin air, later reappearing to ask for refugee status. In its 2005 decision to refuse his request, the Immigration and Refugee Board wrote that "there are serious reasons to consider him complicit in crimes against humanity." Han has appealed that decision.

Defector Fengzhi Li received just as little gratitude from the United States, in spite of all the useful information offered by the ex-agent of the Guoanbu at the time of his debriefing. Li was able to confirm, even in the smallest details, the methods used by Chinese spies everywhere in the world, especially in North America. He was also familiar with the subterfuge used by pseudo-journalists, diplomats, researchers, teachers, and marital partners, together with local informers recruited in the host country. Fengzhi Li's situation is precarious today, since his political status has not been settled and his qualifications are not recognized. Must we conclude that in the pitiless world of espionage, a squeezed lemon is fit for nothing but the compost heap?

Reporters Under the Influence

With each of his immigration hearings, Chen Yonglin made sure to underline the fact that many Chinese-language publications in countries around the world are controlled by the Chinese government. There are entire media companies whose business model depends on advertising revenue from Chinese state companies, or private sector companies closely linked to the state. A certain Montreal company is suspected of being one of them.

La Presse Chinoise Eastern Inc. occupies modest premises on the second floor of a rundown building on Clark Street, in Montreal's Chinatown. This newspaper group, created in the 1980s, is owned by a man named Crescent Chau, who was born in Hong Kong.

Chau prints 8,000 copies of his weekly paper, *Les Presses Chinoises*. The edition dated November 3, 2001, contained a violently anti–Falun Gong insert, paid for by an oddly difficult to locate woman named Bing He. She claims to be a former Falun Gong follower who came to see that the "sect" was nothing but a terrorist conspiracy. Its adepts, she said, perform acts of "bestiality," and their master, Li Hongzhi, has been known to incite them to kill themselves.

Six more pamphlets followed in six more editions of the paper, which became both thicker (in terms of pages) and more rancorous. One wouldn't have known that Bing He and Crescent Chau had received a court order in December, a few weeks after the first anti–Falun Gong issue appeared, enjoining them to cease publishing these inserts or other similar material.

Over two hundred people filed a libel action against the newspaper. When it was refused by the Superior Court in December 2005, eighteen of the plaintiffs appealed the decision and further sued for damages of $100,000 plus interest.

Meanwhile, Crescent Chau re-offended with a special anti–Falun Gong issue in the summer of 2006. Claiming that he acted out of personal conviction and in the name of free speech, he distributed 100,000 copies of the 32-page rant in all the provinces of Canada. There, once again, were found allegations of bestiality and vampirism, and hints of other perversities.

228 DE PIERREBOURG & JUNEAU-KATSUYA

In a May 2008 judgment, the Court of Appeals refused to take
further action against Crescent Chau. The court recognized the
libellous nature of the publication, but hid behind the flimsy pretext that only Falun Gong founder Li Hongzhi was in a legal position to mount such a challenge.

The judge also alluded to the legal notion commonly called
"floodgates," arguing that to accord $100,000 in damages to each
injured party would permit "tens of millions of Falun Gong dis-
ciples throughout the world to obtain similar indemnities."

Here is an excerpt from this surprising judgment:*

> Even if none of the allegations are supported by con-
> crete evidence (allegations according to which the
> movement promotes criminal and perverse practices)
> the judge of the Superior Court finds that the evidence
> offered does not prove that the allegations were false or
> grossly inaccurate, or that they had been published with
> the intention of attracting hatred and contempt.
>
> Taking everything into account, it seems clear that
> the burden of proof concerning the truth of the allega-
> tions lies with the respondents. Moreover, even if the
> authors of the writings had the right to criticize, even
> vehemently, the doctrine of Li Hongzhi and the prac-
> tice of this doctrine by the followers of Falun Gong,
> the authors would commit a libel if, without proof,
> they accused certain persons of criminal and perverse
> acts. We refer in particular to allegations of #1 (money
> laundering, connections with murders and other
> criminals), #4 (women forced into prostitution), #5

---

* The suit has now proceeded to the Supreme Court of Canada.

(bestiality), #6 (?), #7 (vampirism?), and # 13 (violence and cruelty).

However, unless we are mistaken, the dishonest and libellous writings without exception are directed at Li Hongzhi, his entourage, the directors of the movement or the movement itself. However, Li Hongzhi and his immediate entourage are not among those persons who brought these charges.[54]

Chen Yonglin is quite sure that Chinese diplomats in Canada, together with their undercover employees, are responsible for this propaganda operation of *Les Presses Chinoises*. Basing his argument on his experience in the Sydney consulate, Chen is also certain that the campaign was funded and directed from Beijing. This, of course, is what Crescent Chau denies.

As for Bing He, she seems to have beat a hasty retreat to China, where she received a medal for her exploits. A more credible newspaper, associated with the Falun Gong, has repeated the allegations of Chinese espionage and added the information that Bing He was questioned by CSIS before her departure.[55]

Uyghur Terrorists

It's now October of 2006. Night has fallen in Mississauga. A fat black four-by-four pulls up to the curb in front of a small house. Inside the car: three men who will spend much of the night squinting at the windows of the little house and what transpires behind them. Their target: Mehmet Tohti, a thirty-five-year-old official of the Uyghur Canadian Association.

Tohti is frightened. He contacts CSIS and the Ministry of Foreign Affairs. Speaking with certainty, he explains the situation: Chinese agents have parked themselves at his front door in order to intimidate him. His next step will be to move into a condominium with twenty-four-hour-a-day security.

"Me, I'm an international terrorist," he says, in a French that is both perfectly grammatical and perfectly ironic. "Since September 11, 2001, we've been the Chechens of China."

He is sitting in a cozy nook inside a charming Montreal café. It does nothing for his mood. As coordinator of the Uyghur Canadian Association, he needs little encouragement to talk about the suffering of his people. In fact, nothing could stop him.

He begins by describing the Uyghurs and their situation in a remote corner of China's far west. They speak a Turkic language that has no connection at all with Chinese languages. Until 1949 they had no connection with China. But that year the Communist forces, which had just seized power, pushed into the far west and seized control of eastern Turkestan as well. It was given a new name—the Autonomous Region of Xinjiang—and it was soon colonized. It is a vast area of 2 million square kilometres, and today there are approximately as many Chinese Han living there as indigenous Uyghurs: each group makes up about 40 percent of the population. Kayum Masimov, an organizer of the Uyghur Canadian Association, speaks of "cultural genocide" and "forced assimilation." "Whether we're speaking of language, culture, or religion, we have nothing in common with China," he emphasizes.

According to Masimov, the Uyghurs are treated like outsiders in their own land, condescended to as "primitives" or "barbarians." At best they are second-class citizens among the growing number of Han.

The Uyghurs have little public recognition in Canada. This is not surprising, since there are not more than a few hundred of them in this country. There won't be any Hollywood stars publicizing their cause. They'd be happy with a newspaper of their own and a little TV coverage, but there aren't enough of them for those things, either. And, of course, since September 2001, it is not exactly a gift from heaven that they are also Sunni Muslims. Some Uyghurs have even been captured in Pakistan by bounty hunters and turned over to U.S. troops in Afghanistan, who have forwarded them to concrete cells at Guantanamo. An entire people, as it were, who find themselves in the wrong place at the wrong time.

The Americans recognized their mistake some time ago, and have been trying to repatriate the Uyghur prisoners since 2004. A return to China is out of the question, since activist Uyghurs face prison and possibly death. Five have gone to live in Albania. The United States has asked the Canadian government on four occasions to welcome the Uyghur prisoners, and Ottawa has so far refused. This is despite Prime Minister Stephen Harper's professed sympathy for their situation.*

For Beijing, the U.S. blunder in seizing Uyghurs was an undreamed of propaganda opportunity. Since then, this small people, one of the "Five Poisons," has been falsely associated with Al-Qaeda by countries all around the world. Held in the implacable grip of China, they are unable to defend themselves.

Beijing has not hesitated to exploit its advantage. In the months before the Olympic Games, Uyghurs were widely arrested on charges of planning to murder and kidnap Olympic tourists and athletes in the name of their "holy war." The accusations can't be proven, but they were certainly useful for distracting world opinion from the Tibetan revolt and its swift suppression. And it is true that there

---

* In December 2006 the prime minister received Rabiya Kadeer, the president of the Uyghur World Congress—in spite of Chinese protests. Madame Kadeer was nominated for the Nobel Peace prize that year. She was arrested in 1997 during a savagely suppressed demonstration in her homeland. Imprisoned for eight years, she was finally liberated after pressure from the U.S. Senate.

was violence in Xinjiang from the Turkestan Islamic Movement at the time of the Games.* But the group is marginal and relatively powerless. It is not inconceivable, however, that continued Chinese brutality will transform it into a force to contend with.

Canadian citizen Hussein Celil has also paid the price of this campaign of repression. A young imam who had lived in Hamilton, Ontario, since 1999, he was arrested in June of 2006 while visiting family in Uzbekistan and then extradited to China. In spite of much pressure from the Conservative government of Canada, he is still serving a life sentence there. According to his lawyer, Chris McLeod, Celil is yet another victim of China's espionage activities in Canada. As a prominent local Uyghur who often attended candlelight vigils under the windows of the Chinese consulate in Toronto, his movements would have been tracked. At the opportune moment, he was neutralized.[56] Beijing is very aware that the Uyghur movement has no public profile, and intends to keep it that way by seizing any activist likely to give it the kind of irritating prominence currently possessed by the Tibetan resistance.

Celil's fate has made it perfectly clear to Uyghur militants in Canada that they, too, are on Beijing's radar. They have also experienced telephone intimidation and threats against members of their families still living in Xinjiang, as well as computer e-mail attacks.

Mehmet Tohti and Hussein Celil's unpleasant experiences have demonstrated that Chinese agents in Canada have no fear of coming out of the shadows and abusing Canadian citizens when it suits them to do so. Kayum Masimov recounts the story of a sixty-year-old militant in Montreal whose son has already been thrown into a Chinese prison. Since that wasn't enough to silence the man, a

---

* The Turkestan Islamic Movement is located in Xinjiang and has been placed on a list of terrorist organizations by a number of countries.

Chinese official took the additional step of showing up at his front door and offering him a large bribe to give up militant activity.

AIR INDIA FLIGHT 182: THE PANDORA'S BOX NOBODY WANTS TO OPEN

June 4, 1985. A brown Mercury with three passengers inside threads its way into a wooded retreat near the town of Duncan, British Columbia. Talwinder Singh Parmar and Inderjit Singh Reyat open the trunk and take out a package. Then they conceal themselves among the trees. A few minutes later a "powerful explosion" echoes through the area—powerful enough to make a pair of stealthy CSIS shadowers duck for cover and throw themselves behind the largest tree trunk they can find. This is what we get for tracking Sikh extremists, they think, once they are able to think anything at all.[57]

The two agents' next thought is that the noise sounded more like a heavy hunting rifle than an explosion. Although getting photographic evidence was the whole point of their expedition that day, the men forget to take snapshots of the "persons of interest" they were following, who blithely take their leave and head back to Reyat's place.

The bosky little glade is then left in peace for just under a month, until crime scene investigators show up on July 2 and find a short-circuiting device commonly used to detonate explosives. Too late, alas.

June 23, 1986, 2:19 a.m. (6:19 a.m. GMT). Two baggage handlers in Tokyo's Narita Airport die in the explosion of a suitcase registered in the name of L. Singh. Singh has just left flight CP 003, originating in

Vancouver, and boarded an Air India flight to Bangkok. The bomb incorporated a Sanyo tuner (model FMT 611), a Micronta clock, an electrical relay, a twelve-volt battery, and dynamite.

June 23, 1986, 3:08 a.m. (7:08 a.m. GMT). A red-and-white Air India Boeing 747 named Emperor Kanishka is flying 9,500 metres above the Atlantic Ocean, about 176 kilometres south-west of the Irish coast. The cabin is in shadow. In the cockpit, co-pilot Satwinder Singh Bhinder notifies Shannon air control of the aircraft's imminent landing in London. At 3:13 a.m., a dull thud is heard in the cabin, followed by silence. Flight 182 vanishes from radar screens. The aircraft has just disintegrated with the explosion of a brown Samsonite suitcase located in hold number 52, on the left rear side of the fuselage.

The first ship on the scene of the disaster is the *Laurentian Forest*, carrying a cargo of paper from Quebec to Ireland. The crew frantically scans the water, which is coated with iridescent kerosene. Soon, to their horror, they began to discern naked and dismembered bodies amidst the oil and debris. Of the 379 passengers and crew members on Flight 182, only 132 bodies are recovered. Two hundred and seventy eight people aboard the flight were Canadian citizens.

Twenty-three years later, we met François Lavigne in an Ottawa café not far from Parliament Hill. His career as an investigator began in 1983 with the "B" Operations (or "B" Ops) branch of RCMP counterintelligence. Although unpredictable, if not ungovernable, Lavigne also earned a reputation as a forceful and clever agent. His team had about a dozen members, who were kept busy following the clandestine activities of every country actively spying on Canada, excepting Russia, its satellites, and China. That left quite a lot of countries. The department's daily grab bag of activity could range from India to Sri Lanka, with a glance at what the French were up to, and a good hard look at the South Africans, who were aggressively harassing supporters of the African National Congress around the world. A year later CSIS was created. Lavigne was invited to accept a position in its counter-intelligence (CI) branch, which barely existed and needed an experienced hand.

The Air India catastrophe is indelibly printed in his memory, together with the weeks preceding it. But it is the endless years afterward that haunt him. Flight 182 broke his personal life and his career. He is relieved to be asked to speak about it: any conversation helps with his ongoing exorcism of the past. "Guilt about that business has gnawed away at me for twenty-five years. I still see the names, the faces, the mutilated bodies every time I close my eyes."

Where terrorism is concerned, Canadians at best display the wide-eyed detachment of those who find a subject interesting but in no way connected to themselves. Concerning Air India Flight 182, however, we manage something more than detachment: it's been stricken from memory as if it never existed.

It's a surprising display of amnesia, given that Flight 182 was the bloodiest terrorist attack in history before September 11, 2001. And also given that it is incontestably our disaster, planned and carried out right here by a cell of Sikh fanatics belonging to the Babbar Khalsa terrorist group.

Babbar Khalsa was founded in 1981 by Talwinder Singh Parmar. Bob Rae wrote, in his 2005 report on the atrocity it engineered for Flight 182: "There is nothing accidental about what happened here. No internal conflict, no dispute, whether religious or ethnic, and no ideology could possibly justify what took place. Many Canadians believe that it was the events of September 11, 2001 which brought us into the world of modern terrorism. But this happened in fact on June 23, 1985."[58]

Flight 182 isn't just a tragedy. It is also a Pandora's box with the leaden weight of Canada's entire governmental apparatus still sitting on the lid and trying to keep it shut. Concealed inside, apart from the murderers, is the dark history of India itself, in the form of steely-eyed agents bent on settling New Delhi's accounts and prepared to cross anybody's borders in order to do so.

How would Canadians feel if it were known that India's *agents provocateurs* had pulled just one tiny thread in making this disaster come about, or at best had known that it was going to happen and chosen to stand aside? What might Canadians do if they discovered that our authorities had tolerated foreign interference that was bound to spill quantities of blood, for no other reason than to ensure the continued prosperity of corporate interests and the untroubled afternoon teas of our diplomats?

Flight 182 took off from Montreal on the evening of June 22, setting a course for London. There it was to have made a routine maintenance stopover before proceeding to New Delhi. The booby-trapped suitcase was checked aboard in Vancouver by a clean-shaven man of Indian origin wearing western clothing. In his hand was a reservation for Cathay Pacific's Flight 060, Seat 10B, destination Toronto; it had been confirmed by telephone several days earlier in the name of Jaswand Singh. Payment was in cash. The same party had reserved a seat on Flight CP 003, destination Narita, in the name of Mohinderbel Singh. The two reservations were subsequently modified to be in the name of "L. Singh" for the Narita flight and "M. Singh" for the Toronto flight. M. Singh was then to board the Air India Flight 181 to Montreal (Mirabel). This is the flight that would be renumbered "182" for the final portion of its route.

M. Singh, however, was placed on an Air India waiting list in Toronto. For that reason the check-in clerk decided to have the suitcase taken off the airplane. It was already the policy that no piece of luggage could be taken aboard an aircraft if its owner were not also on board. But M. Singh protested long and loudly, and Cathay Pacific's counter agent backed down. M. Singh never got on his plane. Neither did L. Singh, as it turns out.

There were all kinds of blinking red lights in the months and days preceding the explosion. The Mounties, CSIS, the Communications Security Establishment (CSE), the solicitor general, the Ministry of Foreign Affairs, and the high commission in New Delhi all knew something was going on. The Indian government was also alarmed. Two of its diplomats had already been physically attacked in Canada, and there had been threats against its various agencies operating here— including Air India, the national airline. It had asked Canada to close its borders to extremists who came here to raise money and recruits.

More pointedly, Air India's director of security was worried about the safety of its aircraft in Canada. In a telex stamped June 1, 1985—twenty-two days before the disaster—and sent along to the RCMP detachment at Pearson Airport by Air India's Canadian chief of operations, the security director fretted that he had received information "from investigative bodies revealing the probability of acts of sabotage perpetrated by Sikh extremists who intend to place time bombs in aircraft or in registered baggage."

Air India pleaded for reinforced security in every airport where its aircraft operated. The telex was transmitted to every Air India office in the world. Several days later (June 4) it was sent along to RCMP headquarters.

But there it stopped. The officer who read it decided that it wasn't necessary for CSIS to see it. And that was the very day, the very same June 4, that CSIS agents watched Sikh extremists testing a bomb in the woods outside Duncan, British Columbia.

Making matters even more serious was the approaching June 6 anniversary of the massacre in the Golden Temple of Amritsar the previous year. In this great cathedral of the Sikh faith, about eight hundred militants and two hundred Indian troopers died. Tanks fired into the temple, collapsing much of the structure, and igniting a cry for revenge that spread throughout Sikh communities around the world. A few months later, on October 31, Prime Minister Indira Gandhi was killed by one of her Sikh bodyguards. Shortly after this fraught anniversary, new Indian Prime Minister Rajiv Gandhi was scheduled to visit the United States. François Lavigne recalls that there were reports evoking "unspecified threats against India's interests in Canada and elsewhere, including against its diplomatic missions and against institutions such as Air India."

Operational modules at CSIS's Ottawa headquarters had received literally dozens of threat reports between March 29, 1984, and June 11, 1985. Thirteen concerned possible hijackings, suicide-attacks, or bomb attacks—all directed at Air India, either its offices or its aircraft.

The Sikh minority, which makes up less than 5 percent of India's population, originated in the Punjab (which Sikhs call Khalistan), a state of northern India.* Sectarian, political, and social conflicts between Sikhs and Hindus had been ongoing for generations.

---

* In Canada, this community numbers at least 270,000, mostly in British Columbia, Alberta, Ontario, and Quebec.

During the 1980s an extremist fringe sprang up and began to agitate for independence.

We succeeded in locating a senior official of the Indian Intelligence Bureau (IB) who had been in Ottawa at the time, working under cover as a diplomat at India's high commission. Today, Maloy Krishna Dhar has retired to his homeland.* He recalls that he took pains to warn Canadian diplomatic authorities of a specific threat against India's national airline.

"I was an advisor in the security office of the Ministry of External Affairs of India," he explains. "We had received information from Sikh sources, to the effect that Babbar Khalsa International (BKI) and the International Sikh Youth Federation were planning attacks on Indian targets in Canada. There was also information that the BKI was practising with bombs out in the British Columbia backwoods. We shared all of that with the RCMP and the Canadian Ministry of External Affairs' security division. We specifically mentioned, verbally and in writing, that Air India was a major target. But we were not in contact with CSIS."

Maloy Krishna Dhar insists that his sources were not secret agents who had infiltrated into Canada, or local paid agents. They were "Sikhs who did not support the separatists." These particularly included the religious leaders of the Gurdwara, the holy temple, where a copy of the Sikh sacred scriptures is kept.

Dhar's testimony is evasive. But it does confirm the recollections of James Bartleman, a former lieutenant-governor of Ontario who was, at the time, the head of an information section within the Department of External Affairs. A few days before the catastrophe, Bartleman was leafing through the pile

---

* Maloy Krishna Dhar is the author of numerous books. *Open Secrets* in particular deals with the Air India tragedy. He has also written for a number of publications.

of SIGINT (signals intelligence) documents that he received every day from the Communications Security Establishment, the "giant ears" of Canada. And there, he says, he saw a message that CSE had intercepted. It had been sent by the Indian secret service, and it hinted that there would be an attack on Air India on the weekend of June 22–23 .

Bartleman fully understood the importance of the threat, whether proven or not. He immediately sent it along to a senior officer of the RCMP. This was during the course of a meeting of the special interministerial committee on Sikh terrorism. The meeting was held on June 18 at the Ministry of Foreign Affairs.

The officer in question discarded the message, impertinently informing Bartleman that "I've already seen it, and I don't need you to tell me how to do my job."

Twenty-two years later, Bartleman, who had never gotten over the rudeness and unprofessionalism of the officer's behaviour, finally spoke up. He testified before the commission of inquiry led by John Major, and for the first time recounted the appalling tale.

The authorities immediately jumped on Bartleman, marginalizing him and undermining his credibility. During the following days, a number of parties involved in the matter, from CSE to the Mountie who had been present at the June 18 meeting, flatly stated that nothing of the sort ever happened. They also denied ever having seen such a message. Certain parties whispered that Bartleman was getting on in years and his memory perhaps was no longer reliable.

"The CSE document which Mr. Bartleman believes he saw did not ever exist," concluded the attorney general of Canada during his final presentation to the Major Commission.

François Lavigne shared Bartleman's disappointment at his government's conflicting version of events. In his eyes, the warning was real. How difficult would it have been to act on Bartleman's warning? Was this not Air India's only weekly flight? How was it allowed to fly to its destruction after the most elementary security procedures were ignored, one after the other? When baggage was left onboard when its owner was not? When the explosives-sniffing dog had not shown up as expected to check the luggage?

"Moi, je faisais ma job," says Lavigne in good clear "Canadian." "I thought the other guys were doing their job as well. It really isn't that hard to make sure that a flight is safe and secure. What was missing here was any sense of urgency or real danger on the part of the people involved at the time . . . except for a few people like myself, who were brushed off as nutbars."

Lavigne insists, moreover, that nobody was talking about a hijacking plot back then. Rather, the reports and warnings all concerned a hidden bomb—contrary to what India's intelligence services continue to claim.

If nothing else, this dreadful episode shows the price that Canadians pay for their parochial disinterest in the rest of the world. Although hosting a large Sikh community, we know pretty much nothing about the Punjab conflict, its players, and its history. And this is significant. It points to an intractable underlying problem, which is that an organization like CSIS cannot possibly prevent such events unless it possesses a deep understanding of the issues. Like many of our other investigative services, it has instead developed a culture of reaction to what has already happened. It has also repeatedly shown that it cannot manage more than one crisis at a time.

The big crisis back in 1985—so CSIS and the other investigators believed—was the Armenian extremists, who committed multiple acts of terrorism around the world, and had even managed bloodshed on the streets of Ottawa.* That, and the Communists, of course. Assassins from northern India were not the top-of-mind issue.

One of the key names in the Air India affair is Talwinder Singh Parmar. A priest of the Coach temple in Calgary, Parmar had bestowed on himself the title of consul-general of Khalistan in Vancouver. He had been, from the moment he came to Canada in 1970, a prominent activist for the Sikh cause. By the beginning of the 1980s he had founded the Babbar Khalsa International (The Tigers of the True Faith) and was therefore well known to CSIS.

Although most western countries had marked down Babbar Khalsa as a terrorist organization, Canada was extremely slow to take action against it. Unbelievably, the Tigers were permitted to hold on to charitable organization status right up to 1996, and it wasn't until 2003 that they were marked down as a terrorist operation. That was a long time, and Parmar's group made good use of it, sending out charitable donation receipts and piling up money.

We pick up Parmar's trail in India, where he was busy in the autumn of 1981 evading arrest for the murder of two police officers. He made his way to Europe, but not to safety. In 1983 German police locked him up for a year in connection with the killings in India, but they finally had to release him for lack of evidence. By July of 1984 he had arrived in Toronto. The massacre of Sikhs in the Golden Temple of Amritsar had occurred just weeks earlier, and he was greeted by frantic followers who were baying for blood. India knew where he was and tried to extradite him, but with no

---

* In May 1985, a Canadian security guard was killed during an assault on the Turkish embassy in Ottawa by a group of Armenian activists.

success. Even after learning in 1982 that he had been named a terrorist, Canada still cited the absence of an extradition treaty with India as a reason to take no action.

In spite of these frustrations, CSIS placed Parmar under close surveillance and described him as "the most radical and perhaps the most dangerous Sikh in the country, protected by a close circle of similarly minded associates."*⁵⁹ He is still the subject of a Level Three inquiry, which represents the highest level of urgency.

Safe in Canada, Talwinder Singh Parmar promised to avenge his fellow believers. Five months later, in October, Indira Gandhi was assassinated by her Sikh personal bodyguard. In the streets of Vancouver, Parmar's friends found time, between slogan-shouting, to celebrate the glories of "Khalistan." But back in India, hundreds of Sikhs were beaten to death in their villages in retribution for the assassination. No authority was strong enough to halt the downward spiral.

It's late summer 1984, after the attack. In CSIS's Vancouver office, as well as back in the Ottawa headquarters, the staff is working flat out to bug whatever premises Parmar might occupy. But bureaucratic imperatives block their path. There have been problems in the changeover of responsibilities from the Mounties to the newly created CSIS, the biggest being what to do with 110 warrants originally issued to the RCMP. Sorting out the imbroglio takes priority over national security. It also takes nearly four months, because the Federal Court didn't get around to giving force to article 21 of the CSIS Act until mid-March of 1985.

---

* The Sikh extremist movement had at the time a membership of about 350 out of a population of 120,000 Sikhs in Canada.

This was, unfortunately, not the only bump in the road where the Air India investigation was concerned. In fact, so many problems appeared in such a compact and intractable mass that it is reasonable to wonder if it wasn't a cover-up. On the other hand, it may have been nothing more than predictable stumbling and ball-dropping by bureaucrats caught in the muddle of shutting down the Mounties' security service and transitioning its powers to CSIS. The attorney general later testified before the Major Commission that the changeover had been nothing less than "tectonic."

Finally, in November of 1985, the Mounties arrested Talwinder Singh Parmar and Inderjit Singh Reyat. Charges included conspiracy, fabricating explosives, and possessing explosives. But the charges against Parmar were soon withdrawn.

Parmar's disciple, Reyat, pleaded guilty to lesser charges in connection with the victimless explosion at Duncan, and got away with paying a $2,000 fine. He immediately moved to England, where he was arrested in 1988 in connection with the bomb incident at Narita Airport. He was later extradited back to Canada, where he spent ten years in prison for manslaughter, as well as possession and use of explosives.

Two other Vancouver Sikhs, Ripudaman Singh Malik and d'Ajaib Singh Bagri, respectively a Sikh priest and businessman, were arrested by the RCMP in October 2000. Reyat's name was added to the indictment the following year. All were charged with conspiracy, murder, and attempted murder, with regard to both Flight 182 and the Narita incident. There were eight charges in all.

Reyat managed to escape the murder charges, which were withdrawn, but was sentenced to five years in connection with other charges, including perjury. He was to have been the star witness in the trial of Malik and Bagri, but, to the dismay of the prosecution, he flatly refused to answer many questions, and, where it suited him, simply changed testimony previously given to the RCMP. That was in February 2003. By March 2005, after 233 days in court at a cost of $130 million, Malik and Bagri were acquitted by the British Columbia Supreme Court. Judge Josephson found that there was insufficient evidence and a shortage of credible witnesses.

And there you have it! Justice hits the wall, and truth bangs its head. That's all we have to show for the endless hearings, investigations, and reports that filled the hearing rooms and front pages in Canada, India, and Ireland. A great sloppy mess, which added to the suffering of the victims' families. And given what they had endured, it must have seemed as if no time at all had passed before a smiling Reyat walked out of jail on July 10, 2008, a free man once again. The cameras captured his immaculate white tunic, his long and imposing beard, and the plastic bag of personal effects with which he took leave of his cell in Port Coquitlam.

But the saga of Flight 182 was not over. On the first day of May 2006, Prime Minister Stephen Harper named retired Supreme Court Justice John C. Major to head a commission that would "lead an inquiry into the investigative measures taken following the bomb attack on Air India Flight 182." The inquiry's terms of reference stated that "the commissioner shall, in the course of the inquiry, take all necessary measures to prevent the disclosure of information which, if disclosed, might in his opinion cause damage to international relations or to defence and national security."

Given that provision, it's not surprising that nowhere and at no time did anyone raise the suggestion that foreign agents might have been involved in the bombing. Nobody asked: Did these agents know that such a thing was planned? Did they have a role in it? Did Canadian authorities know that police agents from India were present here? Were they identified? Were they under surveillance? These are pressing questions that remain unanswered after twenty-five years and many millions of dollars spent. In March of 2009, at the moment these pages were written, the commission had still not published its report.

People in the undercover world—who, as always, cannot afford to identify themselves—repeatedly make the point that Canada has never tried to ascertain whether agents from India were aware of Flight 182's imminent destruction, and whether, if they knew, they did anything to prevent it happening.

Another uncomfortable detail that keeps law enforcement types awake at night: Why did India's police make no arrests in connection with this attack on their national airline? And why has the homeland terrorist network that supports the one in Canada never been dismantled?

India's Cops and Their Agent Provocateur

The gentleman with the answers to these questions is Parmar himself. But he appears to have been murdered in his cell by Indian police officers in October 1992. This most likely happened during a brutal interrogation. He took his secrets, perhaps very weighty ones, with him to the grave.

In a confession obtained shortly before his death, the authenticity of which is not certain, the former leader of the Babbar Khalsa admitted to a limited involvement in the Air India plot.

But it is also possible that Parmar was an *agent provocateur* sent by the Indian secret service to work undercover inside Canada's "Little Punjab" community. This hypothesis comes from one of our sources. He claims that CSIS intercepted a conversation in which Davinder Singh Ahluwalia, India's consul in Toronto, asked a contact in the Sikh community to arrange a meeting with Parmar. Ahluwalia's office was bugged, and the alleged conversation took place several months before the bombing.

So: a highly placed diplomat tries to arrange a meeting with a man considered to be Terrorist Number One. This is the most gripping thing about the story. This same Ahluwalia, who was regularly involved in louche affairs, had also been repeatedly approached by the Central Intelligence Agency, even in his living room (also bugged), because they wanted him to become their mole in Iran.

In its annual report for 1991–92, the Security Intelligence Review Committee (SIRC) devoted a dozen pages to the study of CSIS's work on the Air India file. Keeping in mind the government's instruction more than fourteen years later to the Major Commission not to reveal anything that might "cause damage to international relations," we should not be surprised that, back in 1992, SIRC went out of its way to slap down CSIS for doing exactly that.

CSIS had endorsed the "allegations concerning repeated interference by a foreign government in the accident," charges SIRC. Here it is relevant to recall that barely five months after the dramatic event, in November 1985, the RCMP fell into line with government policy by judging the allegations to be "without foundation or substance."

In its conclusions, SIRC dismissed the hypothesis of India's involvement in a few sentences and without even mentioning India's name: "We have examined CSIS' evidence in order to determine if an organization or a representative of a foreign government was involved in the destruction of the aircraft. This evidence does not support the theory of a foreign government's complicity in the destruction of the Air India aircraft which undertook Flight 182."

Once more a reasonable person has to suspect that these are false arguments, driven by economic and political pressure, which have interfered with—one might even say contaminated—the search for the truth. India and Canada, both members of the

Commonwealth, have had a relationship of bilateral co-operation in many domains and for a very long time. It's a friendship that has certainly had its highs, but also quite a few lows. This was particularly true when India, which hadn't signed the nuclear non-proliferation treaty, exploded its first atomic bomb in 1974. It was a "first" that very much angered Canada, since we had provided the financing for India's first nuclear reactor at the beginning of the 1960s. The money was provided on condition that the reactor never be used for military purposes.

In February 1987, having chastised the Indian government on many occasions for undercover activities amidst its diaspora population—the activity had reached an intolerable level—Canada at last decided to deal with the matter. Without causing diplomatic waves, the Ministry of External Affairs discreetly showed the door to several high-ranking Indian diplomats. Several of their names were mentioned in the media: Brij Mohal Lal, an ex-army general who had been posted to Toronto; Gurinder Singh, the consul in Vancouver; and Maloy Krishna Dhar, the gentleman from India's high commission in Ottawa, of whom we have already spoken. These were clearly identified as intelligence officers assigned to infiltrate the Sikh community between 1983 and 1987. On the occasion of an official visit to India, then Foreign Affairs Minister Joe Clark politely informed Rajiv Ghandi that his "diplomats" were no longer in good odour in Canada. As Clark spoke, their names were being whispered one by one in his ear by a CSIS liaison agent, himself on the telephone with his colleagues in Ottawa. Naturally it was important to manage appearances and avoid embarrassment, and so no noisy public expulsion ever took place.

But the blacklist in question contained eleven or twelve names of pseudo-diplomats, consular employees, and agents and informers located in Vancouver, Toronto, and Ottawa. It was, in effect, a spy list put together after months of CSIS investigation. And each name on the list came with a substantial biography assembled through investigation in Canada and "trace requests" for information from friendly intelligence agencies in other countries.

To the immense satisfaction of the Canadian investigators, pretty much the entire organization of RAW (India's overseas spy agency) had just been decapitated. When we tried to confront him about this, Maloy Krishna Dhar persisted in brushing off any suggestion of interference or espionage in Canada. "I was never a member of any external Indian secret service," he said, indulging in evasive wordplay. He also denied that his name had appeared on the list or that he had been declared *persona non grata*.

But he let slip one little phrase that implicitly acknowledged that there were RAW agents in Canada "who had been declared *personae non gratae*" at the time of the diplomatic confrontation. He also had the gall to say that he didn't know whether these same agents actually did infiltrate the Sikh community. This is not true. Maloy Krishna Dhar insisted that he was trained only to gather "open" information. Period.

> My job was "open," legitimate. You can ask the agents from [Canadian] External Affairs what that means. It means that I never did undercover work. But whenever my country asked me, I was ready to collect open information, which makes up 70 percent of all information gathering anyway. The other 30 percent comes from confidential sources. Any specialist in the subject will confirm it. It's a universal truth.[60]

Although the Canadian government never bragged about it, it did obtain enough proof from CSIS to conclude that Canadian-based Indian intelligence agents, from both RAW and the IB, had built a network of informers and paid agents and also pressured members of the Sikh community into becoming informers. That made things more difficult for CSIS. Moderate Sikhs, knowing that RAW agents were living among them, were terrified at the mere thought of speaking to anybody from CSIS or the RCMP.

In October 1986, Liberal MP Robert Kaplan, who had been solicitor general from 1980 to 1984 and was well informed on the subject, became concerned about a possible disinformation campaign by India's secret services aimed at discrediting Sikhs living in Canada. He believed CSIS should investigate it.

Even worse, there was proof that Hindu extremists, deported from their country after murderous religious riots at the beginning of the 1990s and now living in Canada, had become spies for India's secret services. The mother country rewarded these good little soldiers for their services with many favours, such as the right to sell products without taxes, to receive all-expenses-paid trips to India, to be offered facilities for commercial exchange, and even to indulge in visa trafficking.

Given all this tension at home, India was not intimidated by Canada's mass expulsions of its diplomats in 1987 any more than it was by the earlier brouhaha around the destruction of Flight 182. Instead, it was caught out a number of times over the next ten years recruiting and corrupting Canadian government officials who happened to be of Indian background—another troubling fact that has been carefully buried by the authorities, in particular Foreign Affairs.

All of this nonsense, considered as a whole, was so infuriating for Canada's secret services that they drew together to oppose the government allowing India to station an official RAW liaison agent in Ottawa.

It wasn't until we laid hands on Maloy Krishna Dhar's book, *Open Secrets* (published in New Delhi in 2005), that we finally got a sense of the extent of clandestine Indian activity in Canada at the time of the Flight 182 episode. The twenty pages he wrote about his mission in Ottawa from 1983 to 1987 should be anthologized in any book about the perfect spy/*provocateur*/manipulator. It's certainly a slap in the face to Canadians and their government.

Mr. Dhar begins by explaining that, from the moment of his arrival in Ottawa (October 1983), High Commissioner Ramakrishnan shared his anxiety about the rise of Sikh extremism. The commissioner admitted that the mediocre "performance of RAW agents" was getting him down: the big problem was their foot-dragging when it came to sharing information with him. And then he added: "I've been brought up to date on your practical expertise. Get ready for another hard slog."

The high commissioner then instructed him to go undercover in the Sikh community, make friends in the temples and get the important people on his side, all the while taking care not to blow his cover as an intelligence officer. Later on, Maloy Krishna Dhar received a list of a dozen or so priority objectives (a classic example of what we call "interference," and one we have seen at play in a majority of the countries named elsewhere in this book). Apart from the three points already mentioned, Dhar was to attempt to to influence the community's activists and agitators, and to recruit informants among Sikh workers who were followers of extremist leaders. It was also his job to sell the Indian government's version of the Sikh community to the mainstream Canadian media and to the members of Parliament. Maloy Krishna Dahr even preens about having continued his "clandestine activities" after the Air India bombing, when CSIS was watching him (he is certain of this because his telephone was tapped).

The rivalry that appears to have existed between the RAW agents and Maloy Krihsna Dhar's clique is also interesting. Dhar feels that RAW smeared him and his associates by suggesting that they were responsible for the expulsion of Indian diplomats in 1987.

The former subcontinental spy never ceases to be amazed by the naïveté of our diplomats, "obsessed" as they were by human rights violations in the Punjab, suspicious of India, and utterly unconscious of the threat posed by Sikh extremism. This misguidedness frustrated New Delhi no end, he writes.

Dhar also holds Pakistan responsible. The country's government not only ramped up its propaganda machine to top speed, it also supported the Sikh separatists in an underhanded fashion (the Punjab was cut in two at the time of the creation of Pakistan in 1947). Dhar claims to have discovered links between agents of Pakistan's ISI, based in Toronto, and Sikh activists in Ottawa, which led him to hide secret microphones on the premises of one of the two groups.

He goes even further, revealing that Parmar, the principal suspect in the Air India affair, took off to Pakistan in 1979 to meet with ISI agents and make a deal with them. Luckily (Maloy Krishna Dhar congratulates himself on this turn), things changed after the assassination of Indira Gandhi and the "sabotage" of Air India's Boeing jetliner.

Maloy Khrishna Dhar was no small player on India's undercover checkerboard. A master spy, he had spent his entire career inside India's Intelligence Bureau (IB) and was its number-two at the time of his resignation in 1996. Dhar, much admired by those who worked with him, participated in a number of delicate operations in the Punjab, in Kashmir, and in Pakistan. We read of the suppressing of uprisings, of counter-intelligence, of arms smuggling, and so on. These operations, which he sometimes describes as illegal and immoral, were initiated by politicians. He was, he says, only obeying orders.

So Dhar was a man accustomed to questionable, clandestine operations, a man of senior rank who was parachuted into Ottawa in 1983 at the very moment when Sikh extremism began to spread. And he spoke the truth when, provoked by our questioning, he testily replied that "spies are even more untrustworthy than people who go around quoting from the Bible."

Today, Dhar, who is much in demand as a commentator on matters of espionage and terrorism, is a late convert to democracy. He says that every investigative agency should have to report to the nation's elected leaders and justify their actions.

The implication here is that political leaders weren't told very much in the past. Of course that might have been guessed by anyone who has studied their incompetence when faced with the vast project of interference and manipulation that was orchestrated by a foreign power on Canadian soil.

The question we must ask ourselves today is why Canada continues to protect India by not compelling it to say what it knew about the Air India disaster.

Consider that François Lavigne was prevented from testifying publicly before the Major Commission by government lawyers who claimed that the questionable activities of India's agents in Canada were not part of its mandate.*

Did India directly orchestrate the bombing? Nobody has brought forward serious proof, and so we won't go any farther down the road of a conspiracy theory.

Nonetheless, when one considers the level of subversion and penetration of the Sikh community by India's IB agency, as described

---

* Lavigne testified privately to the commissioner.

by Maloy Krishna Dhar, as well as the work of the redoubtable and efficient RAW agents (though details are scarce), apart from the troubling information that we revealed earlier, there are only two alternatives.

First, either India really did not know what was being planned, or at best—as its authorities keep saying—heard rumours of vague threats against its official airline, among other entities. But this appears improbable in the light of what we have learned about the professional calibre of its secret services—especially that of Maloy Krishna Dhar, a talented agent who rapidly rose through the ranks of the IB—and the extent of their penetration of the Sikh community.

Or, second, India knew more than it is letting on, but allowed the plot to go forward because it was in its interests to do so; or, at worst, the business got out of control. The chaotic transfer of power from the RCMP to the new CSIS organization also created an environment favourable to the plotters, who aimed both to incriminate the Sikhs and to destabilize Canada. Like many of those we interviewed, we tend to think this is what happened.

François Lavigne endlessly relives and re-examines the Air India affair in his mind. The final revelations from Maloy Krishna Dhar have done nothing to help him recover his peace of mind:

> I saw the kind of "David" I was up against now. And I
> see how easy it could have been for RAW's agents, or
> other people supported by the Indian government, to
> plan such an operation, to encourage and facilitate it,
> without any fear of a response from Canadian authori-
> ties. You need to understand that the stakes were high

and the risk was justified. After June 23, 1985, the Indian government terrorized certain Sikh elements and public opinion became indifferent, if not sympathetic, from that moment forward.[61]

He also issues this warning:

> So I say once again, so long as Canada fails to understand where its interest is, and [fails] to defend itself against threats that really exist, without resorting to petty politics, and without committing resources to issues that are already irrelevant, to the detriment of its real interests, Canada will remain a likely future battlefield. We'll be subject to this kind of nonsense and we'll go on allowing foreign governments to compromise our national security.[62]

IRANIAN MULLAHS AND THEIR ASSASSINS

Canada has had a troubled relationship with Iran for some time now. The most egregious incident was the death by torture in 2003 of Montreal photojournalist Zara Kazemi. This fifty-four-year-old woman died at the hands of Iranian secret police thugs a few days after she was arrested outside a prison in Teheran and charged with spying.

Nearly as bad was the Iranian parliament's investigation, three years later, into the presumed espionage activities of eleven Canadian diplomats working in Iran on behalf of the United States. It also threatened to close the Canadian embassy, which it coarsely condemned as a "hideout for spies." The threats seemed to be connected to Canada's support for a United Nations resolution condemning the unacceptable "state of human rights in the Islamic

Republic of Iran." A year later, Iran actually expelled the Canadian
ambassador.

Canada has always been wary about the activities of Iranian
agents from MOIS (Ministry of State Security, also called VEVAK).
Most Canadians have never heard of this redoubtable and brutal
agency. Here, as in other western countries, its agents are active in
every variety of espionage and proliferation of weapons of mass
destruction, to the extent that most Canadian specialists would
name Iran as the third-largest offender, after Russia and China.

MOIS's great speciality is the intimidation of Iran's diaspora
and the surveillance of dissident organizations, with the intention of
eliminating them altogether (outright asassination was their actual
practice back in the 1990s). This violation of Canada's territorial
integrity is generally carried out by agents working under diplomatic cover as well as true undercover people posing as businessmen,
students, or employees of Iran Air.* They also work through front
organizations, usually cultural ones, and sometimes pretend to be
opponents of their own regime. That's why Iranian-Canadians have
loudly denounced the cultural centre called Fatemeh in Ottawa as a
"house of terror." It opened its doors in 1999 on Robinson Street, on
a 2.3-hectare plot of land sold by the National Capital Commission
to a numbered company belonging to the Iranian government. The
price was $1.6 million.[63]

Fatemeh is an institution clouded in mystery. Its directors, including an eminent university professor who ran for the Green Party in
2007 and 2008, did everything possible to conceal the financial contribution made by Teheran. But it was nonetheless Iran that applied
for a permit in 1999 to build one of the structures on the property.

---

* In Canada, the embassy of the Islamic Republic of Iran in Ottawa shelters about
fifteen secretaries and sub-secretaries as well as an attaché.

Teheran uses a variety of pressure tactics against the 200,000 members of its Canadian diaspora, squeezing them to reveal information about dissidents, and sometimes persuading them to return home. In recent months, for example, certain Iranians living in Ottawa received a remarkably inexpensive offer of two weeks in Iran for $900. The motive behind it was to get them to come to the embassy for a visa or passport renewal, so as to review and update their files. Sometimes, depending on the people involved, embassy staff might even try to recruit them as informers. Students, of whom there are dozens in Canada, will be offered partial payment of their tuition for the same service. Many of them are here to study scientific specialties connected with nuclear technology. Other countries use similar methods.

Unfortunately, as we learned from an Ottawa dissident, Irano-Canadians remember how they were treated by the secret police, whether those of the Shah or the mullahs, before they fled the homeland. They are afraid to contact the Canadian police, and they avoid CSIS especially, when they are the targets of pressure or intimidation. "They don't dare speak out; they have no confidence," says our contact regretfully.

Teheran is adept at selling its message to the Canadian public and its representatives. It also cultivates certain members of Parliament and academics, who are then expected to come out in favour of a rapprochement with Iran. These contacts also help distribute propaganda pamphlets directed against the popular Mujahedin movement (which we'll discuss later).

The Iranians are fond of what the Soviets, in the time of the KGB's Line PR, used to call "active measures"—that is, political warfare. This ranges from standard disinformation through to the fabrication of fake documents that compromise individuals and organizations. Sometimes it is possible to embarrass an entire country.

MOIS's agents received their training in political warfare from first-class teachers, the KGB's experienced practitioners in Moscow.

A favorite Teheran method of moving foreign public opinion on a controversial issue goes by the name "80/20." A good description can be found in a little Farsi-language book published by Tafreshi Jamshid, a former agent of MOIS who fled to Germany. When speaking with a foreigner, he explains, the undercover MOIS agent builds confidence by making sure that 80 percent of his conversation is critical of Teheran. The other 20 percent is an apparently casual discussion of the shortcomings of the regime's opponents. Cynics call this the "80 percent truth, 20 percent lies" formula. The tactic is necessary because expatriate Iranians are so hostile to the regime that a newly arrived Iranian who failed to be critical of it would, in effect, be "outing" himself as a henchman of the mullahs.

A famous MOIS intrigue goes back to 1993–94, during the war in Bosnia. Iranian agents had tried to discredit British diplomacy by writing a false letter, supposedly from the desk of British Secretary of State for Foreign Affairs Douglas Hurd, in which he offers his support to the Bosnian Serbs. Since this was the second time in a very few months that the Iranians had tried the same dirty trick, Great Britain decided on a reprisal. It expelled the Iranian embassy's first secretary in London. Unfortunately the Canadian government does not seem capable of this kind of bare-knuckle response to provocation.

The agents of MOIS must be considered a serious menace to national security, if only because they are trained to use violence to silence opponents of the Teheran regime. They also lend encouragement and material support to named terrorist groups, for example Hezbollah in Lebanon. It is also to be feared that MOIS could do considerable damage inside a number of western countries in reprisal for an invasion of Iran by the United States or Israel.

Does that seem far-fetched? In 2004 the Canadian media happily gave front-page publicity to a high-ranking officer of the Revolutionary Guards who claimed that suicide commandos were ready to attack twenty-nine targets in western countries. Canada occupied a place of honour on the list. Whether this is empty provocation or not, western counter-intelligence agencies take it seriously. They remember unsettling incidents like the expulsion of two Iranian security guards who had been protecting the Iranian mission at the United Nations. The men were deported by the Bush administration after being caught, for the third time since 2003, filming buildings and other infrastructure in Manhattan.

The prime target for Iran's agents here are sympathizers and Canadian members of Mujahedin-e Khalk (MEK). Also known under the name of the Organization of Iranian People's Mujahideen (WIPO), it is a Shia Marxist movement—sometimes seen as secular—which was founded by Iranian students in 1965. It helped overthrow the Shah of Iran at the time of the revolution. But soon afterward WIPO fell afoul of the regime of the Ayatollah Khomeini. After a number of bloody encounters with government troops, the group was outlawed in Iran.

But WIPO's troubles began even before the triumph of the mullahs. In 1986, its chief, Massoud Radjavi, fled to France. Hundreds of its militants crossed over to Iraq and sought refuge with Saddam Hussein. Always the opportunist, the former dictator of Iraq armed the WIPO refugees and turned them into an attack unit to be used in his war with Iran. WIPO's headquarters is still situated in Najaf, to the south of Baghdad.

At about the same time, WIPO was putting down roots in Canada, especially in Montreal.* Its members spent their time fundraising

---

* WIPO's headquarters was a café on Boulevard St. Laurent, which was under CSIS observation.

for the cause and spreading their message and didn't appear to be involved in criminal activity. But they fell under CSIS surveillance nonetheless. A faction within CSIS felt that the group would sooner or later become a violent menace here. Other believed it would not, and that we were wasting our time monitoring it.

Tension notched upwards in April 1992 when a WIPO demonstration outside the Iranian embassy in Ottawa became violent. This was in response to an Iranian army attack against a Mujahedin base in Iraq. There were similar and simultaneous demonstrations against twelve Iranian missions in other countries.

A year later, in June 1993, a security certificate was issued for the arrest of a certain Mansour Ahani, who had obtained refugee status here in 1991. CSIS was convinced he was a MOIS agent who had lied to obtain his refugee status. Ahani insisted that he had been conscripted into a death squad run by the Ministry of Foreign Affairs and told to assassinate WIPO's overseas enemies. He also claimed that he would be executed if deported to his homeland. The lie detectors and interrogators were brought in, because CSIS by then had a good idea that the Iranian was a "trained assassin" and "terrorist" who had been sent to Canada by Iran's security services and implanted into the Iranian community here.

It took time and hard work to send him back to Iran. As often happens, human rights organizations depicted him as a victim and tried to prevent the deportation. For his part, Ahani engaged in protracted guerrilla warfare with the Canadian government, going as far as the Supreme Court, which found against him.

Having run out of legal options, Ahani found himself, on the night of June 18, 2002, sitting in a Teheran-bound airplane on the tarmac of Toronto's Pearson Airport. The counter-intelligence people had finally found the necessary evidence: proof that Ahani had been arrested in Italy ten years earlier, in the company of another

MOIS assassin, Akbar Khoshkooshk, as they worked together on a plan to kill a well-known Iranian dissident.

A few months after his forced return, Ahani told the *National Post* that he had invented the persecution story out of thin air. But even then the U.N. Committee on Human Rights still blamed Canada for its "poor" management of the case. It even suggested that we should compensate Ahani in the event his countrymen tortured him.

CSIS has caught other MOIS agents as well. In 1996, it was Djafar Seyfi's turn to bow to a security certificate and take his leave of Canada. In his case, the evidence was diligently assembled. Less than nine months elapsed between the moment he filled out his refugee application on arriving in Quebec and his hasty return home. Far from being a desperate innocent pursued by bloodthirsty ayatollahs, Seyfi was actually on their payroll. His job was to frighten Iranians in Canada.

During the 1990s, Iranian death squads operating throughout Europe were behind a wave of assassinations. They murdered intellectuals and other opponents of the regime in France, Italy, and Germany, and as far afield as Turkey, Libya, and Iraq.

In October 2005, a dissident group called the National Council of the Iranian Resistance sent out a press release identifying a former employee of Ottawa's Fatemeh cultural centre as a MOIS agent. He had been sent to infiltrate the WIPO organization. The man was a member of the pasdarans—better known as the Revolutionary Guards—who had flown from Toronto to Washington on October 24, where he entered the National Press Club. He was in the company of another Ottawa resident, identified later as a female spy working for the mullahs. This is perhaps the place to mention that WIPO has a fairly good investigative arm of its own.

The two arrested spies were part of a fake-dissident Canadian

group called Pars-Iran, which was supposedly made up of former Mujahedin. It pretended to be opposed to the dictatorship of
Saddam Hussein, but in reality it was part of a propaganda exercise directed against WIPO. Here the Iranians used the same tactic
employed by the Chinese against Falun Gong, which was for its
agents to pretend to be members of a group that the government
actually wished to destroy.

On May 24, 2005, Anne McLellan, Canada's minister of Public
Safety and deputy prime minister, did an immense service to the
ayatollahs in Teheran by putting WIPO on the government's list of
terrorist organizations. The idea—and Ottawa wasn't the only western capital to think of it—was to seek better relations with Iran's
new president, the reformer Mohammad Khatami. The upshot was
that many of the world's democracies agreed to support a government that assassinates its opponents, by calling its opponents terrorists. It was an appalling decision.

In Canada, WIPO had no choice but to disband officially. Its
true believers still hoped their situation might improve. Here, as
elsewhere in the world, they continued an intense lobbying cam
paign on behalf of their cause. In a geopolitical context where the
succeeding Iranian regime of President Mahmoud Ahmadinejad
has become Public Enemy Number One, WIPO has begun to
arouse a certain interest in the chancelleries and information services of western governments—not out of any moral consideration,
but because it has a solid network in Iran.

WIPO's supporters rarely fail to remind the world that they
represent the true political alternative to the rule of the clerics. Why
would the West prefer to threaten a suicidal attack on Iran, a major
military power, when a democratic Iranian group was ready to
take over power there? And aren't the enemies of our enemies our
friends? This logic has begun to be appreciated. England withdrew

WIPO from its terrorist watchlist in June 2008, while the European Court of Justice—in session in Luxembourg—made an order in December of the same year to the European Union's Council of Ministers that the Mujahedin be taken off the list and that WIPO's assets should be unfrozen.

Unfortunately, other countries, such as France—which still energetically pursues the members of the movement—seem disinclined to change their views. This is surely because of pressure brought by corporate interests (automobile manufacturers and oil companies, for example) to whom Iran represents a potentially attractive market. In Canada, WIPO is still banished. CSIS patiently looks on as its supporters demonstrate on Parliament Hill and in the streets of Montreal. (And so do MOIS agents, no doubt!) But WIPO's quest to recover its virginity will have to wait a while longer, since in November 2008 the Canadian government renewed its terrorist status one more time.

PRESIDENT BEN ALI AND HIS TUNISIAN TOUGH GUYS

A conference curiously named "The World Summit on the Information Society and the Right of Free Expression in Tunisia" is taking place in Quebec City. It's May 12, 2005. Mokthar Krifi, a well-known Tunisian lawyer and president of the three-decade-old Tunisian Human Rights League, is giving a speech. Amnesty International has a camera there to film it, not with any idea of immortalizing Krifi, but rather to have evidence to hand over to the Sûreté du Québec (Quebec Provincial Police) in the event the lawyer is attacked. The organizers feel that it's a necessary precaution, because official violence and harassment of the organization in Tunisia is common. It turns out to be quite a useful idea.

Question period arrives. A succession of attendees (a lawyer from Nabeul, a doctor, a citizen) come to the microphone with a strange unanimity of purpose. Each praises the president of Tunisia and denounces the speaker; each is greeted by a round of well-practised applause. The moderator, who writes for the Quebec newspaper *Le Soleil*, repeatedly insists that they must ask a question. Nobody complies.

Another Tunisian seizes the microphone and angrily interrupts the charade, shouting that everything he has just heard is proof positive that Tunisia is a dictatorship with a façade of phony democracy. He hasn't quite finished when the lawyer who previously spoke stands up in the audience and accuses the man who has just spoken of "insulting an entire people."

Another man moves toward the microphone. He introduces himself as the editor-in-chief of a North African (Maghreb) newspaper. Once again, he asks no question. Instead he trots out a short propaganda presentation in favour of the Tunisian government. He also lets it be known that he wasn't impressed by Mokhtar Krifi's defence of the Tunisian people. "You're trying to tear down our country of origin . . . We aren't proud of you, we're ashamed of you, you aren't welcome in the homeland. And who paid for you to come here anyway?" Tempers flare and the room fills with verbal abuse from all directions.

This is beyond strange. Stranger still, however, is the fact that the same scene, with the same actors, hurling the same remarks, was enacted in Montreal just a few days before, at a press conference that came to a rapid close in a torrent of verbal abuse. The subject that day was freedom of information in Tunisia. The first rows were packed with "journalists" from the same newspaper, recalls Jamel Jani, a member of the Human Rights Association of the Maghreb, based in Ottawa.* He disdainfully calls it a "Chinese" manoeuvre, so over-rehearsed as to be obviously fake. "Every time we host a public event a gang like this shows up to provoke people, insulting and intimidating them. I've even heard myself called 'Jamel Jani, son of a whore.' They show up, Chinese style, with flags from the homeland. And guys with cameras. Same thing when we demonstrate in front of the consulate."

Jamel Jani does not mince his words. He is quite certain that this is the work of the Tunisian diplomatic service, pulling strings and doing its best to keep Canadians confused about what is going on in the expatriate Tunisian community. He has, he says, seen the head of security from Tunisia's mission in Montreal at several demonstrations. The several thousand Tunisian students in Quebec, grateful to be allowed to study overseas, are pressured to join in as well. Co-operative businessmen get fat contracts.

Where have we heard this before?

These "Chinese-style" tactics are obvious, grossly obvious, but they work. They get the job done without exposing the government agents who orchestrate it. Quite brilliantly, they force the people opposed to President Ben Ali's police state government to act like sneaky secret police themselves. If they don't want to attract the well-rehearsed saboteurs to their events, they have to plan them secretly. That means that they are limited to e-mailing notices of upcoming actions only to their own militants and a few trusted supporters. The results are a smaller turnout, less media attention, less influence.

Tunisia and Morocco, which together make up part of the region of North Africa called the Maghreb, have long figured on the list of the twenty or so countries most guilty of interfering in Canada's

* Jani has also been a representative of Tunisia's Progressive Democratic Party in Canada.

internal affairs. When Lise Garon, now retired, was still teaching communications at Laval University, she was forced to speak out more than once about the abuse and manipulation of Tunisian students by the Tunisian University Mission in North America (TUMNA). She also condemned the use of "pseudo-journalists" to torpedo public meetings of Tunisian expatriates while the official delegates of that country piously pretended to have nothing to do with it. "It's a systematic practice and it's been in use for quite a long time," says Garon, now a well-known human rights activist. In her view, a majority of Tunisian students who co-operate in this game do so for fear of losing their scholarships.

Since she was well known for her interest in this community, she was not surprised, back in the fall of 2000, to hear from a Tunisian student. Or rather, "an individual who claimed he was a Tunisian student. He phoned me at the office, introduced himself as an opponent of the Ben Ali regime, and asked if he could help out with organizing my Tunisian conferences. I was suspicious, so I decided to set a trap to see what was going on. I suggested he attend an event I was planning for December 8. I have a vivid memory of the day because there was a huge snowstorm. And what did I see when I arrived at the hall? Fifty Tunisian students who were hemmed in on all sides by people quite a bit older than they were. Too bad for them and my so-called dissident, but the program that day was a film about Rwanda!"

TUMNA keeps its offices in the compound of the Tunisian consulate, which is located in Montreal's oldest skyscraper, built by New York Life at the end of the nineteenth century in the Place d'Armes neighbourhood. There are six diplomats working there, more than Tunisia keeps at its Ottawa embassy, supposedly because Montreal contains the biggest enclave of Tunisians in Canada. There is also a small mission in Calgary.

At the end of the consulate's entrance hall is a heavy hard-wood door. Behind it the employees of TUMNA keep themselves busy approving the study grants and tuition exemptions of hundreds of students from the homeland who are scattered across North America. The stakes for these students are high. Because of an exchange agreement between Quebec and Tunisia, about two hundred of these young Tunisians can apply for a complete exemption from the very costly fees customarily asked of foreign students. This can amount to more than $3,000 per year, a significant sum for young people from a poor country. A similar program operates at the University of Ottawa.

The scholarship program is naturally supposed to reward the most serious students, or those who are developing expertise in short supply at home. But our informants tell us that it is used almost exclusively to muzzle the politically recalcitrant, and to encourage general docility.

It is not surprising to find that Tunisia, like many other countries, has an agenda in place for the renewal of passports. One Tunisian dissident waited in the anterooms for literally years before the precious stamp was applied to his papers.

Tunisia's diplomats take a dim view of anybody who suggests that their role in the lives of their former countrymen now living in Canada is not a benign one. "There aren't enough of us to carry on all the activities we're accused of! And there isn't a single security officer in our consulate in Montreal," swears a staffer with whom we had an informal chat. He paints a picture of a small and hard-working team that can barely fill out the paperwork, much less go about shadowing students as they make their way around the city's many campuses.

But, in a moment of that Maghrebian camaraderie that we find so charming, he does allow that some of the local Tunisian dissidents get rowdy. All well and good if he sometimes finds a moment to suggest to the noisiest ones that these noisy methods aren't much to the taste of Canadians.

THE JEWISH DIASPORA, MOSSAD'S RELIABLE FIFTH COLUMN

It's no surprise to learn that Israel's Mossad intelligence service keeps a close eye on expatriate Lebanese associated with the Shia movement called Hezbollah, as well as the few activist groups supporting the Palestinian cause. This is part of the ongoing battle against terrorism.

What gives us pause is Mossad's absolute fascination with Canadian passports, which it steals whenever it can and counterfeits whenever it can't. These documents are handed to its intelligence officers, who then travel freely and without arousing suspicion.

In the fall of 1997 two Mossad killers, tried to murder a Hamas officer named Khaled Mashal with neurotoxins. When they were arrested, they were found to be carrying Canadian passports in the names of Barry Beads and Sean Kendall.

As a consequence, "Canada's government was furious with Mossad, not because they used Canadian passports, but because they got caught," says the former Israeli spy Ari Ben-Menashe, with a crooked smile. This reinforces a similar observation made by Canada's former ambassador to Israel, Norman Spector. Spector has often accused Ottawa of turning a blind eye to this practice, one that is not only scandalous, but also dangerous to the safety of Canadians with legitimate passports who may travel in the Middle East. Spector went even farther than Ben-Menashe, revealing that there had been a secret meeting between CSIS agents and Mossad agents not long before the attack on Mashal.

In spite of this spy-allied-with-spy complicity between the two intelligence organizations, says Ben-Menashe, Ottawa severely restricted Mossad's activities in Canada until Stephen Harper's Conservatives came to power. Did the Israelis do what they were told? That's a story for another day.

That Khaled Mashal was attacked by agents bearing Canadian passports caused quite a stir within the Canadian government. But it was not unexpected, so far as Canada's security agents were concerned. Our agents had been following Mossad's busy spooks around the snowy countryside for some time, and were keeping a secret file called "Mossad Agents in Canada." There were also files on a number of well-known Jewish lobbies.

But there is really nothing for Canada to worry about. It has the good fortune to be one of fifteen or so countries in the world to which Mossad dedicates a special department. And Canada returns the favour by including Israel in the secret list of countries that practise political and military espionage inside its borders. Israel uses pressure and influence on certain communities within Canada, and belongs to the exclusive club of nations who resolve to gather technology by any means necessary, thereby hoping to build even better chemical, nuclear, and biological weapons.

To return to the little blue passports: The Khaled Mashal debacle wasn't the only time that Israeli spies were caught red-handed with the documents. Many members of Canada's Jewish community demonstrate a worrisome willingness to "lend" their passports to Mossad, which then alters them to suit its needs. In 2005, Canada deported to Tunis an Iraqi-Tunisian with a startling itinerary. Hussein ali Sumaida had started his career a couple of decades back working for the terrifying Iraqi spy agency called Jihaz-al-Mukhabarat al-Amma.* The son of a diplomat and an intimate of

---

* Often imprisoned in Tunisia and ill treated, Sumeida secretly returned to Canada a year after his deportation. He was permitted to remain here by Immigration due to the risks attached to another deportation.

Saddam Hussein, Sumaida had betrayed more than thirty students involved in the banned Islamic movement called Al Da'wa. He then became a turncoat, offering his services to Mossad. The organization soon put him on the trail of militants in the Palestinian Liberation Organization (PLO).*

There is also the odd case of Mohamed Essam al-Attar, sentenced to fifteen years for espionage in Egypt in 2007. The authorities there claimed he had been working for Mossad in the years before 2006, even while still residing in Canada.

Al-Attar worked for the Canadian Imperial Bank of Commerce. His assignment was to make sure his Israeli handler knew all about the bank accounts held by certain Canadians of Arab origin. For this service he was paid just over $56,000. What's even more interesting, though, is that Egyptian authorities freely admitted during his trial in Cairo that their agents had been dogging his footsteps everywhere he went in Canada! They took snapshots while he took snapshots of Niagara Falls. They knew every Toronto and Vancouver street he walked down.

Whether any of this was true, or whether it was just a show trial, the al-Attar scandal captivated Egyptians because it looked just like one of those spy films that are so bad they're good. His life was chaotic. He was homosexual. He was an apostate—yes, he had denied the Prophet. Then he wanted to be a Catholic. Next he tried to get hired by the Israelis in Turkey. Then Mossad helped him become a refugee in Canada. Why? So he could recruit gay Muslim Canadian spies. Why would Mossad hire an Egyptian to root around in the computers of the CIBC? Why indeed, when (like the Chinese and their emigrants) the Israelis know that

* Hussein ali Sumaida wrote a book called *Circle of Fear: My Life as an Israeli and Iraqi Spy* (Washington, D.C.: Brassey's, 1994).

they can count on the active and unconditional co-operation of the Jewish diaspora everywhere on the planet. "In Paris, Mossad strolls about, going anywhere it likes in the Jewish community," observes a French counter-intelligence agent, with a combination of amusement and resignation.

There is even a name for members of the Jewish community willing to offer a hand to the clandestine *katsa* (agents) and *kidon* (killers). These helpful folk are called *sayanim*. If a team of assassins needs a car, a car rental agency will oblige; if they need cash, money will appear. And they need never fear a sleepless night; there will always be a hotel or motel manager happy to find them a room.

Victor Ostrovsky, who is Canadian, was also a Mossad officer during the 1980s. He revealed in his devastating book *By Way of Deception* that Mossad had hundreds of *katsas* (intelligence officers) working undercover around the world, and a few thousand employees altogether. Such a system can be viable only with the logistical support supplied by thousands of *sayanim*.

These unconditional patriots are persuaded to volunteer without much difficulty. Mossad plays on the heartstrings of Judaism, and of the sacred call of the Jewish homeland, to which their brothers and sisters have returned after centuries of torment and privation.[64]

A Man for Murky Missions

"I don't spy on Canada," comes the vigorous denial from Ari Ben-Menashe.

Today we're in a chic café on the Rue Laurier in Montreal. We've just explained our mission to this gentleman, and it was a great pleasure, since we'd been stood up so many times before finally laying eyes on him. Such a busy guy! And, in the truest sense of the word, a man who's difficult to grasp. He seems to leap from one airplane to the next, looking in on a Caribbean island, or Russia, or maybe Europe

and Africa—wherever business calls. His cellphone never stops ringing, and on the other end of the line is always somebody you or I
would be surprised to hear from. The man is connected, with a network that reaches into all kinds of spy bureaus and high ministries.

He's a fierce-looking fellow with a little pot belly, but behind
that belly is an appetite that could bend a fork. The espionage writer
Gordon Thomas, a great connoisseur of the shadow world, describes
him as charming and even picturesque. In his books, Thomas often
mentions the military exploits and tangled plots of the man from
Montreal. And why not? The name Ben-Menashe shows up in quite
a few explosive files, and some of them are closely connected to
Canada.

Sprawling on a plush sofa in a magnificent Old Montreal apartment—he calls it his office—his hair in choreographed disorder, his
eyes sparkling with malice, he agrees to tell his story. It starts with
the youthful adventures that taught the spy (now retired, he assures
us) to swim like a fish in murky waters, where survival depends
on unusual alliances made with unusual partners. Listening to his
tales, one is never sure what to believe. But, gradually, a certain pattern emerges. How to put this? In the world of Ari Ben-Menashe,
nobody is ever really an enemy.

His family were Iraqi Jews who immigrated to Iran shortly
before his birth in 1951. His was a cosseted childhood. His father
was the sole distributor of Mercedes automobiles in Iran, a late-
life prosperity made possible by the fact that, as a young man, he
had studied French at the Alliance Française in Baghdad. Then he
moved to Paris, where he obtained a doctorate in Marxist studies
from the Sorbonne.

Ari followed some parts of his father's arc. As a child he studied
at the American School in Teheran and then decided—at the age
of fourteen—to immigrate to Israel. In 1974, with a fresh univer-

sity degree and an Israeli citizen's card in his pocket, he joined the Israeli army. "I was particularly concerned about Iran," he explains. "At the time, we had good relations with the Shah's regime, as well as with the USSR, Europe, and the United States."

Not that these good relations in any way inhibited Ben-Menashe and his colleagues from spying on all these countries' diplomatic missions in Israel, as well as monitoring their communications with each other. Every week the agents of Shin Bet, Israel's counter-intelligence service, headed out to Ben-Gurion Airport to snatch the diplomatic pouch that Teheran sent to its "unofficial" diplomatic representative in Ramat Gan. They photocopied the cryptographic "black book" codes for the week, and put everything neatly back where it was.

Ben-Menashe rose rapidly in the service and was soon working in the Iranian office of the army's SIGINT 8200 unit. There he got the idea that he should be the one to break all the Iranian codes, so they wouldn't need to steal the black books any more. And he did it. "And that," chortles Ben-Menashe, "is how I became a star!"

After that, Israel could study Iran's top secret chit-chat at its leisure, not only at home but around the world.

In 1977 he joined the External Relations Department (ERD) of the Israeli army. Created in 1974 by Prime Minister Yitzhak Rabin, the mysterious ERD is structured around four branches. One carries out surveillance on the military attachés who work out of embassies around the world. Another, whose acronym is RESH, maintains relationships with the secret services of Israel's allies. Because of his background, Ben-Menashe was the obvious choice to take over the Iran dossier when it became clear that the mullahs were slowly preparing a religious revolution.

But his career really began to take off when he met Rafael "Rafi" Eitan, Mossad's director of operations for Europe and one of its master spies. Eitan's CV was very impressive. He was the advisor on terrorism to Prime Minister Menachem Begin, and was also in charge of an ultra-secret backroom unit with the neutral name of Bureau of Scientific Relations, which specialized in the theft of science and technology.

But of course Eitan was a giant chiefly because it was he who captured the Nazi war criminal Adolf Eichmann in Argentina.

There was an electrical connection between Eitan and Ben-Menashe, which is only natural considering what they had in comon: unsavoury personal reputations and a hand in some brilliant operational successes.* Think back to the Promis affair: it was a mere trifle compared to some of Ben-Menashe's other jobs, such as "Irangate." This was the operation in which he and Eitan were up to their armpits in supplying heavy weaponry to Iran on behalf of America and Israel during the 1980s. For better or for worse, it funnelled millions of dollars into the pockets of certain ayatollahs.

Irangate was a truly scandalous business. It gave birth to the "October Surprise" theory, which held that Ronald Reagan's Republicans plotted with the ayatollahs in order to bring about the defeat of Jimmy Carter in the 1980 presidential election. Ben-Menashe believes the plot was nicely tied up and packaged in October, a month before the election, in a salon of the ultra-chic Ritz Hotel in Paris. This was the deal: the United States and Israel supplied weapons to Iran's religious leaders to help them in their war with Iraq, while unfreezing their financial assets, which had been blocked in American banks. The quid pro quo was that Teheran would keep

---

* Eitan was forced to quit after the Jonathan Pollard affair came out. An intelligence officer of the U.S. Navy, Pollard was sentenced to life imprisonment in 1987 for spying on behalf of Israel. Eitan was his handler. Israel stalled for thirteen years before admitting that Pollard was indeed a spy in its service. Eitan returned to prominence in 2006 when he was elected to the Knesset as a member of the Pensioners' Party, a small political party.

the fifty-four hostages from the American embassy under lock and key until after the U.S. elections were over.

The arms traffic was covertly managed by ORA, a shell company started by Eitan and Ben-Menashe, which was based on Wall Street in New York. It generated vast profits from arms shipments, sometimes shuttled through Canada on their way elsewhere. Montreal was a crucial shipping node, says Ben-Menashe, adding the following stunning revelation: "The weapons came from the United States . . . Pierre Trudeau agreed to it after an informal meeting with Israel."

"Did Quebec know what was going on?" we asked.

"Absolutely not!" he cried, bursting into laughter. "And, just because the Israelis knew it would become a huge, huge problem, it wasn't long before they moved the company to Poland."

There is no way to know when Ben-Menashe is telling the truth. But the arms transshipment story is similar to another such arrangement we have learned about. Twice during 2005, a Canadian airport was used to ship weapons and explosives from the United States to a country on the Indian subcontinent that was threatened by a Marxist uprising. The air cargo company involved is based in eastern Europe and is frequently implicated in the arms traffic. Its name appears in a United Nations report on arms trafficking to the Democratic Republic of Congo (after which the company changed its name). So the Eitan/Ben-Menashe operation would hardly be the first time Canada served as a convenient doormat to erase the muddy footprints of arms traffickers.

In the 1980s, the gun-running spy's tawdry business operations were doing well. Things were relaxed enough that he dropped in to Teheran every so often to meet his "friends" and help out with the final delivery details. On these occasions Ben-Menashe went by the rather white-bread name of William Grace, a Canadian businessman.

Whether he liked it or not, it was the name Mossad chose for the Canadian passport it fabricated for him. And gracious, yes, Mossad is fond of our little blue books! And not only for the Iran route. They came in handy for the blood-stained traffic into Nicaragua, where the contras were trying to overthrow the Sandinistas.

Ben-Menashe's luck ran out in Los Angeles on November 3, 1989. There he was arrested, still sopping wet from the shower, for violating the U.S. Arms Export Control Act. Charges included the attempted sale of three heavy-lift Hercules C130 aircraft to Iran. But Israel owns them! clamoured Ben-Menashe, adding that they were stored in Edmonton. And when Israeli lawyers dropped by his cell to suggest that, all things considered, it would be best to plead guilty, he gave them the boot and acted as his own lawyer. Two years later a jury acquitted him.

This was a turning point for a proud man. Israel disowned him, claiming that he had been hired as a low-level translator and had turned out to be a liar. That was enough for Ben-Menashe, who was now a free man. He rebelled. It was time, he thought, to tell the truth . . . his truth. It came out in a book called *Profits of War: Inside the Secret U.S.-Israeli Arms Network*, published in 1992.

"To put it simply, the big thing for me was that I didn't want to get killed," he admits. "[The book] was my life insurance policy." One of the book's targets is media magnate Robert Maxwell, who was Ben-Menashe's "partner" in the sale of the Promis software. Maxwell thought he was stronger than Mossad, with which he sometimes collaborated. But he didn't have enough life insurance, so to speak. On November 6, 1991, six hours after a distress signal from his luxury yacht *Lady Ghislaine*, Maxwell's naked body was found floating in the Atlantic just off the Canary Islands. Ben-Menashe maintains that Maxwell visited Montreal a few days before his death, in an attempt to recover some of the money he had stolen from the retirement fund of the employees of the *Mirror* newspaper. The press magnate was at home in Quebec, which he had often visited during his association with local press lord Pierre Péladeau.

Spanish medical experts concluded that Maxwell's death was accidental. But that, says the Canadian version of Victor Ostrovsky, is false. He advances the alternate hypothesis that Maxwell was executed by *kidons* (professional killers) from Mossad, which was afraid Maxwell was going to go public with what he knew about arms deals.

Editor and journalist Bernard Bujold, who was Pierre Péladeau's assistant at the time, told his boss what happened to his flamboyant business partner. Bujold recalls Péladeau's reaction:

> I remember that we were standing near the receptionist. Pierre Péladeau looked at me and said it was his opinion that this wasn't a suicide but rather that somebody had pushed him overboard. He spoke in a low voice and mimed a pushing gesture. I asked him what on earth he meant by that. So he repeated it, saying that "somebody probably got rid of him" because he was connected with Mossad . . . he was trying to be a double agent. . . . These people don't kid around! . . . Pierre was sure of it: Maxwell was not suicidal.*

Bujold also confirms Maxwell's presence in Quebec less than two weeks before his disappearance: "The last time Pierre Péladeau

---

* Bujold sets out the links between Péladeau and Maxwell in the book *Pierre Péladeau, cet inconnu* (Montreal: Trait d'Union, 2003). See the website www.lestudio1.com.

saw Maxwell was October 24, 1991, at André Bisson's place in Montreal, where he announced the launch of an international newspaper called *The European*."

Ben-Menashe popped up on the radar again shortly after the beginning of the new millennium. Returning from a trip to Australia, he was named in a dark plot to assassinate Zimbabwean president Robert Mugabe. Mugabe blamed the business on his long-time political rival Morgan Tsvangirai, head of the MDC party. At the time, Ben-Menashe was president of a consulting firm called Dickens and Madson, which was registered in May of 2001. According to its corporate registration it is involved in the "production and distribution of films and literary works." One of Ben-Menashe's partners was Alexander Legault, an American living in Canada since 1982 and extradited back to the States in 2008. Charges involved a multi-million-dollar fraud.

According to Ben-Menashe, Morgan Tsvangirai was in the offices of Dickens and Madson on Victoria Avenue in Westmount when the possibility of eliminating Mugabe was first discussed. This was in December 2001. "He offered me $30 million to organize it and kill Mugabe," recalls Ben-Menashe. "When I asked where he was going to get all that money, he said: 'The British government will pay.'"

What Tsvangirai didn't know, and what Ben-Menashe claims, was that he had installed hidden microphones and miniature cameras throughout the office. He planned to send the tape to an Australian television journalist, in hopes that it would be broadcast before the Biennial Commonwealth Summit, to be held in March 2002 in the Australian city of Coolum. "Most of the heads of state had attacked Mugabe," he says, by way of explaining his plan. "Tony Blair, for example, had called him a dictator and praised the democratic qualities of Tsvangirai . . . Great Britain, Australia, and New Zealand wanted Zimbabwe expelled from their organization. The only one who showed any common sense was Jean Chrétien, who said he had to wait for the results of the election."

During the following weeks, Tsvangirai fiercely denied having anything to do with such a plot. Instead he accused Ben-Menashe of inventing a fake *coup d'état* in order to discredit him.

Rumour has it that Tsvangirai was actually in Montreal to pay Ben-Menashe a fee of half a million dollars to create a lobbying campaign on his behalf in North America. Without doubt the Zimbabwean was not aware that his mortal political enemy Mugabe had already hired Ben-Menashe as a consultant. Tsvangirai was later tried in Zimbabwe on charges of high treason, and was acquitted. And this in spite of the fact that Ben-Menashe testified against him, for which he received a thank-you note of $1 million from Mugabe.

"I don't care how many millions of dollars you offer me," huffs Ben-Menashe. "I would never kill anybody, especially a chief of state."

Ben-Menashe's office on Victoria Avenue has been deserted ever since. Nor is there any sign of life in the office tower on René-Lévesque Boulevard where another of Ben-Menashe's companies operated. It dealt in grain shipments and was apparently legitimately registered. But people working elsewhere in the tower say the offices were empty except for occasional visits by Ben-Menashe himself. Another dead letter box.

A good man when things were rough, some say of Ben-Menashe. Fantasist, fraud artist, and mythmaker, say others. He took pleasure in cultivating his myth, it seems, and you couldn't meet him and remain indifferent to it. But security services worthy of the name don't make a habit of using manipulation and disinformation to achieve their goals. That's probably why Israel has piously claimed that that Ben-Menashe was a small player in its grand scheme of things, if he played any role at all.

But doubt persists. How could he be a nobody, a "man of infamy" (his own favorite self-description), seeing the amount of energy that Israel has devoted to attacking his book since it was published? Just like Victor Ostrovsky, who published a payback book and was immediately denounced as a "traitor."

"They can say anything they like about me," opines Ben-Menashe, "but it's a fact that I worked for the government of Israel."

He was also on good (perhaps privileged?) terms with the Canadian government, to the extent that he agreed to be debriefed by Foreign Affairs experts and CSIS agents after returning from one of his many trips abroad. He also hints that he still acts as an occasional go-between in matters of diplomatic delicacy.

Ben-Menashe is not the only all-purpose handyman and dirty-job artist who has found gainful employment in the shadows. Arcadi Gaydamak has a remarkably similar CV. An Israeli-Canadian businessman, Gaydamak was sought by French police in early 2009 in connection with an extensive arms trafficking operation in Angola a decade earlier. Nearly $800 million in helicopters, warships, Russian assault tanks, AK-47 rifles, and other death-dealing toys left their factories and made off to Angola, thanks to this happy possessor of a Canadian passport. They ended up in the hands of President Dos Santos during his struggle with the UNITA rebels.

And, just as happened with Irangate, millions of dollars in commissions were tossed about like wedding confetti. Gaydamuk was obviously part of this so-called "Angolagate," whose network included members of the Israeli, Russian, and French spy services, handshake relationships with some Russian mafiosi, vodka-tippling with an oligarch or two, not to mention a few "special services" on behalf of the French government to liberate two French pilots seized by the Serbs in Bosnia in 1995.

Ben-Menashe's Irangate and Gaydamak's Angolagate both have all-star casts. Gaydamak's marquee included a former French préfet, a French minister of the interior, a son of deceased French President François Mitterand, and the author Paul-Loup Sulitizer, among others. They all ended up in the prisoner's box during a sparkling little trial that took place in Paris in 2008 and 2009.

Gaydamak, Ben-Menashe, Ostrovsky. Three who rubbed their peers in the Israeli secret service the wrong way and are still paying for it.

CHAPTER 007

The Techniques of Espionage

"Corruption is our protection. Corruption keeps us safe and warm.
Corruption is why we win!"
—Danny Dalton in *Syriana* (2005)

The security director leaned forward in his chair. It was hard to explain this to people outside the profession, but he loved chatting about industrial espionage with his colleagues. The enemy was clever, and who knew what it would come up with next?

Of course he was speaking from a privileged position, being the top dog for security in one of the biggest aeronautical corporations in North America. His foes were the high-end snoops who spent their time probing the perimeters of his industrial parks. In dealing with them, it didn't hurt that he had an excellent relationship with his government's security services: they kept him up to date on the background of foreign visitors, especially the occasional visitors who wished to "negotiate" or arrange exchange programs, and who might eventually prove to be spies.

One thing that made him a little uneasy was the extra vigour with which certain countries had been pursuing economic espionage lately. His people were finding spies in everyday commercial delegations they'd never had trouble with before. The security man had been around for a while, and his mind was sharp. He accepted that he wasn't going to catch every one of them, but at least he had the support of his executives and was able to attempt to catch the spies.

There had been two particularly ingenious incidents, and his mind often strayed back to them. One involved a Chinese delegation that had asked to visit the research division working on advanced ceramic tiles for jet engines. It was commonplace for business partners and possible clients to ask for these visits. But the Chinese hadn't asked in years, which was understandable given their country's reputation for economic espionage and theft. They knew that nobody wanted to see them. Times had changed, however, and the head of security had begun to feel it. Competition was fierce, and the directors of his company were obsessed with grabbing more market share. Security was not so much on their minds these days.

And then there was the fact that this particular Chinese company had asked for an "official visit." That was serious. It meant they were "studying" the possibility of a partnership or joint venture with his corporation. This didn't mean much to him personally, but he had certainly noticed how the board members started babbling excitedly about the size of the Chinese market. They were like teenage boys asking the homecoming queen for a date.

The security director wasn't happy about any of this. He had called for new measures to make sure the visitors didn't take any "souvenirs" for the trip home. In addition to previous measures, there would now be a voluntary personal search, a blanket rule against taking pictures, and a strongly enforced rule that electronic gear had to be checked in the lobby. Of course security personnel would accompany the visitors everywhere they went.

But the security boss was still anxious. He'd made time to join the Chinese visitors personally for their tours of the plant. He'd kept his eyes open as well, and he'd noticed something odd. It was the shoes. Nobody's shoes stay completely clean walking around a factory, of course. But the Chinese engineers' shoes were remarkably dirty. Stuff from the floor seemed almost to jump onto them. And one guy appeared to have breadcrumbs that clung improbably to his rather long tie.

The security man was a quick thinker, and he made up a rule on the spot that required the visitors to remove their shoes before moving on to the next department. The shoes were rushed to the lab, where he was amazed to learn that one of them contained a magnet that grabbed scraps of metal from the factory floor. As for the visitor with the exceedingly long tie, who had the annoying habit of leaning into garbage pails filled with scrap metal, they'd had to confront him. Damned if he didn't turn out to have a magnet in his tie as well.

This was the strangest example of reverse engineering he'd ever seen. The plan was clearly to take the precious scraps back to China and find out what chemical elements in what proportions had gone into fabricating them. These "visitors" meant to rob his company blind.

The second case had set him back on his heels even more. It was a classic manoeuvre out of a spy novel, but he hadn't thought it really could be done. A Japanese delegation consisting of six people had come to visit his company's design team. They had gone out of their way to flatter the team leader who'd invited them, marvelling at his "genius" and "hard work."

Then they'd asked if they might see the plans of one of the company's new technologies. Of course, it was understood that no photos could be taken.

But the visitors had a scheme. They had agreed in advance that four of them would concentrate on the blueprints while the others distracted their hosts with conversation. These four individuals had planned to study the document very carefully, agreeing to divide it into four quadrants. Each would memorize his own quadrant as completely as possible. As soon as the visit was over they raced back to their hotel, where they copied the plan as nearly as they could remember it.

Not all the details were there, but—as hoped—they'd nailed down enough for the specialists back in Japan to crack the puzzle. Their competitor's prized innovation was now in their pocket. The American company didn't suspect a thing until, several months later, the Japanese company came out with "its own version" of the product.

With a sinking feeling, the security director realized that the Japanese could not have caught up with his company's research simply through hard work or lucky guesses. Since they were safely out of the country by then, there was nothing he could do to find out more. So he brought the matter to the attention of the government counter-espionage service. After a good deal of investigation, the agency discovered how the visitors had done it. By intercepting the phone conversations of as many senior people in the Japanese company as possible, they snagged an exchange between two engineers. One was happily explaining to the other exactly how the amazing deed had been done.

This time the security director could honestly say that he hadn't seen it coming.

Although these stories seem improbable, the techniques described in them were actually used. Very creative methods, to say the least. There are as many ways of tricking people as there are tricksters— from the tracking devices for sale in spyware stores to the employment of the world's oldest profession (spying itself being probably the second oldest). And, as our examples show, new scenarios are being invented all the time.

It's important, in thinking about spying, to enumerate the different methodologies and understand them individually. For the purposes of this book, we need look at only two broad varieties of espionage: spying for advantage (meaning, to steal commercial, political, or military information) and spying in order to crush dissidence. These enterprises are different in objective and approach. We will also limit ourselves here to talking about spying as carried out by human beings (HUMINT). Technological espionage (SIGINT) is a different subject, and we will mention here only the different scenarios in which it may be used.

COLLECTING LEGAL INFORMATION

There is a popular belief that spying is always covert. But professional spies always look first to see how much information can be had in a perfectly legal fashion. This is especially true of competitive or economic intelligence gathering. Anybody can gather information that's freely (and even naively) offered by business enterprises. You can dig for it on the Internet or in a company's annual report, or in newspaper reports or specialty newsletters. It's generally agreed that when a security agency hands over its strategic analysis, 75 to 80 percent of the report will be composed of information from open sources.

The balance, what we might call the "added value," is the toughest to obtain. This is where the spy's finely honed sense of what is relevant in the mass of open information becomes useful. We sometimes speak of information gathering as a gigantic puzzle. The analyst doesn't always know what the image is that she's trying to reconstitute. The cleverness is in assembling all available clues and then making an inspired guess at what the whole picture should look like.

There's a difference between "information" and "intelligence." Information is what you collect during your research. Intelligence is the outcome of a process. This is the formula we use to describe how intelligence is produced:

Information + Analysis = Intelligence

The intelligence is the final product. You don't gather intelligence, you produce it.

We realize that we're making this point with a sledgehammer, but it's an important distinction, because it leads to unexpected insights. The most difficult for the non-professional to accept is this one: that you can't really protect yourself against a spy by locking your information in a steel box. The only thing that really works is to educate your employees as to exactly where, when, and with whom they can bring forth this information. Some information, of course, will always come out. The idea is to make it impossible for a hostile interlocutor to turn those scraps into intelligence. In the world of business, this comes down to knowing how to sell what you have, but refusing to sell it at any price.

YOUR INTERNET SITE

The unwelcome information gatherer will visit your website long before they visit you. Most websites are gold mines for spies. They will happily check out your services, your products, the neighbourhood where your offices or headquarters are located, how many people work for you, what kind of job positions you're trying to fill, who's on your board, how good the graphic quality of the site is, who your suppliers and distributors are, and contracts you bragged about. The competent investigator will soon know how big your operation is, its strategic direction, and its weaknesses.

For example, a certain American company was trying to enter the Australian market, but the Australian authorities systematically refused permission, year after year. Why? Because a simple Internet search told government analysts that the American company had signed a partnership deal with Singapore Telecommunications Limited. Now, SingTel is notorious among intelligence agencies around the world because it spies on everything that's carried over its equipment and shares the intelligence with the Singaporean government. To let the American company operate in Australia would have been tantamount to opening Australia's classified files to the authorities in Singapore.

Finally, the American company was advised that it had to modify its arrangement with SingTel before anything could happen. Once that was done, negotiations were soon underway for a profitable contract with Canberra.

EVERYBODY ELSE'S INTERNET SITE

Your competitors are interested in much more than your website and any useful government websites. They're also interested in anybody who might have written something about your company.

This could include journalists, pressure groups, unhappy former employees, companies you work with, or even your very good customer who feels like telling the world what they sold you or bought from you, and whether or not they're going into partnership with you.

A Canadian pharmaceutical company that manufactured drugs for a number of larger brand-name companies was bedevilled by a leakage of information on the Internet. When they finally tracked it down, they were very surprised.

It happened that this company had an admirable and generous program of hiring student interns. Their program let young people gain experience of their future profession, and gave the company the satisfaction of making a positive contribution to the community.

Admirable as it was, it backfired. One of the interns had produced really first-rate work. And being a diligent student, she wrote a full report for her professor once the internship was over. This was part of the academic program, and she did it in all innocence. And since the professor had asked her to submit it to his website, she did so. There it was, immediately available for the whole world to see.

None of this was improper. In fact, the pharmaceutical company knew all about it. But it had no internal policy systematically insisting on a review of the report before the student published it. In a spirit of youthful openness, the young woman's unreviewed report described every detail of her work environment, including the company's product lines and even the clients for whom they were being manufactured—clients who now found out that they were competing with each other!

Even worse, her supervisor at the pharmaceutical factory was so pleased with her work that the young woman was given the opportunity to work on product development. The company was developing a new drug that it hoped would dominate a segment of the market. This strategic coup had been in development for several years and cost many millions of dollars. The product was top secret . . . until the inexperienced intern started writing about it. The company paid dearly for its oversight. The new product did not do as well as hoped, and the embarrassing breach of client confidentiality caused the manufacturer to lose several large customers.

COMMERCIAL SHOWS

The big garden show or car show attracts the public, but it also attracts specialized firms that sell information gathered from the companies participating in these events. It's the perfect time and the perfect place. There, the visitor/spy finds a team of your company's best marketing people, and they're avidly looking to do well at the show. They're handing out bags chock full of pamphlets, photos, samples, and a thousand and one clever items intended to promote the company's products and services. A practised visitor can quickly pluck anything useful in the booth, including "samples" you weren't actually handing out but failed to nail down. Nobody would deny that these are useful events, but you want to be careful that they're useful to you and not to your worst enemy.

DIRECT SOLICITATION

It's legal for any company, including foreign ones, to approach you because they want to explore a possible purchase or joint project or even a partnership. The approach is often made by a diplomat from their country working on their behalf. In fact, it's part of a commercial attaché's job to identify companies that might want to do business with his country. Again, there is nothing illegal in this. But a company that has been approached might become enthusiastic about sharing information it normally wouldn't share, or permit visitors to examine sensitive sites. As we saw earlier, this can be an expensive blunder. You need to know how to control the movements of your visitors and make sure your employees are well coached about what they can and cannot say.

ECONOMIC, INDUSTRIAL, AND MILITARY ESPIONAGE

Espionage is invariably about getting a strategic advantage over an opponent or competitor. Illegal in itself, it invites the commission of further illegal activity: deliberate arson, theft, bribing your employees, bugging your telephones, and even—it is far from unheard of—assassination. Here is a sampling of some favourite methods.

UNSOLICITED REQUESTS FOR INFORMATION

This is the most common technique. It happens when a company receives an unexpected request from another business, or a diplomat, or a person desiring information about its products or the company itself. This can be innocuous, but it might be an early warning of aggressive steps to come. Eventually, the contact asks for additional information. Then they ask if they can visit. The more serious they appear to be, the more the company's employees become co-operative. In an honest transaction, being co-operative is a good thing. But if the party making inquiries has another agenda, everyday helpfulness might be disastrous.

The foreign company or agency might hire a local consultant to approach you. This person might also have been asked to make a list of all the companies working in a specific domain, which is a way for the foreign operation to look around and see what's what. The consultant will want to know about products, personnel, suppliers, and anything else pertinent. He or she might inquire about a group visit to your factory. Everything the consultant learns will go straight to the government or security service that asked for it.

MEDIA VISITS

Watch out! This is the second-most-popular trick. Foreign agents show up in the guise of a television crew working on a documentary about a particular industry—yours. This is an almost irresistible proposal, because the company approached right away imagines a great whack of free international promotion coming its way. Quite a few foreign undercover services have filmed with complete liberty inside a target corporation and walked away with important information. Sadly, the film is never seen by the public, only by the competition.

Film crews and associated journalists will show up with all manner of equipment (cameras, microphones, booms, lighting). Almost all of it serves directly to capture additional information. It's a multidisciplinary menace, combing HUMINT, SIGINT, and IMINT.* The camera will pick up scraps of conversation, the sounds of machinery, and various other noises that can be used as a reference base, or what is sometimes called "Ground Truth." When compared with the imagery on the film, sound and other types of input can be used to verify earlier information or to help build a theory about what is going on in the factory in question. An agent can also use specialized film stock: for example, infrared or heat-sensitive film. Other devices can be attached to a camera to

---

* Human intelligence (HUMINT), signals intelligence (SIGINT), and image intelligence (IMINT).

record the temperature, or take air samples, or read the spectrum of the ambient light. This becomes MASINT (Measurement and Signature Intelligence).

This kind of operation is not always undertaken by a company or country trying to play catch-up. It may well be an entity that has a dominant position in your company's industry, and wants to cement its advantage by knowing whether you have had any break-throughs that might threaten it.

THE CARE AND FEEDING OF MOLES

From the undercover agent's point of view, there's no replacing human sources. Of course, it's possible for a foreign agent to infil-trate a company, but it always takes a lot of time, and the results are often not the ones he'd counted on. Sometimes it makes more sense to recruit a person already working there. This is the classic "mole": somebody with an in-and-out swipe card who knows pretty well which of their fellow employees have access to which infor-mation. And since everyone in the targeted workplace knows the mole already, they trust him or her. She can go quietly about her job, picking up bits of information here and there. And when the time comes, her contact (the person we call a "controller") can ask her to do specific jobs. These might include identifying other potential moles, or even carrying out precisely targeted acts of sabotage. In a way, the mole is the perfect double agent.

Before attempting a recruitment, the spy-master builds a psy-chological profile of the person he's interested in. The part that really interests him is the inevitable weakness or sensitive area that might lead the potential mole to an act of betrayal. To identify it, recruiting agents have a useful acronym that sums up the four great areas of human vulnerability. Whatever brings the potential mole to cross the line invariably fits into one of them: money, ideology, sex, or ego/emotion. The acronym is "MISE."

How do recruiters find the weak point of a particular person? They study them with a practised eye. Is this party covetous, always longing for something he doesn't have? Or is the person an ideologue, angered and embittered by the company's views and corporate behaviour? Or does he have sexual desires—or sexual preferences—that aren't easy to satisfy? Those are the first three. Everything else fits into "ego/emotion." This is where we find the person who wants revenge for a perceived slight she has suffered within the corporation; or else he is vain, believing himself brighter than everybody else and wanting power commensurate with his self-image.

Once the bait is taken, the mole cannot change her mind.

The biggest danger for the recruiter is a poor analysis of the desired mole. Say the recruiter has settled on which button to push, and pushed it. But he has misjudged, and the person in question finds the internal resources to say "no." That's when the recruiter finds himself in very big trouble. It's not just that he's wasted months of time and effort. Now the person he hoped to turn into a lovely mole is a fully equipped viper. And it's all his fault. She knows who he is, and right away the counter-espionage service of the country whose language and culture he's spent so much time learning is hot on his trail. The aborted mole will have told the counter-espionage folks everything she knows about him, and he has to hightail it to the emergency exit. If he doesn't get there fast enough, he will be formally deported as *persona non grata*.

Even before attempting a recruitment, the spy-master should know exactly what he is trying to find out. Then he has to figure out who has access to it. Out of that group, he must now identify the individual likeliest to be recruited. This means building up a detailed file of personal information on all the potential targets, learning the particular weakness of each, and then finally selecting the likeliest candidate.

Certain foreign services have specialists for this job. China has agents called "talent spotters" who do nothing but identify susceptible individuals. Once the person is chosen, a different agent steps in to do the actual recruiting. The target never knows who chose them originally, only the person who approached them. And that's the only person in the network with whom they will ever have dealings. This is their controller.

For counter-espionage agencies, the toughest kind of mole to deal with is the one who has been trained to carry out a long-term project. These moles are agents themselves, in that they receive training on how to use a false name when applying for work with, say, a government agency. On other occasions they simply use their own name. In August 2008 we learned of a case in which Japanese authorities arrested a Russian agent (of the old KGB, now SVR) who was himself Asian and had apparently worked for Russia for more than thirty years. The man had usurped the identity of a Japanese man named Ichiro Kuroba, a dental engineer who had mysteriously disappeared in 1965. The authorities still don't know the real identity of this KGB agent, but they know that he got a job with a Japanese weapons manufacturer and stayed there for three decades. His wife, who was Japanese, never suspected a thing.

There's an equally interesting case involving a Chinese agent, Larry Chin Wu-Tai, who worked for 35 years for the Central Intelligence Agency as a translator. During that time he betrayed a fair number of CIA undercover agents in China, all of whom were executed. Chin also got access to large amounts of secret information. His value was such that a spy from the Chinese Ministry of State Security had been specially trained to snatch Chin and get him safely out when the moment came.

Now we come to the specifics of how this kind of thing is done. If the mole is important enough, the agency will do almost anything to save him. The spy watching over Chin, for example, was a Chinese intelligence officer named Mark Cheung, who had studied theology and parish duties so that he could impersonate a Catholic priest (in real life back in China he had a wife and child). He actually worked for a number of years as a parish priest in south-east Asia in order to create a "legend" (a background history) for himself. He eventually moved to New York to be near Chin, taking up spiritual duties as a priest in the Church of the Transfiguration, located in the Chinese quarter.

But in the end, after all the years of preparation, Cheung did not have time to accomplish his mission. Chin was arrested and committed suicide in his cell using a plastic bag.

BLACKMAIL

A spy's bag of tricks is full of all kinds of things, but blackmail retains its perennial popularity. A secret service will invest considerable energy in putting an individual in an awkward spot, the kind where there's no way out short of betraying one's company, one's government, or even one's own best interests. The possible scenarios are infinite but can usually be described as corruption, seduction, or the exchange of sexual favours.

The whole thing often occurs during a holiday or business trip abroad, when the vacationer or travelling executive is alone and even disoriented. Depending on the individual's personality, he might also be tempted to take risks, reasoning that nobody can know about it since he's in a place where he doesn't know anybody. A useful policy for the person who finds himself in this situation: If it seems too good to be true, it's probably neither good nor true.

Private enterprise and government agencies have learned that the best way to protect their employees from blackmail is to give them awareness training before they leave, and debrief them when they come back. This allows the employee to admit an indiscretion and get help if need be. The human resources department of many a corporation now subjects employees to periodic security checks, with additional checks when the employee returns from a trip abroad.

THE "WALK-INS"

Occasionally an enterprising individual will, like Faust, sell himself to the devil. This individual will approach a foreign service or corporation and offer to make a deal. This is not, however, as easy as it sounds. You're not going to be accepted simply because you walked through the door. Foreign intelligence services are very suspicious of potential traps or "sting operations."

An infamous case that caused a great deal of harm to Canada was that of Gilles Brunet, an RCMP officer during the 1960s and '70s. His code name was "Tango." According to KGB General Oleg Kalugin, who was Tango's controller, it was Brunet himself who first approached the KGB. What he had to offer was substantial. He would undertake to neutralize the Mounties' counter-espionage department as well as its information-gathering abilities, and he would do this over a period of years. And who would suspect him, given that he was the son of an RCMP assistant commissioner?

Brunet should have been discovered earlier, since his lifestyle was well beyond the means of any RCMP officer. But he was popular with his supervisors. Later, he tried to make himself untouchable by delivering shocking revelations to the Keable Commission: this is how the world learned about illegal sabotage carried out by the RCMP to undermine the Parti Québécois. In retrospect, it's clear that these acts of sterling virtue were actually part of Brunet's plan to destabilize and neutralize Canada's entire counter-espionage mechanism, which he did.

OPENING THE MAIL

Steaming an envelope is neither as old-fashioned nor as uncommon as one might think. In Canada it is sometimes risked by private detectives, but not often, because it's a criminal act with heavy consequences. It's also easy to get caught doing it. But none of this applies once you leave Canada. Certain national security services simply open all the mail that comes from foreign countries, plucking confidential corporate information and occasionally uncovering a juicy traitor or two.

A Canadian company that learned about this, to its sorrow, had been invited to tender for a contract worth more than $100 million, in Turkey. The only competing bid came from France. Once its own bid was ready, the Canadian company hired a reputable international air courier service to make sure it arrived safely. When the employee in charge of managing the bid did a routine check to make sure that everything was in order, he was dismayed to learn that the package had not been delivered. The courier company had no explanation. Unfortunately it also had no liability, since the contract stated that it could not guarantee delivery overseas.

The courier company offered to resend the package at its own

NEST OF SPIES 299

expense, but the sender no longer felt confident that it would get through. The sender quickly prepared a second parcel, knowing that the deadline had almost arrived. This time a different courier made the delivery, and the package arrived . . . late. The deadline had passed, and the Canadian company was disqualified.

Some weeks later, the Canadians received news that the French contender had been awarded the contract. Strangely, their proposal had very similar features to those offered in the Canadian proposal. The officers of the Canadian company couldn't help but wonder whether the French government had intercepted the package containing their bid. And it's quite likely that it did. Intercepting packages is an everyday thing in France, and it's done on a large scale by the state security services. Had the Canadian company bought a round-trip airfare to Turkey and sent an employee with the $100-million bid, it would have been an excellent investment.

GARBAGE PICKING

What a glamorous business we have here! From dumpster-diving to the delicate sifting of monsieur's kitchen scraps, the trained agents of a nation's lofty secret service organizations rub elbows with gumshoes and peepers from back-alley agencies. It's always amazing to see the kinds of stories that show up in the newspapers, where top-secret corporate material ends up in the worst possible hands. (Consider, for example, the case of WestJet and Air Canada, discussed in Chapter 003, in relation to industrial espionage.)

In the uncertain game of espionage, the other person's wastebasket is the nearest thing to a sure thing that we have. Every company must know where its sensitive paperwork is at any time of day, and there must be a clear policy stating when each document will be destroyed, and that it must be destroyed by burning or shredding. A document might look out of date and irrelevant to a company comptroller, but it's a treasure map so far as an industrial spy is concerned.

In this day and age, it is surprising how often an expert goes in to evaluate a company's security measures and finds that it doesn't own a paper shredder. What could be cheaper and easier to buy? Even the smallest bare-bones startup can afford a fifty-dollar shredder that will do a perfectly acceptable job.

One exception to this rule that every executive should know: Don't purchase any shredder, costly or not, that slices pages into thin longitudinal strips. These can always be glued back together, especially when nobody thinks to jumble the strips before throwing them out. Get the diagonal-cut model.

Other companies might decide to contract document management and destruction to an outside specialist. But the normal rule of business applies: contractors want to maximize their profit, and this task is far too important for cheese-paring. Remember the adage that says you are never so well served as by yourself. At the very least, if there has to be an outside contractor, the manager must insist on having an employee witness the destruction and ensure it is done properly.

EXCHANGES OF ENGINEERS AND TECHNICIANS
This is a reliable and popular method of slipping one's agents into a targeted competitor's operation. When a delegation arrives at your front door, it will contain a number of spies with a tightly designed plan for stealing information. Sometimes these delegations are made up entirely of spies.

This is the moral of an unfortunate tale told by a well-known Canadian corporation, dominant in its market, that accepted an offer to build a partnership with a Chinese company. As a condition of the arrangement, the Chinese bosses insisted on sending a team of twenty-five engineers and technicians for a lengthy working visit to their Canadian "partner." Considering the stakes, the CEO of the Canadian enterprise disregarded his security director's warnings and pleas.

The security man, seeing that there was no way to change course, decided to do the next best thing and prepare an elaborate reception for the guests. They would work in a facility well removed from the company's secure areas, with strict controls on the visitors' movements and hidden cameras everywhere. Certain databases were blocked, and company security people were assigned to escort the visitors everywhere they went. The visitors' workplace did not contain a single photocopier, and the telephones could not make long distance calls. What more could anyone do?

As soon as they arrived, the Chinese visitors were told exactly what the situation was: no freedom of movement, no printer, no copying, no USB keys, and above all no access to restricted databases.

Three days later the visitors were politely invited to repeat the entire information session. During that seventy-two-hour period the Chinese engineers had broken into each and every one of the forbidden databases.

Less than a day after the second information session, a hidden security camera recorded a Chinese technician busily taking photographs of a computer screen full of confidential information.

So far, so bad—but at least familiar. What really went beyond all limits in this episode was the reaction of the company's CEO when the "visitors" were unmasked. This occurred at a board meeting where the CEO was present. When the security director had finished exhibiting the evidence and drawing his conclusions, the CEO asked to speak. He curtly informed the security director that his comments were "immoderate" and that the presentation was "not exactly what we were looking for." In effect, the company did not want to know what was going on. The security director was later warned that "fear mongering" was bad for his career.

FRONT COMPANIES

Quite a lot of foreign security agencies use front companies. It's a sophisticated and costly undertaking, but the benefits it returns down the road make the expense well worthwhile. Chief among these is the ability to ignore the laws of the country in which the agency wishes to operate, and to avoid embargoes on the exportation of desired technology. They are a useful "honeypot," in the sense that investigators get stuck trying to figure them out while the operators behind the front company can't be reached. It's not surprising that we see more and more of them: China may have implanted as many as ten thousand in the United States and Canada. Russia has a hundred, and Iran a few dozen. There is no reason to think they are alone in using the technique.

The Financial Transactions Reports Analysis Centre of Canada (FINTRAC) reported in 2008 that it had located a network of spies working in Canada since 2002. By setting up and doing business through front companies, they had bought more than $35 million of technology over a five-year period. The information had immediately been forwarded to another country.

It's deplorable that FINTRAC chose not to reveal the name of the country that was pulling the strings in this operation. As in the case of the company executive we have just discussed, it seems likely that there was corporate pressure on FINTRAC to avoid embarrassing a foreign power that might retaliate with trade and commercial barriers. Obviously, little thought was given to other corporations that desperately need to know which country was behind the spy network. How are they to protect themselves?

Since we always enjoy filling the potholes that federal cleanup crews never get to, let's just say, with a wink and a nod, that Iran is well known for its use of front companies when it is interested in that kind of technology. If your business is involved with nuclear research, high-pressure pipes, or special gauges or pumps, the previous sentence is directed especially to you.

It's not surprising that so many countries use front companies. It's as close as they can come to laying hands on restricted information without technically breaking the law. To understand how this works, consider the August 1980 case in which the Mounties arrested three Montrealers linked to a Pakistani scam to skirt the embargo on materials essential to making weapons-grade uranium. Embargoed reversers and condensers manufactured by General Electric were bought in the United States by a small Montreal electronics company. This company was (and still is) run by a prominent member of Quebec's Muslim community. The plan was to ship the devices through Dubai to Pakistan. But fortunately the merchandise was seized at Mirabel Airport moments before being loaded on a cargo plane.

Credit for this remarkable bust goes to Canadian diplomats posted to Islamabad who alerted the RCMP to an impending visit by a pair of fake Pakistani diplomats. These two men claimed they were sent to verify the books of the Montreal consulate on Drummond Street. In reality, they were officers of Pakistan's nuclear energy agency. Shadowing teams reported that they never once actually visited the consulate where they were supposed to be working. They spent their time at the front company. It became clear that their real job was to steal technology that was under embargo.

Serious as the matter was, the outcome was yet another law-yers-and-courtrooms judicial farce. The three accused got off on twelve out of thirteen charges. When the Court of Appeal then decided that there had to be an entirely new trial, the Crown attor-ney's substitute in 1988 signed a nolle prosequi against two of the three and the Montreal company—meaning they got off scot-free. The owner of the company defended himself tenaciously, declar-ing that the incriminating parts were intended to be used in a textile factory.

For the Canadian agents who brought the affair to light, how-ever, it was a positive outcome. "The whole idea of it was to rattle them," said one, some years later.

It's not easy to identify a front company. That's why legitimate companies and government officials have to be extremely alert and pay attention to security warnings from lawyers or CSIS. The intel-ligence agency doesn't yet offer this as a service to business, but perhaps one day it will have the foresight to become more proactive on behalf of our beleaguered entrepreneurs.

TECHNOLOGY THEFT, TECHNOLOGY COPYING

This is the quickest way to get one's hands on a company's indus-trial secrets. There are innumerable ways of doing it—as many as there are thieves. But it's important to remember that an employee is often involved when information walks off the premises. This seems to be true in about 75 percent of cases. That's why it's so important to have a hiring policy that calls for a background check of anybody applying for a job, however junior. In the operations of the CIBC, one of the country's largest banks, it's standard pro-cedure to repeat the background check every time an employee is promoted to a sensitive position. The policy costs money, but it is far more costly if even a single act of information theft becomes public. Especially in the case of a bank, the damage to a hard-earned reputation could be almost irreparable.

For smaller companies, and companies working in sectors where public perception is less important than it is for banks, it's not necessary to be so obsessively vigilant. But there are simple steps to take, which can prevent a lot of future trouble. The company can, for instance, ask the job candidate to drop by her local police station and get a document certifying that she has no criminal record. It costs around $25, and it can be obtained only by the individual concerned. An employer has the right to demand it, and can offer to reimburse the fee as an incentive. This is the low-cost approach to getting a background check. Of course, the absence of a criminal record hardly guarantees that the person is a paragon of virtue, but it does keep the actual criminals away from your front door. And it tells your other employees that you care what sort of people they are being asked to work with.

So far as copying somebody else's product is concerned, one of the notable scandals of recent years concerns the Ontario-based Research In Motion (RIM) company, creators of the famous BlackBerry personal assistant technology. This clever new device attracted Chinese attention. China Unicom didn't so much as blush when it put its "RedBerry" on the market in 2006. This kind of imitation is the most insincere form of flattery.

INFORMATION DESTRUCTION

Sometimes, when stealing looks like too much hard work, why not just wreck the thing instead? Believe it or not, a competitor can make a considered judgment that destroying the innovator's information will leave him (the competitor) in as good a position as if he had stolen and copied it. It also has the advantage of being a sure thing, as opposed to the uncertainties of bringing out a copy and getting laughed at because you called it a "RedBerry."

This kind of economic warfare is practised by both corporations and governments. The simplest form is the cyber-attack. Once a virus or a Trojan horse has been launched into the competitor's information system, it's possible to damage every copy of the proprietary software.

Then there is the tactic of eliminating the researchers. We wish this were a tongue-in-cheek way of suggesting they be bribed, but we are in fact talking about murdering them. The pharmaceutical research industry has a remarkable reputation for brutality. The development and marketing of a single new medication costs on average $800 million, which means that a professional killer's $50,000–$60,000 tab is just so much small change once the competing company's two or three lead project researchers have been identified. In Russia these kinds of contracts are almost standard business procedure. Valentin Stepankov, who is the undersecretary of the Council for Russian Security, has publicly admitted that there were more than 5,000 contract assassinations in his country in the year 2003 alone. More than half the victims were business owners or executives.

In countries where getting away with murder isn't quite so easy, there are less drastic alternatives. A Taiwanese company eliminated a competitive threat from an American counterpart by simply offering to double the salaries of its lead researchers. Out of the five scientists in question, four jumped at the opportunity. In one fell swoop the Taiwanese acquired all the strategic knowledge of its competitor, and struck a fatal blow to the U.S. research group.

INTERCEPTING ELECTRONIC COMMUNICATIONS

Once the exclusive preserve of the sophisticated thief with access to an excellent laboratory, a whole new generation of "gadgets" can now be purchased on the Internet or in the so-called spy stores that have sprung up in major cities. Since these are affordable, the do-it-yourself spy business has exploded in the last few years.

Let those who can afford it continue to build cars with flamethrowers and to train dolphins as assassins. For the rest of us, high-tech spying has been modestly democratized. Swiss researchers at the University of Lausanne have shown that it is possible to "sniff" the electromagnetic signals given off by most common devices, usually by measuring the electrical current consumed, but sometimes by actually detecting the energy signal of the minuscule component itself. The clever Swiss have demonstrated that they can read information contained on devices as far as twenty metres away, including material recorded on eleven common USB and PS/2 keys sold between 2001 and 2008.

Electronic snooping in foreign countries is much more common and more casual than it is in Canada. Some national security services simply call the hotel where a foreign delegation is going to stay and arrange to drop by and bug the premises from ceiling to floor. When the visitors arrive they find that their room has already been selected. The custom decor includes cameras, microphones, and electronic bugs that can be remotely switched on and off. The former Soviet bloc, demonstrating a rare sense of practicality and efficiency, simply designated certain hotels for foreign use exclusively, and customized them accordingly. The joke was, "In Russia, you don't watch television, the television watches you!" Now that Putin and the ancient artists of the KGB are running the show in the new Russia, we should expect more of the same, but hopefully with better jokes.

We're not being entirely facetious here. This kind of thing still occurs, as the director of a major Canadian company recently learned. For once setting aside their legendary tight-lipped tradition, CSIS investigators demanded an urgent meeting with him before he left for Europe. The timing was important, because he was scheduled to participate in an important brainstorming session concerning the European market for his business products.

The Canadian agents had something important to tell him. They had learned that the executive's telephone and mobile phone had been tapped for some time by a European security service, one of whose national companies had made detailed plans for grabbing his company's share of the market. The scheming company was privately owned, but like a lot of European enterprises it worked hand in hand with the national security service in order to dominate its market sector. It also used private investigators prepared to break the law.

There was worse to come. On arrival, it seems, our gentleman would be greeted at the airport by his patiently waiting European counterparts, good people who had no doubt already arranged for him to sleep in a thoroughly "soundproofed" hotel room. The Canadian executive was simply stupefied.

Now he had to learn what to do about it. By way of elementary self-defence, said the security people, he should absolutely not use his own mobile phone during commercial negotiations. "It's better to buy a prepaid cellphone without a subscription as soon as you get there," he was advised. And this wasn't even one of the ethically challenged countries that had been dominated by Communists and fascists for most of the twentieth century. This was one of Europe's reliable old powers. Clearly not so reliable any more.

There are specialized businesses that know how to inspect offices, automobiles, and private homes. They often work with businesses that have learned that "threat agents" are testing their external security but need help identifying them. These are often low-profile businesses that have invested a lot of money in cutting-edge technology. The company hired to identify the threats might prefer to work at night time, after the client business has shut down, because experience has taught them that during the daytime there are moles, and the mole would warn his controller that the place was going to be swept for listening devices.

BREAKING INTO HOTEL ROOMS AND AUTOMOBILES

Quite a few travelling executives think it's impressive to go about carrying high-level business information that actually hasn't got a thing to do with the trip they're taking. Like Boy Scouts, they want to be prepared for everything. Unlike Boy Scouts, they're going to have their pockets picked. Whether their information is recorded on a disc, sitting in their laptop, stored in their BlackBerry, or just stuffed into an attaché case, it hasn't occurred to them that they need to keep an eye on it twenty-four hours a day. In less than no time, a capable team of thieves with electronics expertise can copy their papers and drain their laptops. Even the worldliest executive can fall victim to such a theft.

Consider the Russian spy-diplomat who came visiting some years ago. He had adopted some Canadian habits. He especially enjoyed the convenience of dropping off his clothes at a dry cleaner in the mall. One day, during the few minutes that it took him to park the car, carry his things to the cleaner, drop them off, and return to his car, a number of things happened. Canadian operatives disabled the car alarm, jimmied the lock, opened his attaché case, photographed the documents inside, put everything back where it was, closed the doors, and locked up the car. Is there a hack spy-film writer who wouldn't feel honoured to watch those guys at work?

FOREIGN INTERFERENCE

Around the world, many businesses are in the habit of co-operating with their national spy agencies. Western businesses are no exception. We all naively associate this behaviour with the traditional "bad guys," especially China, Russia, and, since the mullahs took over, Iran. Lately, though, it's hard not to notice that western businesses are out slumming in the same neighbourhoods. For the past twenty years, England, France, and the United States have admitted that they are instructing their espionage services to go on the offensive. This is because they have belatedly recognized that commercial negotiations don't take place in some Adam Smith fantasy of an ideal marketplace. They have to protect their national interests, and that means protecting their great national corporations.

REMEMBER, NINE-TENTHS OF AN ICEBERG IS UNDER WATER . . .

The underhanded methods mentioned so far are just a small sampling of what is taking place. International spies, just like the fraudsters who can be found in many corporations, are imaginative when it comes to making off with proprietary secrets. Back in the 1970s, a mole was discovered inside the enormous American defence contractor called TRW. Among other things, TRW had a contract to receive secret messages from overseas on behalf of the U.S. government. The traitorous employee, Christopher Boyce, was the son of an FBI agent. This is the detail that made the story so irresistible to Hollywood, which turned it into the movie *The Falcon and the Snowman*.

Boyce had for many years been a walk-in and a voluntary mole working for the KGB. Part of his testimony to the U.S. Senate Committee on Security and Information was a charmingly simple little story that shows why the human factor will always be the weak link in security. Boyce, it seems, liked to enjoy himself by thinking up new ways of slipping information out of TRW's campus. One day he asked a security guard to help him carry a houseplant from his desk to his car. Inside the pot he had hidden a pile of microfilms, which were now on their way to his Soviet controller.

Who'd want to live in a world where you can't help a guy with his houseplant? But we do.

CHAPTER 008

How to Protect Yourself . . . a Little Better

Genius resides in the capacity for evaluation of uncertain, hazardous, and conflicting information.
—Sir Winston Churchill

There is a new threat, a real one, and during the years ahead it will very likely become even greater than it was during the Cold War. Nowadays it arises from inside our society as much as it does from outside, and, like Proteus, it changes shapes and methods and can be hard to spot. An effective response is impossible so long as our governments and legislatures lack the will and capacity for action. And without leadership, our police and investigative services can't do much.

This means that chief executive officers, if they want anything done, need to roll up their sleeves and do it themselves. These days there is scarcely anybody outside the corporation who is in a position to protect its hard-won proprietary information. And even if the authorities awaken from their long sleep, every citizen, particularly those employed in cutting-edge industries, will still have a role to play in the workplace. The executive suites also need to take the matter more seriously.

At the same time, it's not reasonable to expect everybody to become a security expert. Fortunately, there are relatively simple steps you can take that can shrink the problem somewhat. In a few cases, do-it-yourself techniques can eliminate it altogether.

Our intention in writing this book was always that it should be more than a simple tallying of important battles won and lost in the world of espionage. And don't look for a prophet with a booming voice, returning from the desert to announce the end of the world—or even the end of intellectual property rights. We feel that this is a manageable problem, and we want to offer readers a constructive and practical approach to dealing with it. For that reason, this chapter is addressed to senior executives, their security people, and every employee who wants to do their bit to make the workplace more secure.

THE METHODICAL APPROACH

It's the age-old game of predator versus prey. The predators, who don't usually wear trench coats these days, are out testing the defences and looking for the weak point, the thin wall that yields when pushed. But evolution teaches us a lesson about predators: you don't have to kill them—all you need to do is make yourself harder to eat. In other words, make it difficult for them, and they will go somewhere else.

At the same time, if your company has developed a unique product or promising line of research, then it's going to be harder to discourage a spy. You will need to prepare a good defence. Not to do so will prove very costly.

Here are the three principles we work with:

• Proactive is better than reactive.
• More security doesn't mean better security.
• Your organization's culture and values are a far better defence
  than lockboxes and alarms.

Using these principles, you'll be in a good position to decide which security consultant and which proposed measures are worthwhile, without becoming a specialist yourself. Think in terms of better quality security, and don't be seduced by more security equipment and more guards. Put another way, if your consultant keeps bringing the conversation back to gadgetry and electronics, beware: he or she may be little more than a manufacturer's agent looking to sell the gear. Call it the "gear-through-fear" approach.

Every enterprise needs some security equipment, of course, but it can never be a panacea. And before spending a nickel, the company's executives and security staff must analyze the kind of threat they are confronted with. Otherwise, you're playing football with a catcher's mitt.

Six Important Steps Toward a Spyproof Workplace

These six steps will be useful to a company's senior executives. They will give you a framework for thinking about the problem. As a bonus, they will also help you size up the specialists you're going to have to hire.

1. Recognize that there is a threat.
2. Adapt your business practices to the new reality.
3. Perform a Threat and Risk Assessment (TRA) to identify your vulnerabilities.
4. Make corporate security an executive-level responsibility.

5. Create a permanent and ongoing program for employee training and awareness.
6. Demand periodic security checks and audits.

1. RECOGNIZE THAT THERE IS A THREAT.

In a business where each executive already has more than enough work to do, there's a temptation to ignore hypothetical questions, especially about industrial espionage. "See no evil, hear no evil" seems to be the motto. But imagine for a moment that your intellectual property is in somebody else's hands. Or that your competitor suddenly knows everything about your strategic projects.

In our experience, the most difficult thing to fight is not the espionage itself, but rather the persistence of some CEOs in ignoring the facts. Even when the proof is in front of them—whether it be a snippet of film, the names of compromised employees, actual events, or sworn testimony—they can't bring themselves to acknowledge it.

The weakness of people who have fought hard to get to the top is that they find it hard to admit that there are aspects to the business they can't handle. But security, by definition, requires specialists. If executives don't acknowledge that, then there's a tendency to dismiss those who raise the alarm as paranoid, or as grifters trying to make work for themselves, or as being the guy with the hammer who thinks everything is a nail. There's also a lurking fear that if the worst proves to be true, it's the chief executive and his officers who will take the blame.

If you're still reading, however, you might be one of those with a healthy survival instinct. Perhaps you've even begun to think of commercial self-defence as a sound strategic investment.

You've become proactive.

Those for whom security is just another cost are condemned to act only when catastrophe strikes; that's the reactive mode. And for them, it's only a matter of time before it does. On the other hand, those who understand that security is a strategic investment, something that will heighten their stature with the public and with their business partners, are proactive managers. They're demonstrating that they understand international events and the threats these present. They also demonstrate good sense by acting *before* a crisis, which is always less costly than repairing the damage afterward.

To better understand the difference between proactive and reactive management, look at the following figure. The solid black line indicates a normal level of company activity, while the solid grey represents a minimal level of activity. Whenever a crisis of

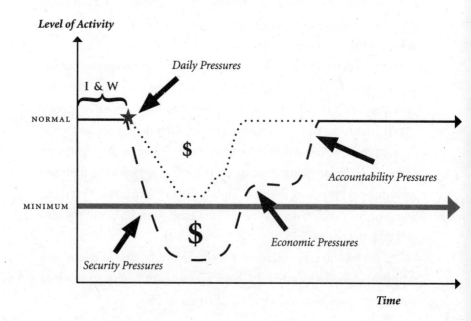

any kind occurs, a business normally sees a drop in productivity.*
Depending on the severity of the crisis and the level of preparation,
the shock may continue for days, weeks, or months.

When it comes to crisis management, a majority of security companies offer services that are implicitly focused on the "after-the-crisis"
model. These will include a business resumption plan, a series of
backup options or contingency plans, emergency measures, a rapid-
response team, and so on. These represent sound business practices,
but they're only relevant *after* the crisis. A company must also have
a plan to fight the crisis at the moment it occurs. Without that, the
damage will take longer to fix and the financial cost will be greater
(see the "reactive" approach, represented as a line of dashes). If the
company's directors wait for a crisis to happen, they will incur maximum costs to return the operation to a normal level of activity.

On the other hand, if the crisis has been anticipated (with a well-
prepared system that sounds the alert while the threat can still be
intercepted), it can be contained and followed by a rapid recovery.
When it's over, the financial loss will be modest, or at least reduced.

Common sense tells us, of course, that a crisis can't always be
averted. This was obviously the case with the September 11, 2001,
attacks. And on a more local and comprehensible scale, there was
the remarkable ice storm of 1998, which shut down the entire
city of Montreal. A crisis prepared for, however, is still a crisis
reduced.

2. ADAPT YOUR BUSINESS PRACTICES TO THE NEW REALITY.
Oddly enough, economic/industrial espionage is less a question
of security per se than of business practices and enterprise culture.

---

* It doesn't matter what kind of crisis. If it's sufficiently serious, the unprotected
enterprise will founder.

Everything comes back to information management and the quality of the personnel. Given the omnipresent awareness of electronic issues, this is perhaps the place to underline that we are not just talking about information technology (IT) security or computer security. They are just one piece of the puzzle. The real question is whether the company communicates its business philosophy to all of its employees, and whether that is reflected in human resources practices (from hiring to firing). The key is enterprise culture.

This in turn brings us back to the human factor, always the weakest link. It can be either the problem or the solution, depending on how it is handled. At the end of work each day the departing employees walk past the cameras on the walls, the guards at the doors, and the bars on the windows. This does nothing to diminish the fact that when they reach the parking lot they still have a considerable amount of corporate information in their heads (and sometimes in their briefcases). Information management means managing all the information. Here is a list, by no means exhaustive, of the ways that strategic information can leave your building like smoke up a chimney.

- Employee lunchtime conversations in the park, or hanging out in a local café after hours, where conversation can easily be overheard.
- Marketing fairs, colloquia, conferences. Your most valuable employees are likely to be the best trained and most specialized. They love to talk about their work, but most people aren't knowledgeable enough to hold up the other end of the conversation. Now imagine one of your scientists, far from home, standing around in your booth at the technology fair when a charming person tells him that he's just been longing to talk about cytoplasmology, it's his personal passion.
- Somebody new comes into your employee's life. Here we will

risk the wrath of the politically correct by pointing out that an administrative assistant's knowledge of the company is still inversely proportional to his or her status. In other words, he or she knows a lot but doesn't get much respect. Except from this charming new colleague who just popped up out of nowhere . . .

- Those interning students and visiting expert delegations.
- The foreign delegation that is terribly excited by the prospect of a joint venture with your company, even though you've never seen them before.
- The disgruntled employee.
- The "problem player" employee who is over his head in debt, or has a gambling problem.
- The chatty marketing department, which thinks that the more they say the more they'll sell. Take a good look at what's in those brochures.
- If we stop the list here, you can probably add a few of your own.

But just as the employees are best situated to leak corporate information, they are also best situated to protect it. If the employee notices senior people speaking discreetly on the phone, and being careful not to copy sensitive material, he or she will develop similar reflexes. If a manager takes the precaution of calling security, even if the problem doesn't seem major, then the employee will learn that it's okay to check with security if she sees anything dubious. A company like that has already built the larger part of its security protection. Security alertness has to start with top management and filter down to the factory floor. Remember: security is everybody's business.

3. PERFORM A THREAT AND RISK ASSESSMENT (TRA) TO IDENTIFY YOUR VULNERABILITIES.

Nobody can claim to be making use of their security program if they don't know what kinds of threats the company faces. All too often one sees the "standard" program, which is nothing but a copy of the sort of thing that people think they are supposed to buy: the camera, the electronic scanner at the entrance (access control), corporate anti-virus software—in short, the copycat version of a reactive "sitting duck" security system. And it gets worse when people start buying additional gear to confront the latest urban legend or the scary headlines in yesterday's newspaper. Some security salesmen have fear-mongering down to a fine art: they might even bring along a scrapbook full of scary headlines. None of this adds up to good service for you.

If you are serious about this, your first step should be to arrange for a periodic Threat and Risk Assessment, or TRA. Without it, both you and your security people are working in the dark. There is really no better way to get a methodical and objective sizing up of your situation. The TRA will, for example, do a detailed reading of the physical environment in your office or plant. Periodic readings of this sort let you monitor anything that changes, including things that shouldn't be changing.

Here's a way to be certain that the people doing the TRA are doing it properly. In its simplest form, there should be two elements to the procedure:

- Threat To: identify the sensitive elements of your operation that must be protected.
- Threat From: identify where the threat is coming from, or who wants to hurt you (often called "threat agents").

The first threat is a matter of common sense, and relatively simple. Nine out of ten security companies—the people already working for you—have the experience and good sense to be able to help specialists identify the sensitive components, key individuals, or intellectual property that require protection.

Unfortunately, the second element is much more difficult. Here, it's fair to say that nine out of ten conventional security companies can't assess the "Threat From." They don't have the expert knowledge to say who or what country or what corporation or even what environmental danger might be a threat to your operation. These threat agents can come from inside as much as from outside the company. They can be a person, a group, a social condition, an economic context, or even an environmental danger. You need specialists who can analyze information gathered in your operation and create useable intelligence.

It's only when the two elements are put together that you will obtain a useful understanding of where your company is vulnerable. The following graphic explains this process of superimposing layers of analysis. It shows three steps:

1. Assess the "Threat To."
2. Assess the "Threat From."
3. Assess your vulnerability.

"Threat To" Assessment   *"Threat From" Assessment*   *Vulnerability Assessment*

4. MAKE CORPORATE SECURITY AN EXECUTIVE-LEVEL RESPONSIBILITY.

All too frequently, security is relegated to middle or lower management without any serious support from higher up. Of course we don't mean to suggest that senior management should be operating the security system. But at whatever level the operational work is done, managers must regularly review it, be knowledgeable, and keep abreast of new developments. An adequate block of time must be set aside in each meeting of the executive committee to discuss security, inquire about new technologies, and deal with any concerns expressed by the staff. Senior managers need to accept that this is a permanent leadership role. If the security staff feels that senior people are just going through the motions, morale will be undermined.

Hydro-Québec is a large state corporation that learned this lesson when a television report revealed the chaotic state of its security department. In record time, management created a special executive security committee and despatched it to fix the problem. The outcome was so impressive that the special executive committee on security became a permanent security committee.

While this is a useful example to keep in mind, it isn't one that can necessarily be transposed onto a smaller organization. But even a small company should assign responsibility for security to a single executive who can report at weekly meetings.

5. CREATE A PERMANENT AND ONGOING PROGRAM FOR EMPLOYEE TRAINING AND AWARENESS.

As mentioned earlier, the human factor is the weakest point in a security system. There is no way to change the fact that confidential information leaves the building every time employees walk out the door. They're the problem, but they can also be the solution.

Almost all staff members want to be helpful and hope to do their jobs well. They're open and forthcoming. But this, unfortunately, is the problem. These are the attitudes that a spy will exploit.

In everyday life, most of us know that we can only go so far in trusting another person before they may be tempted to take advantage of us. But it's not easy for an employee to adapt those instincts to the workplace. How can the employer help them to do so? It's not enough to organize a security workshop every now and then in the belief that that will do the job. A really good program comes into play the moment employees are hired, and follows them even (in some cases) after they leave the company. The idea is for the employee to develop a security reflex through appealing to his common sense and intelligence.

Security policies that rely on threats and discipline don't accomplish much. It's been shown in studies that a workplace climate of integrity and responsibility brings better results: the employees are more loyal, more eager to suggest improvements to the program, and more committed to a good workplace environment. This doesn't mean that managers have to weaken their authority. Remember, trusting employees doesn't prevent you from controlling them as well.

So, a well-thought-out program will convince the employees to do their part and even to help improve the program. This is important, because every security program has a series of lines of defence, each overlapping and reinforcing the others. If one line of defence is compromised, you can count on its overlap with the next lines to generate a timely warning. The closer you approach the heart of the organization, the tighter the lines. The employees are one line of defence. That's why a program based only on technology and technicians gives you the illusion of security rather than security itself.

Here are a few ways to get started with a program of education that will give your employees the "reflex" we have talked about.

- **Check out the employee's history before hiring.** Don't believe everything you see in a CV. It's not hard to check out the academic degrees, the former employers, the criminal and credit record, and whether the person has been involved in civil lawsuits. And you should always contact the references given. Some firms have experts to do these checks, but in most cases it's just a matter of a designated staffer picking up the phone. In some cases, even the prospective employee can help. Take, for example, the matter of a criminal record. As noted earlier, the employer has every right to ask the canidate to get a police document certifying that he has no convictions. Most companies will sensibly refuse to hire anybody with a criminal record. It also helps employee morale to know that the company won't ask them to work alongside somebody who has committed criminal acts. Other statements can be checked out with a telephone call or, means permitting, by hiring an agency to do it for you.
- **Have the candidate sign a confidentiality agreement when hired.** This impresses on the new hire how important company information is. And if the employee later betrays that trust, the written agreement might provide grounds for legal action. Note that it's important that it cover a reasonable period after the employee leaves the company, long enough that anything he or she knows will lose its value by the time the agreement expires. Some human resources people feel that it makes sense to limit confidentiality agreements to certain categories of employees. And while it's true that some will have access to more confidential information than others, we

still feel that everyone should be made to sign such an agreement. This is because you can't control the flow of information inside the company. We are constantly amazed at what is known by secretaries, janitors, and mail room clerks. In fact, they're often the best sources!

• **Organize an information session for new arrivals.** Most companies devote a few hours to welcoming a new employee and showing him or her around. There's often a sit-down orientation session as well. This is the best time to impress upon the new person, who wants to become part of the corporate family, how important it is to report suspicious activity and be careful with strategic information. If your internal security service has a more specific program, make sure the employee is sent to attend it. If your company is too small for that, make sure the human resources director takes a moment to talk to the new hire. Don't be afraid to share information about threat agents with employees. That will impress upon them the seriousness of the issue.

• **Arrange for periodic refreshing of security awareness.** There are many ways to keep staff alert to any risks. Company instructors or invited specialists can arrange formal sessions. An internal communiqué can be sent to every employee. Or managers can insist on a review of the subject during routine meetings. You can even try a poster campaign. The important thing is, whatever you do, do it again. And again.

• **Remind departing employees about the rules of confidentiality.** Just as at the moment of hiring, on termination of employment you must impress on the soon-to-be-ex-employee that she has signed an agreement. Also, that it has a nondisclosure provision that will remain in force for a time after her departure.

6. DEMAND PERIODIC SECURITY CHECKS AND AUDITS.

Security programs are no different from any other company program, in that they periodically need to be examined and adapted to new developments. The rapid evolution of computer viruses illustrates a wider truth: security threats of all sorts are always evolving. Each company will know how sensitive its information is relative to what the competition is doing, and that should dictate the frequency of upgrades. But in general, once a year is sufficient. If the company has its own security service, obviously they should be responsible for this. At the same time, enterprises of all sizes must remember to involve their audit department in the security upgrading program. This ensures that the upgrades will actually be done, and done on schedule.

Here are some additional suggestions for making your security more effective:

- **Review the employee's file every five years.** A lot changes in five years. It's healthy for any business that owns proprietary intelligence to check with employees and make sure the system is still working properly. If it is, that's terrific. If not, this is the time to find out who is having problems, or has noticed any kind of deficiency. For some smaller companies such an ambitious review might not be possible. In that case, prioritize: agree on who's in charge of the most sensitive information, and follow the above procedure with them. Senior officers of the company should remember that they're not just there to cheerlead the staff. The executive suite may have security problems too. It's normally where the most sensitive information is held, and any problem that appears there is likely to be a serious one.

- **Always know where your outbound e-mail is going.** Younger employees in particular are always look- ing for ways to advance their career, which of course is legitimate. But you don't want them doing it at the company's expense. So be aware that some of your competi- tors might advertise a position just to lure some of your employees to an interview. The new position might or might not be real. The real purpose of the encounter is to winkle as much information as possible from your employee, who—unaware and anxious to please—might try to impress the potential new boss. That means sharing information they should have kept to themselves. Company e-mail accounts are not personal accounts, so you are entitled to find out what appears on corporate e-mail.
- **Designate one employee to be in charge of security.** Not every company can afford to hire a security service. If this is the case, it's very important to confide the responsibility to a employee, and let everybody know that this is the go-to person for security issues. Employees won't report security problems if they don't know who to talk to.
- **Create a records system that indexes past incidents and draws attention to repetitions**. In a short time period there won't be many serious incidents. But it's important that employees be trained to report everything suspicious, even if it's in the "well, it was kinda strange, I'm not sure" category. This creates a detailed ongoing record, and that's important because an attack is often prepared over a lengthy period of time. This is when tiny irregularities will appear, and the amber lights begin to flash. They are your call to battle.

- **Store documents after use, and keep desktops clear.**
  This isn't always going to be easy, but it has the great benefit
  of letting your security people see at a glance if anything sensitive has been left out on a desk.
- **Purchase lockable filing cabinets for confidential files.** You
  don't have to put everything into a strongbox or locked
  cabinet, but if you have a research file or marketing plan that's
  worth thousands or millions of dollars, it's not extravagant
  to put it someplace where the cleaning staff can't get at it.
- **Buy a shredder and use it.** We mentioned earlier that it's not
  uncommon for thieves to rummage for information in the
  garbage. Government secret service agents are notoriously
  good at this. A diagonal-cutting shredder will address part
  of the problem. If you've got too many documents to deal
  with, have them picked up by an outside contractor, but make
  sure that your representative is present to witness their
  destruction. There are cases of spy agencies that set up
  bogus document-destruction companies. The customers of
  these companies are literally handing over their secrets to
  the competition.

A list like this can't foresee every possible situation. You must
customize your program to suit the needs of your unique operation.
Remember, though, you don't really know what you need until a
Threat and Risk Assessment (TRA) has been prepared by a professional. And once your system is in place, don't let anyone on the
staff think that the security department can do the job by itself. The
old adage "Security is everybody's business" is not a cliché. Security
should be part of every employee's job description.

CHAPTER 009

The New Face of Espionage

*One ought never to turn one's back on a threatened danger and try to
run away from it. If you do that, you will double the danger. But if you
meet it promptly and without flinching, you will reduce the danger by
half. Never run away from anything. Never!*
—Winston Churchill

Far from receding, espionage is on the march in Canada once more.
As elsewhere, it is increasing here at a startling rate. If it weren't for
the current emphasis on terrorism, which preoccupies the media
and pushes espionage onto the back page, this extraordinary development would be better reported.

The players in this latest version of the Great Game are largely
familiar faces from the recent past. But, in the words of a serving
senior CSIS officer, "It's no longer a game of East against West, or
the United States against the USSR. It's a game of all against all."
Information theft is now a global phenomenon, and more complex,
with a host of new players and strategies. The threat, then, is difficult to grasp in its entirety.

Not long ago, Japanese authorities revealed that they were having to refuse visas to more and more Russian visitors, who were found to be connected with the SVR and GRU intelligence agencies. In a related development, in August 2007, Geng Huichang was named China's minister of State Security. The fifty-eight-year-old is also the supreme boss of its intelligence services. Remarkably, he spent his entire career as a specialist in economic intelligence. To those who follow the dossier, this is proof positive that China means to commit even more resources to purloining other countries' technology and economic information.

The current near-collapse of the world's economy doesn't help the situation. Espionage thrives on chaos, and in a multi-polar world both government and private enterprise will find themselves under attack by entities that mean to seize what they have, or else sabotage their work. Compared with the staggering cost of research and development, many countries find that spy agencies are very affordable; this is true for developing countries as well as G8 countries hit hard by the economic crisis. In addition, they deliver the pirated technology quickly. The upshot is that some countries will have to adopt a form of economic protectionism to safeguard their valuable research. This might, in turn, lead to sluggish and inefficient commercial exchange.

Another possibility is that some economic slowdowns will be planned and predatory. This will give predator countries more time and opportunity to "inspect" commercial shipments and correspondence and to strip useful information from them. Protectionist rhetoric will be used to conceal the growing use of commercial espionage. Governments and enterprises that have already yielded to the temptation of spying will make use of the coming chaos to enlarge their operations. Press secretaries will silently rehearse the rebuttal they will use when questioned: "We have the right to defend our interests."

Political espionage will not go away either. China is driven by powerful historic impulses to seek a greater economic and political role in the world, and will continue suppressing dissident voices, as well as stealing technology and subverting foreign governments to expedite the theft. It has several generations of experience in the stealthy arts, and its intelligence agencies are preparing long-term plans for the coming decades. Globalization will quicken the pace of its economic expansion into the markets of the world. A history of humiliation gives China strong motivation, and it has limitless manpower.

Nor is Russia standing in the wings. Today, more than 80 percent of its ruling elite has served in its spy services, army and police. Vladimir Putin is a former KGB colonel and has encouraged his country's rapid regression to brute force methods. But one wonders if Russia ever really left them behind, given its evident craving once again to become Great Russia, so as to inspire the fear and envy that it enjoyed during the Soviet period. It goes without saying that, like China, Russia will pursue espionage and suppression without scruple.

The friendly countries aren't resting on their laurels either. America and Europe are in the grip of an unprecedented credit crisis, and have already concluded that the best response is to become more aggressive in protecting their interests. This means, unfortunately, that they will finance ever-larger clandestine operations to be sure of having the advantage when signing commercial treaties.

Brutish countries like Iran and Syria are unlikely to be economic competitors, but will certainly continue to explore new ways of terrorizing their own people. As population growth continues to outstrip economic growth, they will fall back on even more ruthless methods. And, the world being as it is, they will redouble their determination to acquire nuclear weapons.

Back in the fall of 1996, Peter Schweitzer, expert on national security and fellow at the Hoover Institute, told a U.S. Senate committee on economic espionage that FBI research had turned up evidence implicating 57 out of 173 countries in the theft of high-tech research. A hundred of them had also used taxpayer money to acquire American technology.[65] About the same time, Australia estimated that it was losing $18 billion (AUS) yearly due to economic espionage.

A further insight is to be found in a 2001 study by the American Society for Industrial Security (ASIS), PricewaterhouseCoopers, and the U.S. Chamber of Commerce. It showed that espionage-related losses in 138 of the Fortune 1000 companies amounted to $53 to $59 billion between mid-2000 and mid-2001, which represented a substantial rise.* About the same time, FBI Director Robert S. Mueller III told the National Press Club that it estimated a total loss of $200 billion annually to the United States.[66]

Looking at the progression of technology theft since the 1990s, this shows an increase of over 200 percent.

WHITHER CANADA?

It's not easy to find out how much Canada's head-in-the-sand attitude to economic espionage is costing us. As far as we know, there hasn't been a serious study of the matter since the one released in 1996 by CSIS. That report amply documented a loss to Canada of $10 to $12 billion per year. We have to rely on more current American studies to infer what Canada's losses today might be. They will certainly be greater than before. Even cutting the U.S. figures in half, we come up with $20 to $30 billion annually. Unfortunately, we can't confirm these figures.

In light of what we learned in preparing this book, we feel that

---

* The study is called "Trends in Proprietary Information Loss."

it may be time for some thoughtful self-scrutiny by Canadians. Unsavoury events have been taking place in plain view in this country since the Gouzenko business—a lifetime ago. We need to face the fact that we are a desirable target, and likely to become more so. The naïveté and timidity of successive governments since the 1980s—at all levels, from federal down to municipal—have given us a false sense of security. Complacency of any kind is costly. This kind costs jobs and money.

We shouldn't deceive ourselves that anybody is about to tackle the problem. Since the fall of the Berlin Wall, Ottawa has set the subject aside. Nobody of influence deals with it; sadly, even the destruction of the World Trade Center was pushed down on the agenda. CSIS's spy-chasers are demoralized, and it doesn't brighten their day to see their meagre remaining resources draining away to the counter-terrorism units. And if, through some miraculous event, a spy is actually arrested, he need only pass through the mills of our justice system, which grind hardly anything at all, before resuming his trade somewhere else.

It's hard to get an idea of the scale of the problem. In a world awash with information, this is one of the few areas where shame ensures that information will remain scarce. Companies that have been successfully attacked do not want publicity. They're deeply traumatized, but they're not likely to tell Oprah about it. The difficulty, to begin with, is that they might be legally liable to share-holders for losses. They fear that the general appearance of incompetence will not endear them to suppliers or customers, either. And they're quite right. This kind of truth-telling is costly. In addition to alienating commercial partners, they might also see their subsidies and tax privileges re-examined by the authorities.

Still, it's not edifying to watch the business elite bobbing and weaving to avoid involvement with government security services.

It's just as bad in Europe. Rémy Pautrat, former director of France's DST security service and current president of the Institute for Study and Research in Enterprise Security, said this in an interview with us:

> Directors of small and medium-sized companies have little awareness of the importance of industrial security. Their research is stolen, but they pay no attention until it's too late. . . . We note the same negligence with respect to upgrading information systems. Only a quarter of [French] corporations have installed even an average grade of protection against this scourge. They're not interested and they're not involved. Until disaster overtakes them.

We see this behaviour repeated in Canada. It's ironic and even saddening to see that corporate leaders don't come knocking at the doors of CSIS or the Mounties until after a crime has been committed. They seem to believe, gazing into their empty vaults, that something can still be done for them. But Rémy Pautrat's observation holds true here as well: after the theft, there's no way to turn back the clock. Your research is in somebody else's hands. You may hope for satisfaction in seeing the malefactors punished, but on the rare occasions when a spy does get caught, the sentence imposed, if any, is very light. It certainly has no correlation to the immense harm the criminal has done.

Our lack of sympathy may appear unkind, but it really is time for Canadian business to face facts. The corporate community must acknowledge the scale of the problem and demand public assistance in fighting it.

Here are the areas where something can be done immediately:

- Learn about what you can do to bring the problem to the attention of political authorities. The time of "see no evil, speak no evil" is long past.
- Demand that the Senate undertake a national study of the matter. This will give specialists a forum where they can educate the public and raise support for further research, both in the academy and on the shop floor. This is also where business leaders who have paid no attention to the problem can find out what they're up against, and what kind of help police authorities can provide.
- Help draft a law on economic and industrial espionage that contains appropriate penalties. This must be a stand-alone law, not a few clauses hidden in another legislative proposal that may have little to do with the problem.
- Draft a law or amendment to the Criminal Code that will make it easier to jail foreign agents who commit commercial espionage or harass and intimidate members of their cultural communities.
- Lobby for the RCMP to train and employ officers with special training in commercial espionage. These should be mandated to work with CSIS, which does not have authority to arrest miscreants.
- The ministries of Foreign Affairs and International Commerce are notorious for blocking the prosecution of spies from countries we do business with. You can demand regulations that will bar these ministries from such interference. Only then will Canada be able to send a clear message to the world that we no longer tolerate commercial espionage. It may even be necessary to return to the massive public expulsions of diplomat-spies that we saw in the 1980s. Bureaucratic careerism, not to mention chasing after the

336 DE PIERREBOURG & JUNEAU-KATSUYA

business of countries that would rather steal the goods from us, has no place in matters of national security.

- The business community needs to ask CSIS to be more forthcoming and more committed to investigations. We'd do well to return to the former program of encouraging enterprise awareness and collaborating with the private sector. It's time to end the habit of silence and bring in a new paradigm, in which information sharing with the private sector is a top priority.

- Help to create, fund, and manage information repositories where business leaders can educate themselves concerning threats to their particular sector. Such an institution was opened in the United States in 2000. The Information Sharing Analysis Centers (ISAC) provide an excellent model for Canadian business. The current American model does have its limitations, and would need to be modified for Canadian environment. But it would give our business sector a quick strategic boost.

- Increase CSIS's management accountability by allowing agents to meet with the organization's inspector-general and to file a complaint with full immunity and independence when necessary.

Should We Create a Service to Spy on Others?

If our allies and our faithless friends keep on robbing us blind and passing the loot bag along to their own corporate sectors, should we do likewise? Is turnabout fair play? Do we need to create an aggressive overseas spy service like the CIA, MI-6, or Russia's SVR, which means going much farther than we presently do? Should we give CSIS more robust powers to protect our country? This is an unpleasant question that keeps coming back, however much we wish it away.

Creating an offensive secret service would take us well beyond the economic issues it might help to solve. It would have serious political repercussions. To begin with, such a service would cost a good deal of money and become a significant line item in the federal budget. A service operating overseas could cost between $125 and $250 million per year. A country of comparable size with an offensive information agency is Australia, which allocated $162.5 million for it in 2007.

Another consideration is that, politically speaking, creating such a service would change the rules of the game. It would put in play Canada's current good reputation as a non-aggressive nation. The mandate of CSIS is to defend Canada within Canadian borders, and it has the authority to operate abroad only when investigating a case that originates on Canadian soil. This kind of agency meets with universal approval, since every nation must agree that it has the right to protect its national interests within its own borders (how they go about it is another matter, of course).

The decision to do without an aggressive spy service has been useful to Canada up till the present time. Of course, there have always been those who feel that we have thereby made ourselves dependent on others, especially the United States, for crucial information gathering. But this argument doesn't bear up under close examination. How well, in fact, have America's spy services done their job? The record shows that they consistently failed to anticipate what we now understand to be the great events of recent history: the fall of the Soviet Union, the nuclear testing done by Pakistan and India, the rise of Al-Qaeda, the rapid growth of China, and the return of "Greater Russia." Canada's intelligence services predicted all of these events.

This has a good deal to do with America's spy culture, which operates "on the ground" and relies obsessively on technology for information gathering, to the detriment of HUMINT, or human sources. Really effective secret services regard human sources as "the hard point of the diamond." Put another way, Americans tend to have their nose stuck to the tree and don't see the forest. Which country, then, depends on which?

Canada has in fact been very helpful to other countries by sharing our advanced strategic analysis with them. This is one reason why, despite our relatively small population and military forces, we have often been a strategic intermediary and even an arbitrator in great international conflicts. Lester B. Pearson said that "Canada is the smallest of the big and the biggest of the small." In the field of intelligence, we stand tall.

It's a strong, pivotal position to occupy, but we have recently forgotten how to use it to our own advantage. We still have the reputation of being a nice crowd to hang out with, but we need to think seriously about how much that is worth. Because it's a sure thing that, the moment we endow ourselves with an aggressive spy agency, we will no longer belong to the Nice People Association. American kids abroad will no longer disguise themselves with a maple leaf on their backpacks. Foreign border guards will look at our passports and see "spy." We will henceforth be seen as a threat by others, and that is the reality we will have chosen.

Is it worth the price? For us, the answer must be no. It would, in our view, be a strategic blunder; the loss would outweigh whatever might be gained. Our experience tells us that a costly and aggressive clandestine service will not bring us any data that could not be procured just as well by sophisticated analysis.

Analysis is the key to success. But we have lost the analytic cutting edge we once possessed. In fact, several federal ministries were once capable of it, but the heavy personnel cutbacks during the Mulroney era eliminated the expert strategic analysis groups.

They have never been replaced. These superb teams were the eyes and ears of the federal government. Without them, our leaders have become hesitant and vulnerable.

There is good historical evidence to prove the value of strategic analysis. The current world champion in this fine art is Japan's Ministry of International Trade and Industry (MITI). It was created shortly after the Second World War, at a time when the country, having suffered years of bombardment culminating in two savage nuclear blasts, was under foreign occupation.

And yet, largely due to MITI's matchless ability to gather and analyze information, Japan became a leading world economic power in less than twenty-five years. The ministry was nothing less than a gigantic analytical box that compiled data from Japanese government agencies, embassies, industries, and private companies, and then distributed the resulting analysis where needed. Government czars, working closely with the country's industrial leaders, were able to give Japan a strategic national vision that got the country back on its feet and pointed it in the right direction.

Being Canadian, we are modestly obliged to say that Canada is, of course, not Japan. But leadership is leadership. Vision is vision. And it has been far too long since we have seen either in this country. There is no better time than now, when a deep economic crisis calls out for leadership, to get on with it. We can no longer trust our future to myopic Mr. Magoos who don't care to see beyond the next election.

WHAT TO DO WHILE WE'RE WAITING

The situation we've tried to bring to light in this book can't be changed overnight. Canada will, for the foreseeable future, continue to be the more or less helpless hunting ground of roughshod and roughriding international spies. And yet the spies are not the problem. The problem is our attitude and the stance we adopt to confront them.

It is time to adopt a profound change of outlook and behaviour. Those who occupy the heights of government must find the courage to look at the big problem and show the rest of the world that we have the will to eliminate foreign spies and covert theft in our country.

The private sector will also need to change its corner-office thinking and organizational culture. It must understand that hidden cameras and anti-virus programs are no kind of serious protection at all. Employee quality and highly developed employee reflexes are what's needed. Once these are in place, the whole country will benefit.

Nobody has ever found a way to make the world stand still. Change must continue, and in our world it is certainly going to become faster and more aggressive. Overpopulation is now a universal catastrophe, with massive and uncontrolled human migration, depleted farmland and natural resources, collapsing aquifers that will need thousands of years to regenerate, and powerful nations whose instinctive response to these problems is to try to grab what belongs to others. Yes, Canada has a choice: we can be swept up in this great change, or we can be swept away by it. We must face up to the great forces at work in today's world.

Perhaps you've heard it said that life is like a parade. Some of us are in the parade, twirling our batons and stepping high. Others watch it pass by and wish in their hearts that they were in it. Canada has every right to be in the parade; our marshals and our marching bands are ready. We need only step off the sidewalk and stride proudly.

GLOSSARY A

Spy Jargon

Agent in place: An agent who works on behalf of a foreign country within another government or one of its diplomatic missions. These agents may be citizens of the country they are spying on, or may be double agents.

Antenna (or station): A group of intelligence agents working together in another country who, as a rule, work out of a diplomatic mission in order to mask their illegal activities. This kind of group is called a *rezidentura* (residence) by the Russians. It usually includes an officer called the station chief (or, by the Russians, the *rezident*). This person keeps the group informed of what's going on at headquarters and assigns the group its duties.

Bottomfeeder (fish of the great deeps): A Chinese metaphor describing a sleeper agent.

Classified information: Information or intelligence classified as confidential, secret, or very secret.

Controlled technology: Technology controlled by a state to prevent other states from acquiring it. This is generally used for military technology and also for dual-use technology.

Controller (handler): An agent who manages a clandestine source. This is generally a human source (see HUMINT), but the term may also designate the agent who manages a technical source (see TECHINT).

Co-optee (collaborator): An individual who co-operates with a foreign spy by supplying strategic information, sometimes confidential but not necessarily secret in nature. The co-optee's motivation is usually tied to ideology or the hope of personal gain. A co-optee may, for example, be used to collect information on a group of dissidents from the homeland. He may also spread propaganda while pretending to express personal opinions.

Counter-espionage (counter-intelligence): Measures taken to neutralize aggressive espionage by another country or by a competing company or organization.

Dead letter box: A location where a message or parcel for a spy is hidden. This is usually in a public space, such as a library or a tree trunk. The message or parcel might also be casually dropped on the ground or in some other hard-to-spot location. The item is meant to be picked up quickly without attracting the attention of counter-espionage agents. The dead letter box also permits agents to communicate with each other without arousing suspicion.

Defector: Any person, but commonly a spy or diplomat, who transfers her loyalty from one government to another. A defector is usually debriefed by the host country's spy service for whatever useful information he might possess. The famous defection in 1945 of the Soviet cipher clerk Igor Gouzenko in Ottawa revealed for the first time the scale of Soviet espionage and compelled western spy services to change their philosophy from the ground up. In this case, a single defector is often credited with starting the Cold War.

Diplomatic bag: Correspondence, sometimes in a bag but possibly in a container of any size or material. It is protected through international diplomatic agreements; notably, it may not be opened or inspected by border guards or police officers. The package or object is described as "diplomatic mail." It is routinely exploited by diplomat-spies to keep in touch with their homeland headquarters, and to transmit clandestine information that they have gathered or to receive equipment, from listening devices to weapons.

Double agent: A spy who pretends to work for the government or security service of his country, but in reality is acting on behalf of a foreign government and transmitting secret information to it. This can also refer to an agent who infiltrates a particular community within a country by pretending to be a sympathizer.

Dual-use technology: Technology developed for civilian use but which can be converted into military technology. This generally falls under the category of controlled technology or "control goods."

Economic espionage: A government or its intelligence services may undertake espionage to acquire commercial or economic information, from a company or a foreign state. This kind of spying is often confused with industrial espionage, a term that applies only to spying by one private corporation on another. The distinction is important when, for example, a government opens a front company that is in fact part of an economic espionage operation by that government.

Espionage: The act of illegally obtaining and communicating information. A spy works secretly and outside official channels, generally on behalf of a foreign government agency that operates in violation of international and diplomatic agreements. Espionage is increasingly popular within the private sector as well, where it usually involves the theft of commercial information (see *Economic espionage* and *Industrial espionage*).

Front company: A business that is registered by a spy agency in order to mask its undercover operations and to help in obtaining restricted technologies, intellectual property, and other confidential information through illegal means.

Ground truth: Basic information that can serve as a reference to evaluate information obtained by satellite or by other means, including HUMINT, SIGINT, IMINT, and even MASINT.

HUMINT (Human Intelligence): This refers to information obtained through men and women who agree to carry out espionage, whether as moles, informers, or double agents.

Illegal agent: An undercover agent working on behalf of a foreign government. Unlike a posted agent, this kind of spy has no diplomatic immunity. Both types of agent are "officially" forbidden.

IMINT (Image Intelligence): This term covers both conventional photographs and satellite imagery.

Industrial espionage: This occurs when a private-sector company illegally spies on another private-sector company in order to steal proprietary information or to learn about a competitor's economic strategy. It is sometimes hard to distinguish from economic espionage. Both are criminal activities.

Informer: Any person who agrees to turn over confidential and strategic intelligence. The term is usually used in conventional police work rather than intelligence work, where the term "source" is preferred.

Intelligence: Sometimes called "classified information," intelligence is the product of collecting, evaluating, and interpreting information from open or confidential sources. There are four varieties: SIGINT (Signals Intelligence), HUMINT (Human Intelligence), OSINT (Open Source Intelligence), and IMINT (Image Intelligence). It is usually created for the use of political leaders to resolve definite questions and help in decision-making. "Intelligence" is not raw information; it is the result of analyzing raw information. A concise definition: INFORMATION + ANALYSIS = INTELLIGENCE. The sole purpose of intelligence is to empower decisionmakers.

Legend: A term used within the spy profession to describe a false identity that also contains a fictitious life history of the person concerned. It is usually based on the name and family history of a child who died young in the country where the spy is trying to operate. The child's story then becomes the spy's cover identity, with "official traces" in government records. If necessary, the spy will live in one or more countries before arriving in the target country in order to leave "traces" that legitimize his legend, should a suspicious government decide to investigate him.

Liaison officer: An intelligence agent whose identity is open and declared, and who works as the official representative of his agency to foreign agencies. His job is to encourage the sharing of information. Sometimes such an agent may be officially integrated into a foreign agency for a specified period of time.

Line (of a *rezidentura* or residence): "Line" is a term used to describe a department of a Russian spy agency. Different lines are identified by letters of the alphabet, which also designate the different functions of the departments. For example, Line N manages networks of illegal agents in a target country where the spy service operates; Line X specializes in science and technology theft; while Line PR gathers political intelligence through collaborators or co-optees and also spreads propaganda in other countries. Line RR specializes in electronic intelligence (SIGINT), while Line KR handles security and counter-espionage, including catching double agents and bringing in defectors.

MASINT (Measurement and Signal Intelligence): A sub-product obtained by the analysis of disparate elements such as SIGINT, HUMINT, TECHINT, IMINT, and OSINT. It combines all of the above kinds of information to produce a technical output that can verify or refute hypotheses developed by looking at the other sources individually. Example: air samples (MASINT) taken in a certain place can reveal the local manufacture of chemical weaponry or, in the case of private-sector companies, the kinds of products being produced.

Mass collection process: This is an information collection technique used only by Chinese intelligence services. It makes use of most Chinese citizens travelling outside the homeland, who are forced to bring home information on people they meet and places of interest (universities, government offices, research centres, etc.). They are also obliged to keep a record of people they meet who have strong views on China, whether sympathetic or not. These individuals may later come under surveillance or be approached for recruitment.

Mole: A spy who works inside a government, a foreign agency or a company using his or her job as a cover and giving secret intelligence to a foreign state. May be a sleeper agent.

OSINT (Open Source Intelligence): This refers to the gathering of publicly available information from open sources, including newspapers, commercial pamphlets, government reports, the Internet, and so on.

Persona non grata: This term describes anyone expelled from a country for activity "incompatible" with diplomatic status. Such activity is nearly always espionage. The deported person's name will be circulated through the intelligence services of allied countries and that person will no longer be able to work as a diplomat. Sometimes he or she may no longer be able to get foreign visas at all.

Posted agent: A spy with an official diplomatic cover within the embassy of the country he works for. He is in direct communication with his agency headquarters at home and takes orders for intelligence gathering and offensive operations. In the course of his work he will use his diplomatic immunity to contact, recruit, or obtain information or access to people in an "official" manner. He may also approach people in a clandestine fashion. The use of posted agents is forbidden by the Vienna Convention on Diplomatic Relations.

Recruitment: Procedure followed by an intelligence service in order to induce a person to collaborate and to furnish strategic/confidential information.

Reverse engineering: Procedure used by a corporation to dismantle and discover the technical details and design of a competitor's product in order to copy it.

Rezident **(resident):** A Russian term; the senior officer among a group of spies working out of an embassy or consulate. Very rarely, the rezident is also the ambassador or consul herself.

Rezidentura **(residence):** Offices inside a Russian embassy or consulate used exclusively by secret agents. The *rezidentura* may be divided into several departments (see Line: *Rezidentura*). The word *rezident* is used exclusively for the station chief, who is the highest authority within a *rezidentura* and usually has diplomatic immunity.

SIGINT (Signals Intelligence): Information acquired by intercepting electromagnetic signals, e.g.: radio waves; satellite transmissions; telephone calls; faxes; telemetry; and electronic messages (e-mail).

Sleeper agent: A foreign spy who is sent to a country where he remains inactive for a number of years. He is not in contact with his controller, who generally works in a diplomatic mission. When finally contacted, he furnishes intelligence to the agency that he really works for. Sleeper agents can remain inactive for many years, which makes it very hard for counter-intelligence officers to locate them.

Source: Includes all sources of information, whether human, technical, or open. The term is often freely used in conversation in order to conceal the source of the information or the means by which it was obtained. For example, to admit that one uses a "technical source" immediately reveals that the party in question is using electronic observation devices or listening equipment. For Human Source, Open Source, and Technical Source, see respectively HUMINT, OSINT, SIGINT.

Station chief: Highest-ranking officer of a station group operating in a foreign country. The station chief usually poses as a diplomatic employee in one of his country's overseas missions to conceal his identity. The title is mainly used by the U.S. and other Western countries.

Talent spotting: Intelligence gathering carried out by agents or by collaborators (who may not be aware of what they are doing) with the aim of identifying people susceptible to being recruited as moles or agents.

TECHINT (Technical Intelligence): This refers to intelligence concerning the capabilities of a foreign country's military establishment.

Threat agent: This describes any form of security threat, whether emanating from an individual, a group, a situation, a social climate, or a condition (such as avian flu). Threat agents are usually identified through a Threat and Risk Assessment as part of the Threat From analysis.

Threat and Risk Assessment (TRA): A specialist assessment of an industry or corporation's security system, identifying its weak points. An assessment should have three components: Threat To, Threat From and Vulnerability Assessment (see Chapter 008).

Undercover: A false identity adopted by a spy that allows him to do his job without being identified.

Volunteer or "walk-in": Somebody who contacts a foreign country's intelligence service and volunteers to give it classified information. This kind of treason is often motivated by money, or revenge, or by strongly held political views.

Vulnerability assessment: A complementary analysis of Threat To/ Threat From (see Chapter 008). Only when these two categories are superimposed can the analyst get a useful picture of the weak points of a company's security system. This in turn allows the analyst to recommend the best use of the company's security budget. It is the only way of empirically improving a company's security rather than simply enlarging or augmenting it.

GLOSSARY B

Security Services

This is not a glossary of all the security services in the world, but rather a short list of those that operate in Canada. Many of the foreign organizations do so secretly, but others participate in legitimate exchange programs, in which investigative or liaison agents are attached to the staff of their diplomatic missions in Canada. We should underline, however, that most of the agencies listed here have, at one time or another, carried on clandestine operations in Canada.

CANADIAN ORGANIZATIONS

CCIRC (Canadian Cyber Incident Response Centre): This organization reports to the Ministry of Public Safety Canada. Its job is the permanent surveillance of cybernetic threats. Its mandate is the protection of essential infrastructure against cyber-incidents and the national coordination of all actions taken against cybernetic threats. CCIRC is an integral part of the Government Operations Centre.

CSE (Communications Security Establishment Canada): This agency collects and analyzes all telecommunications. Created in

1947 as the Telecommunications Authority, its existence was not officially acknowledged until thirty-four years later. CSEC's mandate is to monitor foreign communications, especially those intended to be received in Canada. It is forbidden by law, however, to listen to messages sent by Canadians.

CSIS (Canadian Security Intelligence Service): This is the information agency responsible for investigating threats to national security both inside and outside Canada. It was created in 1984 after the McDonald Commission recommended dividing the RCMP's authority so as to create a civil investigative agency. CSIS responsibilities include investigating espionage, terrorism, and sabotage, and reporting to the federal government on these matters. It derives its authority from the Canadian Security Intelligence Service Act. It has no authority to arrest: that authority remains with the RCMP.

FINTRAC (Financial Transactions Reports Analysis Centre of Canada): Created in July 2000, FINTRAC is responsible for financial intelligence in Canada. It gathers, analyzes, and makes available financial analysis concerning suspected money laundering and the financing of terrorist activities. In 2008 it had 329 employees and a budget of $51.1 million.

RCMP (Royal Canadian Mounted Police): As Canada's federal police agency, the RCMP investigates and carries out operations against organized crime, terrorism, and drug trafficking. It was also Canada's national security agency until that responsibility was transferred to CSIS after the McDonald Commission reported on RCMP abuses in the 1970s. Since September 11, 2001, the RCMP has been largely responsible for investigating terrorism.

SIRC (Security Intelligence Review Committee): An independent organization in charge of supervising the activities of CSIS, SIRC's mandate is to ensure that CSIS operates within the law. It reports to Parliament, and thereby to the Canadian public, every year. At the present time, no similar agency exists to supervise the RCMP.

FOREIGN ORGANIZATIONS

ASIO (Australian Security Intelligence Organisation): Charged with internal security, this organization's responsibilities include espionage, sabotage, political extremism, and foreign interference. It is authorized to operate overseas when necessary to internal investigations. ASIO has the power to investigate but not to arrest, a power that remains with police forces. It has a formal agent-exchange program with CSIS and keeps an agent posted in Ottawa.

ASIS (Australian Secret Intelligence Service): This is an external information service that collects human-sourced information (HUMINT). Its mandate is to protect Australia's vital interests overseas through counter-espionage and also through spying on behalf of the Australian government.

CIA (Central Intelligence Agency) (United States): An external intelligence service, the CIA guards against threats to national security. It has four branches. These include the National Clandestine Service, which recruits informers and carries out secret operations overseas, and the Directorate of Intelligence, which produces special reports on matters of interest to the U.S. government. The CIA is officially not permitted to arrest anybody within American borders, that authority being reserved to the FBI.

CIS (Chinese Intelligence Service): Generally referring to all intelligence agencies in China, it includes Ministry of State Security (MSS or Guoanbu), Office 610 (especially created to neutralize Falun Gong and other activists) and the United Front Work Department (UFWD). China has an impressive arsenal of intelligence services that are active not only inside their country to control dissidence and to protect the State against any dangers but are also very active abroad in a very aggressive and proactive manner. The People's Liberation Army (PLA) has units in all three great divisions—army, navy and aviation. The Central Committee of the Communist Party plays a major part in planning the activities of all the intelligence services by choosing the strategies considered necessary to support the State. What is perhaps unique to China is the fact that the Western intelligence services consider the news service New China News Agency (Xinhua) an active branch of CIS. The Chinese Ministry for Foreign Affairs, although not an official agency responsible for the security of the state, is very active in support of the intelligence services. However, in China all government departments, media agencies and academic centres are infiltrated or used in other ways by CIS.

CISEN (Centro de Investigación y Seguridad Nacional) (Mexico): This is Mexico's internal and external intelligence agency. Because of the country's growing drug problem, CISEN works closely with law enforcement agencies against organized crime and drug trafficking.

DCRI (Direction Centrale du Renseignement Intérieur) (France): This is a police agency that reports to the Ministry of the Interior. Created in 2008 with the amalgamation of the Direction de la Surveillance du Territoire and the Direction Centrale des Renseignements Généraux, the DCRI is responsible for France's economic security. It deals with espionage, foreign interference, political extremism, and terrorism.

DGSE (Direction Générale de la Sécurité Extérieure) (France):
An external intelligence service responsible for collecting and analyzing electromagnetic information (SIGINT) and human-sourced information (HUMINT), the DGSE also carries on clandestine operations in other countries to advance French interests.

DRS (Département du Renseignement et de la Sécurité) (Algeria):
The DRS is a domestic and external intelligence-gathering agency with responsibilities including counter-espionage, internal security, and intelligence collection. It is suspected of using torture.

DSE (Direction de la Sûreté de l'État) (Tunisia): This is a service responsible for national security, the war against terrorism, and surveillance of dissidence both inside and outside the country. The DSE is known to have carried out operations in Canada against Tunisian dissidents. Both it and Tunisia frequently appear on the Amnesty International list of organizations and countries that employ torture and arbitrary detention.

DST-France: see DCRI

DST-Morocco (Direction de la Surveillance du Territoire-Morocco): This is a domestic and external intelligence agency. In the past the organization specialized in political espionage. Today it is also known for its involvement in joint operations with allied foreign intelligence agencies.

FBI (Federal Bureau of Investigation) (United States): The FBI is a police agency that investigates crimes committed within the United States. It has Legal Attaché offices in more than seventy cities outside the United States, including Ottawa, Toronto, and

Vancouver. These offices are responsible for the safety of Americans and work to minimize harm to Americans when crimes are committed abroad. They also investigate some international crimes.

FSB (Federalnaya Sluzhba Bezopasnosti) (Russia): The name means Federal Security Services, and the organization ensures public safety. The FSB succeeded the KGB after the fall of the Soviet Union and then the FSK in 1995. Its activities include counter-espionage, economic crimes, anti-terrorism, and surveillance. It is believed that at least 75 percent of Russian political leaders today have in the past worked for the FSB or the KGB.

GDI (General Directorate of Intelligence) (Iraq): This internal and external intelligence agency operated at the time of Saddam Hussein. The GDI had a number of directorates, of which Directorate 9 was the most important. Its specialties were sabotage and assassinations carried out in foreign countries.

GRU (Glavnoje Razvedyvatel'noje Upravlenije) (Russia): This organization's name means Central Intelligence Administration, and it functions as a military intelligence service. The GRU gathers human-based intelligence through illegal agents and through military attachés posted in Russian embassies. It also oversees electromagnetic intelligence and satellite imagery.

GSD (General Security Directorate) (Syria): An internal and external intelligence agency, the GSD has three branches: Internal Security, External Security, and Palestinian Affairs. The External Security branch's activities are similar to those of the CIA.

IB (Intelligence Bureau) (India): This domestic intelligence service is charged with counter-espionage, anti-terrorism, surveillance of communications, and making sure that the government's point of view is heard in the media. Once responsible for external intelligence, it yielded this job to RAW in 1968.

Intelligence Directorate (Cuba): Formerly known as the DGI, this is an external intelligence service that collects information and does analysis. Cuba has the third-largest UN delegation, and half of its employees are considered to be Intelligence Directorate agents. Starting in the 1990s, the agency expanded its economic espionage activities with a view to improving Cuba's economy.

ISI (Inter-Services Intelligence) (Pakistan): This domestic and external intelligence agency monitors foreigners, the media, diplomats, and active political groups inside Pakistan. It intercepts communications and carries out aggressive secret operations. It is suspected of passing confidential information to the Taliban and of being a "state within a state" in the sense that the government is no longer able to control it.

KGB (Komityet Gosudarstvennoy Bezopasnosti) (Russia): The KGB is a secret police and intelligence agency that operated from 1954 to 1991 before being dissolved and replaced by the FSK and later the FSB. The KGB was responsible for intelligence collection and secret missions both inside and outside Russia. It was especially known for the brutality of its methods where dissidents were concerned, and it developed an impressive spy network during the Cold War.

MI-5 (Military Intelligence, Section 5) (United Kingdom): MI-5 is a domestic intelligence agency in charge of counter-espionage, the war against terrorism, and investigating national security threats. Although MI-5 generally operates on British territory, it has been known to carry out operations in other countries. When this occurs, it works closely with the UK's external spy service, SIS. This agency has an agent exchange program with CSIS and maintains an agent in Ottawa.

MI-6 (Military Intelligence, Section 6): see SIS.

MİT (Millî İstihbarat Teşkilâti) (Turkey): Focusing on domestic and internal intelligence, MIT leads counter-espionage operations overseas and shadows groups with Communist, separatist, and fascist tendencies.

MOIS (Ministry of Intelligence and Security) (Iran): MOIS is a domestic and external intelligence-gathering service. While little information is available, it is known that MOIS replaced SAVAK, the former security agency, after the Islamic revolution of 1979. Overseas MOIS personnel are usually attached to embassies or consulates as posted agents or Ministry of Culture representatives. MOIS also has illegal agents posing as students, academics, journalists, and business men. The agency is suspected of having ordered the assassination of overseas Iranian dissidents toward the end of the 1990s.

Mossad (HaMossad leModi'in v'leTafkidim Meyuhadim) (Israel): Its Hebrew name means Institute for Intelligence and Special Operations. An external intelligence service responsible for gathering human-based information (HUMINT), special operations, and counter-terrorism, Mossad is specially active in Arab countries, but also in western countries and within the United Nations. Its activities include espionage by both illegal agents and posted agents, sabotage, targeted assassinations, and psychological warfare.

MSS (Ministry of State Security) (China): This intelligence service manages counter-espionage, surveillance of political dissidence, and overseas information gathering. The MSS is also very active in economic espionage. In 2003, the FBI estimated that 3,000 Chinese companies operating in North America were chiefly concerned with coordinating economic espionage activity.

NIB (National Intelligence Bureau) (Sri Lanka): A domestic and external intelligence agency founded in 1984, NIB handles all the intelligence needs of the army and the police.

NIS (National Intelligence Service) (South Korea): This external and internal intelligence service was earlier known by the acronyms KCIA and ANSP. The NIS investigates threats to national security and gathers intelligence overseas, in particular military secrets. It also manages domestic counter-espionage and in particular fights industrial and military spying.

NSA (National Security Agency) (United States): The NSA is an external intelligence agency responsible for gathering and analyzing electromagnetic information (SIGINT). The NSA created the ECHELON network, a worldwide alliance of countries that monitor telecommunications, including Canada, Australia, New Zealand, and the United Kingdom. Its official mandate is to protect America from attack, but the NSA has also been accused of carrying out economic espionage on behalf of the United States.

NSB (National Security Bureau) (Taiwan): An internal and external intelligence agency, the NSB's chief duty is to inform the government of recent developments around the world, in China, and inside the country. It has the authority to carry out intelligence gathering. But in Taiwan law enforcement is strictly reserved to the police agencies.

NSS (National Security Service) (Armenia): This intelligence agency carries out the government's national security policies. Many of its espionage operations are concentrated against Turkey and Azerbaidjan, which are both political adversaries.

Office 6–10 (China): This specialized external intelligence service is charged with tracking groups critical of the Chinese government. Little is known about this organization. According to two Chinese defectors, it was created on June 10, 1999, with the mandate of infiltrating and gathering intelligence on dissident groups. Its particular target is Falun Gong.

RAW (Research and Intelligence Wing) (India): RAW is a foreign intelligence service in charge of intelligence gathering, secret operations, and the fight against terrorism. Created in 1968, it is most active against Pakistan and other neighbouring countries.

SB (Special Branch) (Malaysia): An internal and external intelligence service attached to the Royal Malaysian Police, the SB has seven departments and emphasizes the gathering of technical, economic, and political intelligence.

SIE (Serviciul de Informatii Externe) (Romania): This external intelligence service, created in 1990, protects national security and Romania's interests overseas.

SIS (Secret Intelligence Service) (United Kingdom): This is the external intelligence service also known as MI-6. The SIS carries on clandestine overseas operations and collects intelligence. It is officially charged with carrying out economic espionage.

SVR (Sluzhba Vneshney Razvedki) (Russia): The organization's name means External Intelligence Service. The SVR works overseas, monitoring communications, collecting intelligence, and carrying on economic espionage. It is the successor to the First Branch of the KGB after the dissolution of the Soviet Union.

SZRU (Sluzhba Zovnishn'oyi Rozvidky Ukrayiny) (Ukraine): An external intelligence service, the SZRU is mandated to collect and analyze political, economic, military, scientific, technological, and ecological information.

TC2 (Tổng cục 2 Tình báo quân dôi, or Second Central Commission of Military Intelligence) (Vietnam): An internal and external intelligence agency in charge of collecting and analyzing information, particularly of an economic, diplomatic, political, scientific, or technological nature.

United Front Work Department (China): A department of the Central Committee of the Chinese Communist Party, the United Front Work Department maintains contact with Chinese citizens who work overseas and calls on them to provide information that may be useful to China.

VEVAK (Vezarat-e Ettela'at va Amniat-e Keshvar) (Iran): See MOIS, the Ministry of Security and Intelligence.

NOTES

Chapter 001: *How the "Tired Old Whore" Became a Brand-New Menace*

1 *Manchester Evening News* website, "Full speech by director-general of the security service MI-5," 5 November 2007.

2 Auditor General of Canada, "Modernizing the NORAD System in Canada—National Defence" (Chapter 006), May 2007, website: oag-bvg.gc.ca.

3 Roger Faligot, *Les Services secrets chinois, de Mao aux JO* (Paris: Nouveau Monde, 2008).

4 Andrew Christopher and Vasili Mitrokhine, *Le KGB contre l'Ouest, 1917–1991: Les archives Mitrokhine* (Paris: Fayard, 2000).

5 Constantin Melnik, *Les Espions: Réalités et fantasmes* (Paris: Ellipses, 2008).

6 Pete Earley, *Comrade J: The Untold Secrets of Russia's Master Spy in America After the End of the Cold War* (New York: G.P. Putnam's Sons, 2007).

7 Stewart Bell, "Return of the spying game," *National Post*, 7 June 2007.

8 This sentence paraphrases André Dalcourt, "Le Consulat sovietique, une grosse PME de l'information," *Journal de Montréal*, Friday, 16 January 1987.

9 Andrew Christopher and Vasili Mitrokhine, *Le KGB contre l'Ouest, 1917–1991: Les archives Mitrokhine* (Paris: Fayard, 2000).

10 Normand Lester, *Enquêtes sur les services secrets* (Montreal: Éditions de l'homme, 1998), p. 35.

11   Constantin Melnik, *Les Espions: Réalités et fantasmes* (Paris: Ellipses, 2008).

12   "Espionnage au Quebec? Phillip Edmonston défend un montarvillois contaminé." Press release dated 16 October 1991. Authors' archives.

13   Claude Allaire, "Michel Bordeleau, alias Mikhail Bordelov," *Journal de Montréal*, 27 September 1989.

14   Réjean Tremblay, "Michel Bordeleau, l'URSS il en revait . . . il y a goute." *La Presse*, 25 February 1990, p. 8.

Chapter 002: *Paul William Hampel*

15   Federal Court dossier DES-3–06. The summary is dated 20 November 2006.

16   "Russia steps up espionage," JID website www.janes.com, 3 December 2002.

17   Andrew Christopher and Vasili Mitrokhine, *Le KGB contre l'Ouest, 1917–1991: Les archives Mitrokhine* (Paris: Fayard, 2000).

18   Mark Tighe and Mark Paul, "Canada claims an Irish boss is top Russian spy," *Sunday Times*, 26 November 2006.

19   CSIS website.

20   André Noel, "Sur les traces de Hampel," *La Presse*, 27 December 2006.

21   André Noel, "Le dossier traine en longueur," *La Presse*, 19 December 2006.

22   Andrew Mitrovika, *Entrée clandestine: Crimes et mensonges dans les services secrets canadiens* (Montreal: Trait d'union, 2002).

23   Miller v. Canada, 2006 CF 1446, 30 November 2006.

24   Miller v. Canada, 2006 CF 1446, 30 November 2006.

Chapter 003: *Even Our Friends Are Spying On Us*

25 Ian Fleming, "James Bond is a highly romanticized version of a true spy. The real thing is . . . William Stephenson," *The Times* (London), 21 October 1962.

Chapter 004: *Chinese Espionage*

26 CSIS, "Opening of the Confucius Institute," ref. BR 2006–7/27. From the collection of Fabrice de Pierrebourg. (See photo section.)

27 The Senate Standing Committee on Defence and Security, Ottawa, 30 April 2007.

Chapter 005: *Cyber-Surveillance*

28 "China and the Internet," a paper published in September 2006 on the CSIS website.

29 Gordon Thomas, *Histoire secrète du Mossad, de 1951 à nos jours* (Paris: Nouveau Monde, 2006).

30 Quoted from "China and the Internet," a paper published in September 2006 on the CSIS website.

31 Roger Faligot, *Les Services secrets chinois, de Mao aux JO* (Paris: Nouveau Monde, 2008).

32 Sophie Clairet, "L'US Cyberspace Command s'organise," *Diplomatie* magazine, Number 32, May/June 2008.

Chapter 006: *Foreign Interference*

33 Fabrice de Pierrebourg, "Une Façade pour les Tigres Tamouls," *Journal de Montréal,* 6 May 2008; Stewart Bell, "Tigers sought $3-M from Canada," *National Post,* 6 May 2008.

34 "L'Espionnage au Canada," Study 2006–7/01 and 01 (a), 1 May 2006. Authors' archives.

35 J. L. Granatstein and David Stafford, *Spy Wars: Espionage in Canada from Gouzenko to Glasnost* (Toronto: Key Porter Books, 1991).

36 Roger Faligot, *Les Services secrets chinois, de Mao aux JO* (Paris: Nouveau Monde, 2008).

37 Tom Zeller, Jr., "House member criticizes internet companies for practices in China," *New York Times,* 15 February 2006.

38 Extract from the report, on line on the SIRC website: www.sirc-csars. gc.ca.

39 Secret CSIS report, "Demonstrations Against the Olympic Games," BR2007–8/07a. 16 August 2007. From the archives of Fabrice de Pierrebourg.

40 "Harper remains firm with China," *La Grande Époque,* 21 November 2006.

41 Chinese Embassy's Statement on the Issue of Falun Gong, 2006/07/26.

42 Holly Porteous, "Commentary Number 72: The Strategy of the United Front from Beijing to Hong Kong," CSIS website: www.csis-scrs.gc.ca/, Winter 1998.

43 Roger Faligot, *Les Services secrets chinois, de Mao aux JO* (Paris: Nouveau Monde, 2008).

44 The MP3 file on which it was recorded, as well as part of the English transcription, are available on the website of WOIPFG and *Epoch Times* (en.epochtimes.com/news/8–5-24/70954. .html).

45 Dossier A-289–00; Reference 2001 Federal Court of Appeal 399, The Ministry of Citizenship and Immigration (appellant) versus Yong Jie Qu (respondent). Federal Court of Appeal website (decisions.fca-caf. gc.ca).

46 Dossier IMM-1571–00: Reference 2003 CFPI 741, Haiquan Yao versus the Ministry of Citizenship and Immigration. Federal Court.

47 Roger Faligot, *Les Services secrets chinois, de Mao aux JO* (Paris: Nouveau Monde, 2008), p. 163, 106n.

48 Bill Gertz, "Embassy unit works to block Falun Gong broadcast license," *Washington Times*, 17 April 2007.

49 "Broadcasting Public Notice CRTC 2006–166, 22 December 2006." CRTC Website, www.crtc.gc.ca.

50 Matthew Little, "Chinese consulate meddling in Calgary show, says host," *Epoch Times*, 24 April 2008.

51 Jan Wong, "Feeling the long arm of China—the consul general is making sure politicians know where her country stands," *Globe and Mail*, 6 August 2005.

52 Laura-Julie Pereault, "La Chine a le monde à l'oeil," *La Presse*, June 9, 2007.

53 Statement of Chen Yonglin, "Falun Gong and China's Continuing War on Human Rights," Committee on International Relations, House of Representatives, 109th Congress, 21 July 2005.

54 Kulun Zhang and seventeen other appellants versus Crescent Chau and La Presse Chinoise Eastern Inc. et Bing He. Dossier 500–09–016312–068. Judgment handed down by the Appeals Court of Quebec, 13 May 2008.

55 Mark Morgan, "Montreal newspaper a voice for Chinese regime," 6 July 2007. Article located on the Internet site of the *Epoch Times*.

56 Cited by Charlie Gillis, "Beijing is always watching," *Maclean's* magazine, 14 May 2007.

57 Stewart Bell, *Terreur froide: La filière canadienne du terrorisme* (Montreal: Les Éditions de l'Homme, 2004).

58 "The report of the Honourable Bob Rae, Independent Advisor to the Minister of Public Safety, on outstanding questions with respect to the bombing of Air India Flight 182," 2005. The report is available on the website of the Ministry of Public Safety Canada.

59 "Final Observations of the Attorney-General of Canada," vol. 1 of 3, p. 52, website of the Commission of Inquiry into the Investigation of the Bombing of Air India Flight 182, www.majorcomm.ca.

60 Correspondence with the authors.

61 Interview with the authors.

62 Interview with the authors.

63 Kathleen Harris, "Dissidents fear 'house of terror,'" *Ottawa Sun*, 21 February 1999.

64 Testimony of Rafi Eitan, former senior officer of Mossad, quoted by Gordon Thomas, *Histoire secrète du Mossad, de 1951 à nos jours* (Paris: Nouveau Monde, 2006).

Chapter 009: *The New Face of Espionage*

65 Peter Schweitzer, "Remarks to the American Senate on security and information," October 1996.

66 William McQuillen, Bloomberg News, 21 June 2003; quoted from a presentation to the National Press Club, Washington, Friday, 20 June 2003.

BIBLIOGRAPHY

Bell, Stewart. *Terreur froide: La filière canadienne du terrorisme interna-tional* (Cold terror: how Canada nurtures and exports terrorism to the world). Montreal: Les Éditions de l'Homme, 2004.

Ben-Menashe, Ari. *Profits of War: Inside the Secret U.S.–Israel Arms Network.* New York: Sheridan Square Publications, 1992.

Cherkashin, Victor, and Gregory Feifer. *Spy Handler: Memoir of a KGB Officer: The True Story of the Man Who Recruited Robert Hanssen and Aldrich Ames.* New York: Basic Books, 2005.

Christopher, Andrew, and Oleg Gordievski. *Le KGB dans le monde 1917–1990* (The KGB in the World, 1917–1990). Paris: Fayard, 1990.

Christopher, Andrew, Vasili Mitrokhine, and Philippe Delamare. *Le KGB contre l'Ouest, 1917–1991: Les archives Mitrokhine* (The KGB against the West, 1917–1991: The Mitrokhine Archives). Paris: Fayard, 2000.

Dhar, Maloy Krishna. *Open Secrets: India's Intelligence Unveiled.* New Delhi: Manas Publications, 2005.

Earley, Pete. *Comrade J.: The Untold Secrets of Russia's Master Spy in America After the End of the Cold War.* New York: G.P. Putnam's Sons, 2007.

Faligot, Roger. *Les Services secrets chinois, de Mao aux JO* (The Chinese secret service, from Mao to the Olympic Games). Paris: Nouveau Monde éditions, 2008.

Melnik, Constantin. *Les Espions: Réalités et fantasmes* (Spies: Reality and Fantasy). Paris: Ellipses, 2008.

Mitrovika, Andrew. *Entrée clandestine: Crimes et mensonges dans les services secrets canadiens* (Clandestine Entry: Crimes and Lies in Canada's Secret Services). Montreal: Éditions Trait d'union, 2002.

Ougartchinska, Roumiana. *KGB et cie, à l'assaut de l'Europe* (KGB and Company, the Assault on Europe). Paris: Éditions Anne Carrière, 2005.

Security Awareness in the 1980s: Featured Articles from the Security Awareness Bulletin, 1981–1989. Darby, PA: Diane Publishing, 1992.

Thomas, Gordon. *Histoire des services secrets britanniques* (History of the British Secret Services). Paris: Nouveau Monde éditions, 2008.

ACKNOWLEDGEMENTS

This book would not have been possible without the valuable assistance of numerous individuals.

In particular we would like to thank Yves Bonnet, Roger Faligot, Brian McAdam, Kayum Masimov, Lucy Zhou, Jamel Jani, Lise Garon, Vladimir Fedorovski, Stéphane Handfield, Gérard Pardini, Raymond Nart, Rémy Pautrat, François Lavigne, Maloy Krishna Dhar, Ari Ben-Menashe, Michel Auger, Pablo Durant, Claude Rivest, and Bernard Bujold.

At the same time we must emphasize that many of our sources have been involved in the world of espionage and must therefore maintain their anonymity. We are especially grateful to these people for their confidence in us, and for their generosity in making themselves available whenever we needed their assistance.

Special thanks go to Ray Conlogue for his hard work in translating our text from French into English. Ray took on the daunting task of translating a book covering a difficult topic with very specific jargon. Thanks to him, hopefully not much was "lost in translation."

We would also like to express our special gratitude to Karl Payeur, the formidable young researcher whose skills were immensely useful in our work.

But finally, we must particularly thank our wives, children, and families. They offered their unfailing support and patience, putting up with the lengthy absences that are inevitable in researching a book of this nature. They have all of our love and a great share of our gratitude.